T. p. 1

Nov. 1999

Amateur Soldiers – A history
of Oldham's Volunteers and Territorials 1859 – 1938

K. W. Mitchinson's interest in the Great War stretches back over several decades. He made his first trip to the battlefields of the Western Front in 1971 and has been a frequent visitor and guide ever since.

He lectures on several social and military aspects of the war, regularly contributes articles and book reviews to various historical journals and has recently written an introduction to a reprint of Henry Williamson's *A Patriot's Progress*.

Although born in the South, he has lived and worked in the Oldham area for nearly 25 years. His publications include:

> *Gentlemen and Officers* (Imperial War Museum, 1994)
> *Saddleworth 1914 – 1919* (SHS, 1994)
> *Pioneer Battalions in the Great War* (Leo Cooper, 1997)
> *Epéhy* (Leo Cooper, 1998)
> *Riqueval* (Leo Cooper, 1998)
> *Villers-Plouich* (Leo Cooper, 1999)

and, as co-author,

> *Cotton Town Comrades* (Bayonet Press, 1993).

Amateur Soldiers

A history of Oldham's Volunteers and Territorials, 1859 – 1938

by

K. W. Mitchinson

JADE

Jade Publishing Limited
5 Leefields Close, Uppermill, Oldham, Lancashire, OL3 6LA

This first impression published by Jade Publishing Limited 1999

© K. W. Mitchinson 1999
   All rights reserved

ISBN 0-9518098-9-X Amateur Soldiers – A history of Oldham's Volunteers and Territorials 1859 – 1938.

Typeset by
Jade Publishing Limited, Uppermill, Oldham, Lancashire

British Library Cataloguing in Publication Data
Mitchinson, K. W. (Kevin William) – 1951
    Amateur Soldiers – A history of Oldham's Volunteers and Territotials 1859 – 1938
    1. Great Britain. Army. Infantry – History
    2. Military service, Voluntary – England – Oldham – History – 19th century
    3. Military service, Voluntary – England – Oldham – History – 20th century
    4. Oldham (England) – History, Military – 19th century
    5. Oldham (England) – History, Military – 20th century

    I. Title
    356.1'13'09427393

ISBN 0-9518098-9-X

ACKNOWLEDGMENTS

INFORMATION FOR THIS BOOK came from a wide variety of sources and the author is conscious of the debt he owes to them all. Acknowledgment is accorded to the Trustees of the Public Record Office, the Imperial War Museum and to Oldham Local Studies Library for permission to use material within their archives and libraries. The professionalism and co-operation of Mary Bayliss and Philip Powell of the IWM's Department of Printed Books and of Dr Rod Suddaby and Nigel Steel of the Department of Documents have, as usual, been of immense help. The ladies of Accrington Library and of Oldham and Tameside Local Studies Libraries provided great assistance. My thanks also to the sons of Lt. Col. Fred Hardman for permission to use their father's letters and to the nephew of Henry Lawson for permission to quote from his uncle's *Vignettes of the Western Front*.

When appeals were made in the local press for information regarding men who had served with the 10th, Ian McInnes shared the time-consuming but enjoyable task of visiting many Oldham homes to borrow and copy private papers and diaries. His efforts are greatly appreciated as of course is the co-operation of the relatives of the former soldiers and of the former Territorials themselves who so willingly allowed us access to their documents and memories. They included Maud Brown, David and Sebastian Charlesworth, Matt Cowell, Arthur and Jack Kirkbride, Mrs W. Miller, Geoffrey Stemp, Jim Street, Anne Stewart, George Wright, Jean Wroe.

The Regimental Trustees have made available a huge amount of material from various sources. Special thanks are due to Bob Bonner, John Cleverley, David Rodger and Michael Seal. Major Rodger's means of opening doors and his enthusiastic encouragement has made the author's job immeasurably easier.

Finally, my thanks to several individuals who have assisted in less formal ways towards the production of this book: Eddy Atkinson, Barbara Bramall, Stewart and Sue Cashen, Pamela Daniels, David Geen, Janette Key, Sue Latimer, Helen Mackie, Dr Tony Parker, Molly Phillpotts, Jean Plowright and Nick Tarren.

CONTENTS

INTRODUCTION

ALTHOUGH THIS BOOK has taken several years in the researching and writing, it seemed for two reasons appropriate to delay its publication until 1999. First, the year marks the 150th anniversary of Oldham's incorporation as a Borough; secondly, and perhaps more significantly, the millennium will witness the closure of what has become one of the town's most readily recognised landmarks, the TA drill hall on Rifle Street. The Borough will still retain a TA element within its boundaries but the loss of Rifle Street signals the end of an era stretching back well over 100 years.

The Militia, a part-voluntary and part-balloted band of part-time soldiers, existed long before Oldham attained the status of borough. Ten years after the town's incorporation the Militia was largely replaced by a purely voluntary organisation known, appropriately, as the Volunteers. This in turn gave way to the Territorial Force in 1908, and in 1920 to the Territorial Army. Despite several amalgamations, reorganisations and rebadging, the presence of volunteer or amateur soldiers close to Oldham Edge has been a feature of Oldham's life since the 1860s.

This book attempts to trace the development of the Volunteer movement in Oldham from 1859 to 1938. The central theme of the work is, inevitably, the experiences of the town's Territorials during the Great War. In recent years there has been a huge revival of interest in this war but the role of the Territorial Force in the conflict has been largely overlooked. Studies of individual units have tended to concentrate more on the raising and work of Kitchener's New Armies rather than on the units already in existence in 1914 and, in many cases, fighting overseas before the Pals battalions were even up to establishment. In Oldham's case the Territorials were sweltering in the Egyptian desert weeks before the inaugural meeting to launch the Oldham Comrades battalion was held in the Empire Theatre.

The story of Oldham's amateur soldiers is not unique. By 1914 most major towns had a drill hall housing a Territorial detachment, be it infantry, artillery, Field Company of Royal Engineers or Royal Army Medical Corps ambulance. By the end of the war one of the town's two Territorial battalions had been disbanded and the other was hardly recognisable as a battalion of

Oldhamers. As a consequence of losses and official policy it was, like all Territorial battalions, barely distinguishable from any other TF, New Army or Regular unit. Nevertheless, it was a unit which had served abroad since September 1914 and which had fought in a variety of theatres. It had sustained heavy losses and, as part of the 42nd Division, had been criticised for not performing as well as some in authority had wished. If it did need to redeem itself, it did so emphatically in March 1918.

In the post-war years the reformed battalion became embroiled in political controversy and was the only TA unit to win the *Daily Telegraph* cup for outstanding attendance at annual camp on three successive occasions. By that time it was again a battalion of Oldhamers and a unit of which the town was exceptionally proud. During the Second World War the Borough's Terriers fought in tanks and in an unorthodox assortment of armoured vehicles. Officially honoured by the town in 1954 the 'Saturday afternoon soldiers' have remained at Rifle Street ever since. Now, as a result of the recent Strategic Defence Review, the era of Territorial soldiers in the town centre is drawing to a close.

The bronze plaques on the wall behind the war memorial list the names of nearly 3,000 of the town's fallen. Daily, probably thousands of people pass by them, most not giving a thought to what or whom they represent. Every year in early June between the wars, Oldham remembered the sacrifice of many of its sons near the sun-bleached ruins of a far away Turkish village called Krithia. Perhaps next Remembrance Sunday, if not before, passers-by might give a special thought to those 94 men of the Oldham Territorials who fell near Krithia between 4-6 June 1915. They were typical of the thousands of Oldham's men who in the last 140 years have given of their time, and in hundreds of cases their livelihoods, limbs and lives, for a cause in which they believed or comrades in whom they trusted.

THE VOLUNTEERS AND BEYOND

ENGLAND HAS AN ANCIENT TRADITION of enrolling men either voluntarily or compulsorily in its armed forces. The Saxon levy, the fyrd, was replaced in medieval and early modern times by the militia or by a feudal landlord compelling his tenants to take up what arms they might find on his behalf. The bands of would-be soldiers were at best partially trained and often more of a hindrance than a help. As the technology of warfare developed and the threat of a French invasion increased, Parliament decided to rationalize the existing system in the hope of securing a force of part-time soldiery that could in times of foreign invasion or civil unrest be of some quantifiable use. In Oldham the local Horse and Foot Association appeared during the eighteenth century and from it evolved first the Oldham Volunteers and then the Oldham Local Militia. This last named organization was raised in 1808 and remained in force until the perceived threat from Napoleon had diminished. Although it did consist largely of volunteers, there was also a proportion of balloted men.

The disbanding of the militia in 1816 did not completely frustrate the desire of local gentlemen to don uniform. They played a part in quelling unrest by the inhabitants of the cotton towns afflicted by the post-war slump and those involved in the agitation for political reform. Attracting men of the industrial and commercial classes, the part-time cavalry of the Yeomanry (reinforced if necessary by itinerant squadrons of regular cavalry) were called out on several occasions in the thirty years following the defeat of Napoleon.

It was another Napoleon, the nephew of the original Emperor, who prompted a later invasion scare. Despite fighting on the same side in the Crimea, the Anglo-French alliance was seen simply as an expediency. Once the Russian bear had decided there was little point in continuing what was a particularly futile and unconvincing war, traditional Anglo-French hostility again reasserted itself.

Developments in French naval design, combined with suspicions of Napoleon III's ambitions of empire, caused Britain in 1859 to look to her home defences. No longer quite so secure behind her traditional wooden walls, Parliament announced the creation of a new form of militia. Capitalising upon the contemporary national interest and enthusiasm for rifle clubs, local leaders called for patriotic men to enlist in the new Volunteer battalions. The response was immediate. Up and down the country middle-class men and artisans, resplendent in uniform and carrying arms, could be seen drilling and parading in preparation for a French invasion. By the end of 1860 Lancashire alone had 76 such battalions.

The Volunteer movement in Oldham began in November 1859. A circular letter and advertisement addressed to gentlemen of the town requested their attendance at the Angel Inn where, it was proposed, discussions would be held on the means of creating a local Volunteer Rifle Corps. Records of the meeting have not survived, but it is known that sufficient gentlemen turned up or showed an interest to set in motion the creation of what became known as the 31st Lancashire Rifle Volunteers, the first recruits to which were attested in the Masonic Hall by Nathan Worthington JP on 5 December. Just over one hundred men were prepared to pay the three guineas entrance fee and one guinea annual subscription. This was sufficient to dissuade any but the comfortable Victorian middle-class patriots or their social superiors from joining. In addition to the membership fees, members were also expected to provide their own uniform.

The Oldham Company was commanded by a local solicitor, Captain John Blackburn, whose business office doubled as the Company HQ. He was assisted by Lieutenant Hamilton Greaves and Ensign William Blackburn. Arms were stored for safe keeping in the Town Hall and by early 1860 members were wearing a grey uniform topped by a semi-shako. Enthusiasm was so great that a second and third company were formed the same year. In 1863 a fourth company, known familiarly as the 'Irish Company' was established. This was commanded by Captain Alfred Clegg and officered by two subalterns, Henry Wrigley and Dr Hart. Unfortunately the company seems to have enjoyed only a brief existence for within two years its members were dispersed among the other three companies.

Parades were usually held on a piece of waste land known as the Intake. Crowds gathered to watch manoeuvres and drills, and the companies' activities were frequently reported in the local press.

The wealthier members of Oldham society clearly supported the idea of the Volunteers for in 1861 the 'Ladies' of the town presented the companies with colours and mess silver. The Intake had been purchased by public subscription and an armoury, drill shed and surrounding wall had been built at a cost of £700. However, in case the Volunteer movement should prove to be a passing whim, the drill hall was designed to be easily converted to houses for the working class. To complete the picture of a thriving unit, brass and drum and fife bands were formed, their instruments being provided from the public purse. The fife and drum band fell into disgrace some time later for accepting an engagement without first having obtained the CO's permission. So outraged was he at this slight to his authority that the band was ignominiously dismissed from the corps.

In 1863 the first of what would become many reorganizations took place. The battalion was amalgamated with the 23rd Lancashire Volunteers based at Ashton. The new unit was rather cumbrously called the 7th Administrative Battalion, the Lancashire Rifle Volunteers. Two years later the uniform was slightly altered, but it was changed more significantly in 1871 when the unit adopted the green of the Rifle Brigade and scarlet facings. A further change of name came in 1880 when the word 'Administrative' was dropped. The uniform was altered to infantry red with green facings and in 1882 the Oldham and Ashton battalions resumed their separate identities. The reformed Oldham Battalion became the 22nd Lancashire Rifle Volunteers. Facilities at the drill hall had been improved during the intervening period and a subsequent appeal for funds to pay for the improvements resulted in sixteen citizens each subscribing a sum of £50 or more. The officers of the battalion also chipped in with a combined sum of £1,300. The battalion now boasted Britain's largest single span drill hall. The willingness of the citizenry to pay for the facilities through public subscription was an expression of faith in the town's Volunteer movement and of its future.

Training still largely consisted of marching and drill, interspersed with the natural enthusiasm of the men for rifle practice. The purpose of the former was apparently to get the men to 'march like a wall and wheel like a gate.' Annual shooting competitions were held with prizes of Enfield rifles donated by the officers and in 1868 the battalion was equipped at its own expense with the Lee-Enfield muzzle-loading rifle. Armed with these already obsolete weapons, the battalion took part in a sham fight in Heaton Park against four battalions of regular infantry and a squadron of Dragoon Guards. The regulars, armed with the more recent breech-loading rifles, charged the ranks of the Oldhamers. To the amazement of onlookers, the Oldham Battalion stood firm, repulsed the charge and then turned defence into attack. Although stunned at this impudence the regulars soon rallied and reformed their ranks; in contrast, the civilian observers hurled themselves into the lower branches of the park's trees to escape the *élan* of the Oldhamers' counter-attack.

In the 1880s, as part of the reform of the regular army, the Volunteers again underwent change. The battalion became known as the 6th Volunteer Battalion, the Manchester Regiment, thus beginning the long association of the town's volunteer soldiers with the Manchester Regiment. The men were equipped for the first time with haversack, water bottle and mess tin. This increasing semblance of professional soldiery was reflected in an annual government grant of 35 shillings for every man deemed efficient. Examinations for officers seeking promotion were introduced and battalion specialists were selected for training in signalling, cooking and as a machine-gun section.

The Boer War of 1899-1902 provided a boost to the national Volunteer movement. As misfortune and blunder beset the attempt of the regulars to overcome the Boer guerrillas, the call went out for Volunteers to serve in South Africa. In 1899 the strength of the Oldham Battalion was only some 10% below establishment and over 100 of its men volunteered to go to the Cape. Much prevarication ensued until in May 1900 the first contingent left Oldham to embark for South Africa. As the party arrived at Ladysmith soon after the town was relieved, it assumed it would not see action. The men's assumption proved incorrect and the party, along with groups which followed later, did take part in several small engagements. Lieutenant and Quartermaster Kennedy was commended by his superiors for rescuing a wounded officer at Zant Kop but, with the exception of Private J.Nightingale who probably died of disease, none of the Oldham Volunteers was actually injured or killed. One year after landing at Capetown they were back on a boat bound for the UK and a civic reception in the town. Fourteen years later several of these veterans were to serve with the 10/Manchester in Egypt and Gallipoli.

The first decade of the new century witnessed yet another significant change in the Volunteer movement. Awakened to the increasing likelihood of fighting in a continental war, Haldane, the Minister of War, embarked upon the creation of the Territorial Force. Originally conceived as a means of reinforcing the regular army overseas, Haldane, for political reasons, was later forced to accept a compromise and create the Territorials for home defence. To get his new force started Haldane relied upon large numbers of Volunteers agreeing to transfer from their existing battalion to their new local Territorial one. Much preliminary work and consultation preceded the change of designation from Volunteer to Territorial but in many parts of the country the transition was far from smooth.

In Oldham the strength of the Volunteer battalion had by 1908 fallen to under 700; reports in the town and from elsewhere indicated a marked resistance on the part of attested Volunteers to transfer their allegiance. Reasons for the reluctance varied; they ranged from general resentment at the passing of the Volunteers to annoyance at having to wear a 'T' (denoting 'Territorial') on their uniform. The CO, Lieutenant-Colonel Hodgkinson, even went so far as to criticise the attestation papers. He did however announce that, although the draft proposals for enlisting in the TF were more stringent than those applying to the Volunteers, the battalion's officers were prepared to take the plunge and attest. There was a widespread belief that Haldane would have to ease the conditions of service and, although a compromise was again reached, there were still many who objected to the terms. One of the more common complaints was that recruiting would be damaged by excluding men in the TF from the insurance benefits of the Workman's Compensation Act. Allowing TF soldiers to be exempted from jury service seemed poor compensation for the possible loss of civilian income resulting from an accident incurred whilst on the King's business.

In many towns across the country preparations were in train to announce, with as much publicity as could be manufactured, the transition from Volunteer to Territorial. Although the *Oldham*

Standard was more interested in reporting Athletic's rise to the top of the Second Division and the notorious murder trial of Margaret McNeeney, it did find space to devote several columns to the church parade intended to solicit intercession for the birth of the new battalion. In order to demonstrate the Council's support for the battalion, civic dignitaries by the score attended the service. The Reverend J. W. Orton who, as well as being the vicar of St Stephen's, doubled as the battalion padre stressed how the town's employers could make or break the new formation. Turning his attention to the better off in local society, he declared that the battalion offered a 'grand opportunity for the young men of our leisured classes to become useful to their fellow men instead of frittering away ability, social position and educational attainments in sinful and selfish indulgence'.

The church parade certainly provoked a good deal of interest within the town. The papers declared that the new force should be given a chance and demanded that the Government should do more to encourage membership of the Territorials than it had done for the Volunteers. Haldane had himself been campaigning around the country, his speeches and proclamations finding a home in the columns of both national and local papers. During a visit to Oldham in the previous December he had announced that it was the 'bounden duty of the leisured well-to-do to come forward and, by example and precept, make this alternative to conscription a national success'. To Haldane this was an essential feature of the new formation's role. Strong and influential forces were at work within the country to get conscription introduced: many who advocated the TF did so mainly because they thought it would be a step toward their real ambition of complete conscription. Other supporters believed that a successful TF would eliminate the need for a larger, conscripted, citizen army. Haldane belonged to this latter school of thought. He insisted the Territorials would not merely play at being soldiers but that, given the right financial and moral encouragement, they would become an efficient and vital adjunct to the regular army. Achieving this goal would thus do away with the need for full conscription.

It was all very well for Haldane and his supporters to expound the advantages to the individual and the nation of the Territorials, but the force would prove of little value if employers were not prepared to make it easier for their employees to enlist and fulfil the required number of drills and, more importantly, attend the annual camp. Oldham's Volunteers had first gone to camp in 1879 but until the 1890s such events had been fairly intermittent. This was partly because the Volunteers did not have the equipment to maintain themselves in the field and partly because their senior commanders had little interest in undertaking manoeuvres which might spoil what equipment and uniforms they did possess. When camps did take place, most of the time was spent in drill and in practising the final march past. The battalion's one machine gun was supposed to be pulled on a cart by a mule but, as no mule could ever be produced, the authorities decided it should be replaced by 'an intelligent NCO'. Attendance at Territorial camp was intended to be compulsory; many married men, however, believed this was one step too far. For younger and single men, compulsion did not cause too many difficulties providing they were prepared to sacrifice their two weeks' holiday in order to attend camp. Yet even if they were keen to go, office juniors were usually at the bottom of their employers' holiday priority lists. Oldham was more fortunate than some towns because during Wakes all the mills were closed at the same time. The battalion's camp was therefore usually chosen to coincide with this period. However, married men faced a choice of loyalties. Few family men were prepared or able to spend their entire two weeks' holiday allocation at camp with their comrades rather than at home with their wives and children.

Despite the entreaties of vicars, mayors and politicians, in Oldham the transition from Volunteer to Territorial was disappointing. The improved attestation forms enticed only some 300 of the 700 Volunteers to transfer. The contemporary view was that the town's big employers were not doing enough. It was hoped that Oldham Corporation would lead the way and announce that it would grant extra payments and holiday entitlement to any of its employees who enlisted in the battalion. This was not however the only cause for complaint. One young man who had made the change was dismayed when he turned up on a Saturday afternoon for a shooting competition. Having completed a morning's work, he arrived at the drill hall to discover that not enough officers were present to allow the competition to go ahead.

He blamed the 'neglect by superiors' for the large number of men who had refused to transfer to the battalion and believed there were many who had been similarly disgusted with the attitude displayed by their officers.

Notwithstanding this unwelcome indictment of the battalion's officers, the unit attempted to capitalize on the coverage of the original church parade by maintaining a high public profile. In an effort to attract would-be recruits, 'smokers', dances, 'pies and pints' and even picture shows were held regularly at the drill hall and several erstwhile Volunteers were wheeled out to deliver speeches supporting the concept of the TF. Despite these events and efforts, the battalion was never up to strength. This was by no means unusual as the majority of Territorial units found it difficult to recruit to establishment. The annual camps were often publicised, again in an attempt to attract recruits, but as they were usually held at Alderley Edge rather than the more popular coastal resorts, the response was patchy. Authority might describe them as 'very good for unit morale' and that they 'cannot be too highly recommended', but unless the young men of Oldham fancied themselves in a uniform and preferred to spend their precious holiday under canvas, the exhortations fell on deaf ears.

Low numbers at camp and at drills did not allow for the easy fostering of unit *esprit*. There were regular whist and billiard matches between the officers and sergeants and frequent in-house concerts which did help, but an additional major problem facing the officers and NCOs was how to train an efficient unit and develop morale and pride in the battalion when there was such a regular turnover of members. These problems were further exacerbated in 1912 and 1913 when many men left on the expiration of their initial period of service. For example, in three months of 1913, 116 men were discharged and did not re-engage; later in the year another 39 men left at the end of their service. The departure of these men who had served for four years and had also probably seen some service as Volunteers, left a large hole. In the same period, 94 men either re-enlisted or were recruited. Nationally, about one third of all those who enlisted in the Territorials served for less than one year. Things did improve in early 1914 when 208 men were recruited and only 74 left as time-expired. This haemorrhage did not cause too much alarm in official circles as it was anticipated that in the event of war, large numbers of trained or partly trained men would return to their former units. In Oldham, as in most of the other towns up and down the country, this was indeed to be the case.

On the eve of war Oldham's Territorials were thus somewhat under strength, with perhaps 50% of those attested having served for less than one year. The battalion also had a new CO, Adjutant and RSM. Lieutenant-Colonel Paterson, who had joined the battalion in 1886, stood down and was replaced by Lieutenant-Colonel J. B. Rye. As Territorial units were obliged to have a regular soldier as Adjutant, Captain de Pentheney O'Kelly of the Royal Welch Fusiliers took up his new appointment in early 1914. Surviving evidence suggests that the battalion was, like most Territorial units, run on a fairly feudal system. The men were largely mill hands and their officers were the mill owners or their sons. There were other professional men amongst them – a sprinkling of architects and accountants – but, in the main, the Other Ranks came from the terraced streets and their officers from the leafy avenues. They did, however, have something important in common. Membership of the Territorials was not for financial gain. Some officers might have enlisted for social reasons, but given the ridicule that the public generally heaped upon Britain's 'Saturday afternoon soldiers', most men joined because they believed in what they were doing. It would make life more exciting if you could join with friends and colleagues from the same mill, factory, church or sports team, but the majority did so for patriotic reasons. Those higher in the social scale believed it their duty; those of more lowly rank enlisted because they considered the British Empire was worth defending.

An Egyptian Sojourn

ALTHOUGH ECONOMISTS AND MILITARY STRATEGISTS had long confidently stated that modern weapons had made a protracted major war financially and militarily impossible, escalation of what Austria had intended to be a short punitive war against Serbia into a wider conflict was not altogether unexpected. The existence of alliances and *ententes* had always threatened to involve more powers than any original two antagonists and the German invasion of Belgium provided the flux to weld together a hitherto divided British Cabinet. Here was the opportunity to teach the upstart Kaiser and his upstart nation that this time he had bullied and coerced once too often. Wilhelm's temerarious and boastful challenge to Britain's world and naval hegemony had aroused the nation's wrath (especially during the invasion scare of 1909), and on several occasions since had contrived to jeopardise the *Pax Britannica* and the European balance of power. Britain's long-established policy of opposing the occupation of Belgium by any major continental power meant that the execution of the Schlieffen Plan would bring Britain into the conflict. There were few in Britain who did not believe the cause was just.

In the summer of 1914 Oldham, like the other textile towns of the North-West, was a community confronting financial difficulties. Many thousands of its mill workers were already on short time and the majority of the remainder were on a week's notice. As befitted a town with a history of radicalism, Oldham was at the forefront of the Suffrage movement and in its foundries and workshops the engineering unions were strong. In recent times union activity had threatened to bring the country to a halt; the worsening economic prospects, the continual antagonism between the Commons and Lords and the long-running sore of Ireland caused many people in authority to believe that war could provide the nation with a panacea of patriotic union. Similar sentiments were expressed in all the capitals of Europe. The policy of fostering *pro patria* by those who feared for their own positions of power and influence, were proved to have possessed an astuteness which many of the lower orders only later perceived.

At about 6.00pm on 4 August the orderly room staff of the 10th received orders to begin the mobilisation process.

This procedure had been practised on paper many times and now, when the need for a swift and faultless execution was paramount, the system proved its worth. Telegrams ordering men to report to the drill hall at 6.00am on 5 August went out to the homes of all members. Several NCOs were stationed at the town's principal entertainment palaces to inform any unsuspecting soldier, perhaps with his sweetheart on his arm, that the King required his services in the morning.

By the early hours of 5 August nearly 90% of the men had assembled at the drill hall. Word spread quickly along the streets of terraced houses and a large crowd gathered to watch the martial manoeuvrings of the town's sons. Observers were disappointed because all they could see were sentries with fixed bayonets intent on keeping away anyone who did not have a legitimate purpose for being in the drill hall's immediate environs. One journalist reported that inside the hall the men were behaving in the manner expected of an English regiment: 'No enthusiasm, No Mafficking – they were facing a stern duty with their dogged English way which is never flurried or mad, but wonderfully steady and sure'. Had the journalist been privy to the activities of the battalion's Medical Officer, he might not have been quite so fawning. This extremely harassed individual snarled a curt greeting at a semi-naked NCO and demanded 'You all right?'

'Yes sir', replied the man.

'Well if you're not, you … well ought to be. Get out!' bawled the over-worked doctor.

The hack was largely correct but inside the hall there was an air of great anticipation. By noon, every man had been through his cursory medical examination and kit was in the process of distribution. Here again the system worked remarkably smoothly. What the Quartermaster did not have in store was delivered by contracting firms. County TF Associations were responsible for providing all their units with kit and equipment and on 6 August, when Oldham townsfolk saw their own battalion drawn up on parade, each man had his full requirement. The town was to see much of its soldiers during the next two weeks. Besides daily parades on Oldham Edge, parties of troops went about requisition-ing the necessary number of horses from the streets and stables of the town. As the local yeomanry unit, the Duke of Lancaster's

Own, was also attempting to obtain its transport requirements from similar sources, amused observers often witnessed competition between representatives of the two units for the same horse or carriage. One unfortunate customer at a bank returned from completing his transaction to discover his carriage was horseless; his animals, now part of His Majesty's Forces, were being led triumphantly towards Rifle Street. Lieutenant Fred Hardman's party had the effrontery to commandeer the Chief Constable's horse and later managed to acquire a medical cart in the shape of a governess's carriage and pony. For several subsequent years the cart did sterling service in the Egyptian desert.

During the night of 7–8 August the town's slumbers were awakened by the blast of trumpets. It was merely a test mobilisation but those who were ignorant of its real purpose again congregated at the drill hall. Special trams were laid on for the men and by about 2.00am several thousand expectant well-wishers thronged Rifle Street in anticipation of seeing the men march off to war. The more belligerent amongst them were disappointed and, save for a parade staged to present the mayor with the battalion's colours for safe storage in the Town Hall, the community returned to watching its men parade and drill on Oldham Edge. Like the men themselves, the town was beginning to wonder whether the battalion would ever be employed more usefully. It paraded at the public baths for free bathing and was cheered as the band led it on route marches about the town; everyone agreed it looked smart and did the town credit, but when was the battalion actually going to do something? The British Expeditionary Force was on its way to the continent, the German army was marching inexorably on France, but the Territorials had not even moved to their war station. This frustration is perhaps indicative of the general public's ignorance of the TF's intended role.

As so few people envisaged the TF would ever be required to go abroad, only a handful of pre-war Territorials had agreed to accept what was known as foreign service. Kitchener was one of the several leaders who discounted the contemporary anticipation of a short war and realised that until the New Armies (which more familiarly bore his own name) were ready for the field, the Territorials would have to fill the gap. Some could be used to replace regular battalions garrisoning the Empire, but others, as events in France unwound, would be needed to bolster the shrinking battalions of the original British Expeditionary Force.

In the middle of August Kitchener announced that although he would not send Territorials to Ireland, he required the force to volunteer for foreign service. If 75% of a unit opted for service abroad the men were assured that they would be sent overseas as a battalion or battery. This was a major incentive to TF units who were 'Pals' battalions in all but name. Although they are rarely regarded as emotively as those Pals units raised in later months, Territorial battalions were the precursors of those battalions. Territorials had long enlisted with their friends, work mates, team-mates and school-chums. Once the possibility of a unit being broken up, and its members posted indiscriminately to any other battalion short of numbers, was removed the obvious corollary was to volunteer together for foreign service.

Yet, within this easy, general supposition lay individual agonies. Many Territorials were men of increasing years, married and with good jobs. Patriotism might be an admirable motive but, unless employers were prepared to make up the deficiencies in army pay, not only would the men be exposing themselves to the danger of death or mutilation, their families would also suffer from a substantial decrease in income. Many white-collar and Corporation workers were promised that the difference between their army and civilian pay would be made up but, for the mill workers and the unemployed, the prospect of remaining at home and benefiting from the inevitable boom resulting from government contracts was hard to resist. Whether to put family before loyalty to friends and the battalion was a question on many lips and in many hearts during late August and early September.

In a conversation which must have typified many between friends and comrades in those early fateful days, Lieutenant Fred Hardman and Lieutenant James H. Clegg argued the merits of volunteering for foreign service or staying at home. Both men were in their mid-twenties, married only a year earlier and each with a baby to consider. Initially the two officers agreed that they would make a joint decision to remain at home and help to raise the battalion's second line unit. However, Hardman agonised whether this was the correct option. In late August he wrote to his wife:

They are putting the screws on pretty thick ... and are practically forcing us to go. I am in a terrible fix tonight and cannot tell what to ... do I have my duty to my country and my duty to my baby. If I stayed at home I shall be branded as a coward for evermore and if I chose to go abroad I must ask you to be brave and take on an Englishwoman's part ... if you would just give me your word it would make it so much easier. My mind is in a dreadful state.

Kitty replied that if he felt he must go, he should change his mind and renege on the pact he had made with Clegg. This eased his conscience and Hardman informed the CO that he would go with his platoon to wherever the War Office decided their services were required. Clegg initially remained in Oldham to raise the new 2nd Battalion and joined the 1st Battalion in Egypt at the end of the year. He was killed on Gallipoli whereas Hardman survived the war.

Meanwhile, the War Office had decided that the disparate units of the East Lancashire Division should assemble in a more concentrated area. The first stages of preliminary training were over and, with the Adjutant's frequent exhortation to 'Dubbin your boots!' ringing in their ears, the men of the 10th paraded at 6.00am on 20 August and marched to Bury.

A depot under the command of Captain Booth was left behind; so too was a small detachment guarding the reservoirs at Greenfield. This group aroused the ire of Councillor Dransfield by allegedly taking pot shots at him as he walked along Chew Valley. The puce councillor thundered to Saddleworth Council that these 'trigger happy Territorials should ask first and shoot later'. Those men who marched for six hours to Bury were unsure of the eventual future but were aware that, although they might look like soldiers, there was the certainty of long weeks of hard training before them. Neither was it as yet a full battalion. Despite the re-appearance of at least 80 former members and the enthusiastic volunteers of August, the unit was still slightly under strength. Well over 100 were entirely new recruits who had not yet done any real drill or training. After the Brigadier had addressed the battalion on the need for it to volunteer for overseas service, nearly 240 of its members decided they would not go with it and were put into a separate camp under the command of Captain

R. Smethurst. This exodus, largely of men with at least one year's experience in the battalion, was replaced by another batch of recruits and former soldiers.

For the majority of men, the introduction to active service conditions was miserable. The tents at Chesham Camp almost floated on a sea of mud; rain poured incessantly and the camp degenerated into a quagmire. When the weather permitted, drills took place, but most of the time was spent in marching around the streets of Bury or huddled in leaking tents in sodden clothes. Although the food was considered reasonable and parties of men were allowed evening leave to visit Bury's chip shops, the increasing tightening of military discipline meant that any soldier returning late was crimed and had pay docked. So many rumours abounded about when they would leave and of their eventual destination that, 'We're moving on Wednesday!' became the means by which men greeted each other in the morning. Nevertheless, being in a rain-lashed camp did offer some compensation to at least one soldier. Private John Jowett could not attend court when summoned for non-payment of £5 maintenance to his wife. A not altogether sympathetic magistrate told the unfortunate Mrs Jowett that she should apply to have one shilling deducted from her husband's weekly army pay but should wait until the war was over before suing him for the balance.

Rumours of imminent departure persisted and, upon word of what was again considered to be a definitive judgement, on 8 September scores of families travelled up to Bury to say farewell. On this occasion the speculation was proven to be well-founded. Stories abounded of cancelled train services in the Bury area and these whispers were followed by further conjecture that 100 extra locomotives were being assembled in nearby marshalling yards. These trains did materialise during the afternoon and evening of Wednesday 9 September and, amid some very hurried and no doubt tearful separations, the 10/Manchester and the other units of the East Lancashire Division set off for war. The solemnity and apprehension of the occasion was lifted for a moment when Private Seddon managed to trip or slip in the mud and ended up with his head through the skin of his bass drum.

Having awaited its departure for some weeks, and having exhausted all known superlatives to describe the manner and appearance of the local soldiery, the local press were somewhat dumbfounded when the battalion finally left. Censorship prevented them announcing anything other than that its movement to an unknown destination had commenced. A later short paragraph stating that the battalion had left from a southern port was all that was permitted. Besides the possibility of odd snippets from official communiqués, all the papers could do now was to wait for soldiers' relatives to receive word from their loved ones and pass on the information to the papers.

The 10th arrived at Southampton on the morning of 10 September after what, by wartime standards, was a remarkably quick journey. Although probably very few of the men knew of it at the time, they were later very proud of the fact that they were members of the first complete Territorial Force division to be travelling overseas.

As they waited at Southampton for further orders the men had their first glimpse of German soldiers. Eighty-six prisoners captured in France shuffled past the observing troops. One Oldham officer was not impressed by these representatives of the formerly invincible German army:

> Without exception they hung their heads and looked thoroughly ashamed of themselves.

During the evening of 10 September, 29 officers and 980 Other Ranks under the command of Lieutenant-Colonel Rye VD embarked upon the former mail-steamer and occasional cruise liner the RMS AVON. The battalion was accompanied by eight regular soldiers of its Permanent Staff and its Medical Officer with his five Royal Army Medical Corps orderlies.

The troops on board the AVON, which apart from the 10th included the Duke of Lancaster's Own Yeomanry, the Westminster Dragoons and the 3/East Lancashire Field Ambulance, were more fortunate than some of the others in the division. The convoy consisted of several former cattle transports whose hasty conversion was all too evident to the troops on board. Unlike some of the Lancashire Fusiliers who slept packed like sardines on iron decks, the 10th at least had the comfort of hammocks slung from the deckheads. As the late summer's night began to fall, the convoy slipped anchor and formed up in the Solent.

Escorted by two fairly ancient warships – the pre-Dreadnought OCEAN and the MINERVA, a cruiser of 1895 vintage – the 15 transports made their way around the Isle of Wight. Searchlights swept the seas as bands crashed out *God Save the King* and *Rule Britannia*. Amid the excitement there was also pathos and quiet reflection. As the coast of England was cloaked by the dark of a September night, the men on the AVON sang *Homeland, when shall I see thee again?*

The Channel and the Bay of Biscay welcomed the Territorials in their traditional way. Before long, men were hunched over the rails of the ship and, when rations were served on the mess decks, most of the food tins slid off the tables and deposited their contents over the deck, the men and their equipment. Even the discovery that tins of 50 Capstan Navy cigarettes could be bought for as little as nine pence failed to alleviate the gloom of many. Conditions and stomachs improved as the weather ameliorated and by the time the coast of Portugal was sighted on 16 September, the troops were more settled and enjoying the cruise.

Occasionally the MINERVA would leave her flock to investigate an unidentified ship on the horizon. In those early days of the war, the U-boat menace was still largely an unmaterialised threat but there were fears that a German surface flotilla might have escaped the blockade and be prowling the trade routes.

The troops were kept occupied doing physical drills, kit inspections, sentry duty and attending the odd lecture on military matters. When they could, the signallers and machine-gun section practised their skills but a lot of the time was spent in listening to the band and in illicit gambling. A ship's journal appeared just as the convoy entered the Mediterranean and included so many helpful notes about Gibraltar that some of the troops anticipated a run ashore. As the morning sun poured down upon the rock, the convoy entered the harbour; unfortunately the most Private William Swallow managed to experience of the base's delights was a view of the Old Red House pub through his eyeglass. After eight hours of swinging tantalisingly at anchor, the convoy again slipped out to sea.

The weekly journal reported snatches of war news passed to the ship by wireless. The troops were informed that the German retreat had ended on the Aisne, that the Russians were pressing the Austrians hard in Galicia and that the Prime Minister had announced that Indian troops were now heading to Europe on behalf of the motherland. This last story was confirmed on 22 September when the Lancastrians spotted a large convoy heading towards them; 22 troop ships were bringing Indian divisions to France. As the convoys passed, one soldier on the AVON speculated 'we should never see a sight like that again in a hundred years'. The Oldhamers were certainly impressed by this display of the Empire's unity and returned to their deck swabbing with rather more enthusiasm. Shortly afterwards the cruiser WEYMOUTH, which had escorted the Europe bound convoy, exchanged places with the MINERVA and OCEAN and proceeded with the East Lancashire Division towards Alexandria.

Life on board ship was enlivened by inter-unit cricket matches, regular concerts and by the obvious delight with which the 3/East Lancashire Field Ambulance inoculated the troops against various forms of fever. General boredom and a wish for the journey to end set in as the AVON ploughed its way across the Mediterranean. The whole convoy hove to on 24 September to bury a man of the Duke Of Lancaster's Own Yeomanry who had apparently been kicked by his own horse. A few hours later several men ended up in the AVON's sick bay, allegedly poisoned by rotten potatoes. The beautiful panoramas of the sweeping horizon and the African coast did little to sweeten what for one officer of the Westminster Dragoons was becoming a nightmare of a journey. In a letter posted on his arrival at Alexandria, the obviously sophisticated gentleman complained of having been 'cooped up with the uncouth, clog-dancing men of the Manchester Regiment' for an impossibly lengthy period. Having discovered a means of acquiring after-hours beer, one of the officer's own men had somewhat disgraced himself during the voyage. Arrested in a drunken state and thrown into the cells, the Dragoon was later allowed to perform his turn at an evening concert under armed guard.

While at sea the old eight-company organisation of Territorial battalions was altered to four. This coincided with the arrangement of regular battalions but necessitated the amalgamation of companies which had, since the Volunteer days, enjoyed distinct identities. It also meant that four captains who had previously commanded companies now became, on seniority, second in command. If there was any ill feeling or resentment, for the purpose of unity it would have been well hidden.

Fifteen days after leaving Southampton the men of the reorganised companies spotted the lighthouse of Alexandria. Tugs puffed and fussed about the transports as lines were secured to tow them into the dock. Although most men had long assumed they would disembark at Alexandria rather than steam through Suez to India, there was still uncertainty over whom they might actually fight. Turkey was not yet in the war so was the purpose of their Egyptian sojourn merely to harden them up preparatory to being shipped to France, or were they to be employed in some nefarious duties against possible native insurgents?

Two things especially caught the attention of the Oldham men. The first was the swarm of small boats crammed with Egyptian hawkers which immediately surrounded the AVON; their crews offered what Eric Hickling described as 'all sorts of weird looking things which we have since found out was Egyptian food'. The second was not the glittering domes of exotic mosques, nor the flamboyant splendour of the Khedive's palace, but a clutch of mill chimneys. Incongruous and unexpected, they aroused a great deal of interest amongst Oldham's displaced soldiery. Used to seeing their tapered snouts poking eerily through the cloud and smog of an Oldham dawn, the Egyptian variety stood bathed in the shimmering heat of an autumn morning above the mansions and minarets. From the train conveying the battalion south the men saw seemingly endless cotton plantations beside the track. Familiar enough with the cotton itself, it was the first time the spinners, piecers and weavers had seen the reason for Lancashire's fame and selective prosperity *in situ*.

The train carried the battalion towards Cairo and some hours later the men alighted at a suburb some six miles outside the city. Partially fortified by a 24-hour biscuit ration, the men were employed in unloading equipment from rolling stock. Their next destination was Heliopolis racecourse, but any dreams they harboured of luxuriating on lush grass were rudely shattered when the track was discovered to be sand. Fortunately tents were already erected and as the battalion arrived the previous occupants, the Highland Light Infantry, Gurkhas and 125th Indian Rifles, were on the point of marching out. The Oldhamers were told-off by platoons and then sections and allocated tents. In the previous twenty-four hours they had been issued with biscuits and a small ration of bully beef. Anticipation of a more varied and substantial ration was quickly dashed:

There was very little food. Our breakfast consisted of tea and yesterday's biscuits. Our dinner was boiled beef with pumpkins (no bread or potatoes), for tea we got dry bread and bully beef and tea without milk or sugar. The bread is rotten. It is as sour as can be and as heavy as lead and a brownish colour.

Things did not improve the following day:

Fall in on parade at 5.40 am until 8.30 am. For breakfast, dry bread and tea. The men are very dissatisfied ... Drill this afternoon from 3.45 to 6.00 pm. Dry bread and tea again for tea (sic) ... It is as bad as being in prison. In bed at 9.30 feeling very miserable and fed up.

Notwithstanding the less than adequate food and the spartan accommodation, the men began their training. Khaki drill suits and pith helmets soon replaced the unsuitable woollen serge and field service caps, but adjusting to the heat and dust required more than a mere change of clothes. As they were separated from the trained men, the recruits of August had a slightly less onerous introduction to training; instead of route marches through the uncompromising desert, they were awarded the marginally less uncomfortable honour of drill under the Permanent Staff. The first few weeks witnessed an increasingly demanding programme of route marches and occasional demonstrations in strength to remind the natives of who really ruled Egypt. Brigade marches were followed at the end of October by a divisional parade through the streets of Cairo. During the preceding fourteen days the battalion had marched an average of fifteen miles in the heat of the day carrying sixty-five pound packs. The men's feet were blistered and swollen and the diet remained inadequate, but their appearance at Cairo was reported as presenting a 'magnificent and impressive spectacle'. The GOC Egypt commented that they had 'vastly improved in every way' which was probably just as well, for two days later, in the face of a growing threat from Egyptian nationalists, he declared martial law.

To the troops, little really changed except that they were ordered to provide guards at strategic points throughout the city and were instructed to be armed whenever they left camp. The Egyptians resented the British presence, regularly stoning soldiers returning to camp; troops had consequently always found it prudent to take at least a bayonet with them and never to go out alone. When they did venture out of camp, there were many and varied sights to explore. Expeditions to the pyramids and the sphinx at Ghizeh were especially popular excursions and it was during a scramble on the pyramids on Boxing Day 1914 that Sam Holden fell to his death. Other sights to explore were rock tombs at Sakhara, Cairo's bazaars and an ostrich farm. As it was tempting fate to wander into the narrow streets of the native quarters, most of the men kept to the main thoroughfares and regular tourist attractions. While they might wonder at the marvels of the ancient world and at the breathtaking splendour of the sun rising from behind the pyramids, more mundane aspects of Egyptian life also fascinated some of the Oldhamers.

On arrival at Alexandria they had been pleasantly surprised to discover how smoothly the Egyptian railways operated and in a letter home Alf Hitchen of 'B' Company related how Cairo's tram system was superior to that of Oldham Corporation. Perhaps Jim Donovan was equally impressed and being keen to have a closer look, stepped too close to a passing tram. Whatever the circumstances, Donovan was knocked down and killed. Both he and Sam Holden were buried with full military honours in Citadel Cemetery two days later.

However much the mysterious and exotic sights intrigued the Oldhamers, many would never quite get to grips with the city of Cairo. The Calvinist in them caused some to recoil from its flesh pots and associated debauchery; nevertheless it held strange and forbidden temptations which many found impossible to resist. Although some condemned it with a ferocity approaching fanaticism, others found they could not resist its intoxicating allure. Alf Hitchen thought it a 'splendid (but) an absolutely immoral city', Bradbury, 'excessively fascinating and exceeding wicked'; while Dyer of Royton thought it 'poisoned at twenty paces'. He suggested that they 'ought to burn it down … drinking and debauching … are all (the Egyptians) can think about'.

Initially Swallow described it as a 'very quaint place' but after further investigations thought the sights were 'disgusting ... you pay half a Piasbe to go in a place ... and there you see women doing the can-can with no clothes on at all ... the way they made an exhibition of themselves is disgraceful'. He concluded by declaring 'IT IS TOO HOT TO PUT DOWN HERE ALL THAT I SAW'. In April, Swallow paid another visit. Again, although considering it 'shameful to see women dancing and placing themselves in all attitudes with nothing on but a wee smile', he still could not resist adding 'my word, it is great'. It is to be hoped that Alf Hitchen did, despite his reservations, derive some pleasure from its dubious delights for within a few months the 22-year-old from Yale Street was dead.

There was no such ambiguity concerning the men's attitude towards the natives. The British soldier had never held the Egyptian in quite the same, albeit reluctant respect, as he had many of the natives on the Indian sub-continent. The Oldhamers quickly understood why. To Hitchen they were a 'treacherous lot of rogues' while the normally more reserved Wynne thought that they were the 'greatest thieves and swindlers unhung'. Brigade orders stressed that troops should hold themselves aloof from the natives, but when of necessity the occupier and occupied had to come into contact, Bradbury thought the latter were 'dirty, deceitful and treacherous'; the only way to deal with them was 'to swear back at them'. We can only speculate upon whether the Egyptians were any the wiser or chastened after having been sworn at in what to them was the probably incomprehensible Oldham dialect.

Another group to whom at least several of the Oldhamers took exception were the colonial troops from Australia and New Zealand. Throughout the war the Australians were often regarded by British troops in the same way as were US forces during the Second World War. A brashness and arrogance and a desire to live up to the image of wild colonial boys did not find favour with the more reserved British Tommy. Furthermore, the colonials enjoyed a higher rate of pay than their British counterparts, a detail which they generally made no bones about hiding. Notwithstanding the fact that many of those wearing Australian uniform were British citizens who had only recently emigrated – the economic and political problems of the last decade of the nineteenth century had caused many young men to believe their future lay overseas – they had quickly adopted the attitude of what soon became a stereotype. Fred Hardman's comment to his father probably typified the thoughts of several: 'If these are the pick of them, it's "God help Australia". They think they own the universe'.

New Zealanders, on the the other hand, were generally regarded as quieter and more restrained, with a discipline more akin to the British army than the casual and indifferent attitude toward authority displayed by the Australians. In his post-war series of articles for the *Oldham Chronicle*, Wynne described the arrival of the New Zealanders as an opportunity to discover old friendships and wrote of the 'warm welcome' offered to the antipodean troops. In his unpublished account Wynne noted that the Australians and New Zealanders were 'inefficient in drill and discipline' and that they were 'surprised at the finely disciplined men of the 10th Manchester'. 'Appalled' would probably have been a better word. While there is no better grouser in the world than the British soldier, he has generally been content to complain in word rather than deed. Upon arrival in December the first batch of New Zealanders had not eaten for twenty-four hours. Rather than merely grumble, they decided to forage some food for themselves. The nearby 10th's officers' mess was the obvious target for their raid and, having plundered assorted foodstuffs, the Kiwis retired to their own lines to enjoy their spoil.

While this might have been considered to be a fine example of derring-do and quietly admired by the 10th (which was still largely existing on an unchanging diet of bully beef and biscuits), the activities of the Australians in April certainly aroused a great deal of resentment. The Dominion troops went on a rampage, wrecking bars and brothels and building bonfires of looted furniture in the streets. Various units of the East Lancashire Division were turned out to guard points in the city in case the rioting got out of hand. Although the subsequent Court of Inquiry completely exonerated the Lancashire Territorials, who were also in fact praised by the GOC for their exemplary conduct, the entire division was confined to barracks or camp. This confinement, which in the words of one very disgruntled private amounted to 'punishing us for being good', lasted until the 10th left for Kantara nearly two weeks later. To add to the injustice, the Australians remained at liberty to wander about the town at will. William Swallow had learnt enough about them to realise that if 'they tried to confine them, they would pull the place down and their officers know it. You cannot keep them in for they fear neither man or devil'.

The occasional riot apart, the most common reminiscence of this desert sojourn was the drudgery and sheer unremitting toil. What to the Quartermaster was an 'elaborate and exhaustive' scheme of training drawn up by the Adjutant, developed into the first stage of a programme which was in theory to prepare the Oldhamers for any eventuality. The first significant test came in late October when the battalion was ordered to march through the streets of Cairo as a demonstration of strength during a three-day Moslem festival. The march took in not only the main streets but also the foul-smelling warrens of the native residential district. The broiling heat was too much even for some of the attached regular Permanent Staff; service in all parts of the Empire had not prepared even the toughest of staff sergeants for work such as this – and this was only the start.

Major O'Kelly's developing programme of training usually entailed a march of about five miles with full pack into the desert, entrench a position, charge with fixed bayonets an imaginary line of trenches some hundreds of yards away and finally march back to camp. Marching across the energy-sapping sand for six hours a day caused enormous problems for men's feet; then, before returning home, to have to dig through lava so hard it turned up the edges of the pickaxes tested their stamina to the utmost. The day after one such exercise, 500 of the men, who according to Wynne were the 'pick of the battalion', were told that they had been chosen to line the streets for the enthronement of a new Sultan. Now that Turkey had been tempted into the war on Germany's side, Britain could dispense with any pretence of legality and install a puppet of its own choosing. To honour the event, those selected spent two hours after returning from the desert expedition preparing their kit and were later roused at 3.30am in preparation for the march to Cairo. In case the Egyptians questioned the authority of their new ruler, they stood fully armed for three hours in a biting wind and close to a hostile crowd. The following day it was back to the desert.

In mid-December brigade training began. This was another developing programme which grew more demanding as the days progressed. The Oldhamers were particularly unfortunate. They had first to march six miles into the desert to rendezvous with other battalions of the brigade who had come only a little way from their own encampments. Typical of the daily exercises was that undertaken on 30 December. The battalion was woken at 5.00am for breakfast, kit inspection and company parades. It was scheduled to move off at 10.00am, march nine miles into the desert, entrench, do an attack, march back and arrive at camp about 4.00pm. Kit was then to be cleaned and the normal fatigues performed before the inevitable boiled beef would be served at 7.00pm. On this occasion the demands were too much. The men stopped in the middle of the bayonet charge because they could not run any further. The brigadier made them march back three miles and then start all over again. It was not completed any better the second time of asking but the brigadier decided to call it a day and the men marched back. During the day the battalion had marched and manoeuvred 24 miles with full pack.

Most were too exhausted even to look for the two familiar landmarks which heralded the approach of their camp – the Virgin's Breast (a strange shaped hill), and the Third Tower, an old watch tower on the ancient caravan route to Suez. Wynne observed the men as they returned to camp and, despite their appalling state, decided that they 'undoubtedly showed themselves to be one of the best disciplined and best trained units in the brigade'. Next came divisional training.

Without more than 24 hours' respite, the demands were again increased. On 7 January 1915 the battalion left camp at 7.45am, marched eleven miles into the desert, skirmished for another two and a half miles and then marched back. Dozens of men dropped out but the gruelling regime continued the following day. In fact it went on until 16 January when, because so many men were incapable of marching, the GOC ordered a rest day. The exercise of the day before had been exceptionally severe even for this, the severest of programmes. The battalion had been on the sand from 6.30am to 5.45pm and had covered over 32 miles. Stragglers in droves were still arriving back at camp during the night and even the officers, most of whom had been on horseback all day, were close to collapse; all the hardened NCOs of the Permanent Staff had dropped out well before the Third Tower. When the battalion was dismissed the square, scores of men simply collapsed there on the ground and were carried off to their tents by members of the band. Looking through his rather rose-tinted spectacles, Wynne thought the men bore the experience 'splendidly'. Hardman remarked to his father that 'they are trying to see what the Territorials can do for they certainly have been knocking the stuffing out of us'. On 26 January, just as the official divisional schedule was completed, 15 members of the Oldham battalion were invalided home.

For the great bulk of the battalion, something approaching a respite was now in sight. Having camped for eighteen weeks on the sand at Heliopolis, the 10th exchanged places with the 'Holy Boys', the Ashton Territorials. The Oldhamers now took up residence in Abassia barracks. Although very crowded, the barracks offered the luxury of beds for NCOs and the prospect of an improved diet for the men. Food, or the absence of it, had remained a burning issue. On 5 November the first change in the dinner menu since the battalion's arrival was recorded – roast instead of boiled meat, and a ration of potatoes. Marmalade made an occasional appearance at breakfast and on 11 November the troops were astonished, but delighted, to receive portions of currant pudding.

The improvement was short lived for by 2 December it was back to no pudding, jam, boiled beef and an overall reduction in the ration. Three weeks of bread and jam, broken only by three days of dry bread and cheese and two of dry bread and salmon for tea, caused the optimists amongst them to hope that the good food was being conserved to provide them with a memorable Christmas feast. In that respect the optimism was reasonably well placed. Breakfast at 7.30am consisted of salmon, bread and butter (an almost forgotten commodity), and dinner of turkey, potatoes, vegetables and currant pudding. Under the watchful eyes of Sergeant Trevitt, the cooks toiled for hours over sizzling roasting pans and boiling dixies.

In regular army tradition, officers and NCOs acted as orderlies to their men and were later apparently carried out shoulder high by the cheering troops. The day, however, was not yet complete.

Tea at 6.30pm of ham, chicken, an apple, orange and nuts was followed by a performance from the band and a general sing-song. It was as well that the men enjoyed themselves because for many of them it was to be their last Christmas.

Food apart, the men suffered from a number of ills about which the army could do little. The troops were again asked to volunteer for the hazard of army inoculation, an experience according to Charles Kershaw of Royton that was 'not half cruel and I have another dose to go through yet that is worse than the first one'. The majority did undergo the agony because it usually meant a day off to recover and unpleasant duties for those who declined. However the abiding problems were those caused by the conditions in which the men lived and worked. Poor food caused plagues of boils and 'gyppie tummy', the heat brought rashes, the burning sand blisters and sores to the feet. Within days of camping at Heliopolis the men were covered in lice, in the evenings mosquitoes bit lumps from their faces and the deadly threat of scorpions was ever present. When the men tried to eat, either myriads of flies descended upon the food or hawks, reminiscent of those which so tormented King Phineus, swooped down to snatch the rations from their mess tins. Officers regularly received hampers from home and, by contributing about 35 shillings per week to a mess fund, a variety of food was bought locally and cooked in what one officer described as a 'fairly decent manner'.

The men looked forward to the post from home as it brought not only news of friends and family but also parcels to supplement their meagre rations. On occasions the news could be unwelcome. For example, in October Joseph Hyde learnt that his six-month old daughter had died from whooping cough. Delight upon receiving a parcel soon turned to disgust when it was discovered that recipients had to pay a duty before taking possession of its contents. Depending upon what the parcel contained, this tax would often amount to over two shillings; the sum being deducted from a normal weekly wage of seven shillings. Pay was another constant cause of complaint. A married man had sixpence of his daily shilling stopped as separation allowance and by the time threepence-halfpenny and one and a half pence had been docked for laundry and National Insurance respectively, the man drew only three shillings and one penny weekly. A soldier with two years' service in the Territorial Force could claim another daily threepence as proficiency pay, but service in the Volunteers did not count towards this little extra. The troops were delighted in April to learn that pressure inside Parliament had finally persuaded the authorities to remove the duty on comforts sent from home.

Although the move to Abassia barracks did not presage a life of luxury (even the usually urbane Wynne in a letter to his employers requested that they should not 'imagine we are living in a happy and contented land and have no anxieties') conditions did improve sufficiently for spirits to rise.

There was also the stimulus of potential action against an enemy who could now be identified. The belief that they were only in the desert to harden up before being posted to France had persisted, but in October platoons had gone off into the desert to mount a guard on the wireless station at Abu Babul; in early November the Colonel told the men that they should expect to be fighting the Turks 'within two weeks'.

The regular demonstrations of force in Cairo and the arrest of resident Germans and Turks heightened the suspicion that Suez might become a Turkish objective. This belief was reinforced in early November when Captain Leach and his machine-gun section of 21 Other Ranks were sent to Ismailia for detachment to Indian brigades guarding the canal. Little was heard of the party for some time, but a reserve machine-gun section was formed and began training under Lieutenant Stott. The arrival of more colonial troops, a large guard mounted on the magazine inside the Citadel and on batches of Turkish prisoners of war, the departure of 16 Other Ranks and 17 pack animals under the command of an NCO, to join the Yeomanry on the canal, all pointed to significant developments elsewhere. The return of the machine-gun section and the transport with stories of how they had helped drive off a Turkish attack on Suez, confirmed the belief that the battalion really was now at war.

March was a month of final shaking down and of increasing security against a possible Egyptian rising. Five instructors of the South Wales Borderers who had been with the battalion since Bury returned home, leaving only two, Sergeants Hart and Anlezark (2/Manchester), to complete the training. At a 'smoker' held the night before the Borderers left, Dr Baird, the MO, was rather surprised to see Colour-Sergeant Steward perform a dance involving some rather dainty footwork. For two months Steward had been convincing Baird that his 'sprained ankles' prevented him from doing anything but light duties. A further nine men were invalided home shortly after and Thomas Lally of Renshaw Street became the battalion's third fatality when he died of smallpox. The punishing drills, working and marching over ten hours and eighteen miles a day with no water bottles, continued. Anyone seen attempting to buy an orange from a hawker was liable to be confined to barracks by an officer who was permitted to march with his water bottle filled.

The authorities had been keeping a watchful eye on the progress of the division during the most demanding period of training and on 28 March it marched past General Sir Ian Hamilton in Cairo. Hamilton was making preparations for the Gallipoli landing and wanted to know the calibre of the troops who might fall under his command. Having inspected some ten divisions in the UK before his departure, he remarked that what he called the 'advantage' enjoyed by the Lancastrians of 'fine weather and the absence of billeting' had made them into the best of the divisions he had seen. It was, he went on, 'in no respect below that of any regular division, and declared that it was 'ready to take its place in the first line whenever and wherever it is called upon'. Hamilton had relished commanding a contingent of Mancunians at Ladysmith and ever after took a personal interest in the regiment. He concluded his inspection by announcing that the 'great city is being finely represented in the East'.

Praise such as this usually meant a move. Thousands of the Australians and New Zealanders were preparing to leave for an 'unknown destination' and in mid-April the battalion was told it would relieve Indian sepoys at Kantara. Troops were again vaccinated and one officer and 100 Other Ranks were selected to remain at the base when the battalion moved. None of the officers wanted the job, but eventually Second Lieutenant Joseph Kirk was detailed to command this group of early would-be draftees. The East Lancashire Brigade, to which the 10th belonged, was the first of the division's three brigades to be warned to move at short notice. This was considered to be something of an honour and caused the Oldhamers' spirits to be considerably bucked. The order coincided with the departure of another 31 originals who were considered unfit for further overseas duty; three officers and a draft arrived to replace them from the battalion's second line unit. Major Hardman had already returned to England for family reasons, and Lieutenant Chisholm Taylor, who was still recovering from illness, remained absent from the battalion. Two former privates of the 6th Manchester, the Kirk brothers from Heaton Moor, were commissioned into the 10th and became supernumerary. As Territorial battalions regularly appointed suitable men from other battalions who had a connection with the unit or were recommended by their own colonel, it is probable that the 10th asked for the brothers to be commissioned. There was a great feeling of pride within such units which, unlike New Army battalions, had a tradition to maintain. At least one battalion of the 42nd Division is known to have commissioned British residents of Egypt. In a letter to his father, Hardman insisted that if necessary the 10th would do the same for 'we will not have just anyone from the reserve battalion'. The draft which accompanied the new officers was not considered to be of an adequate standard. It was consequently drilled on the square for a period longer than would normally have been anticipated. This embarrassment caused Hardman to comment that he 'despaired of how the reserve battalion has been spending its time'.

On arrival at Kantara the battalion was divided into detachments and dispersed to guard posts stretching along 27 miles of the east bank of the canal. Lieutenant Griffith and 99 Other Ranks manned an armoured train which periodically puffed its majestic way up and down the line running roughly parallel to the waterway.

For the majority of the men, life was more mundane, albeit demanding. Hardman described the existence as, 'Just like a gramophone record. When you get to the end, you move the needle to commence all over again'.

With such a huge battalion front to protect, even the band sergeant and drummers were called upon to mount guard. Some men were on duty for five successive nervous nights. The desert gave off strange sounds and created seemingly moving, ghostly shadows. For inexperienced troops the hours of darkness could be very trying and the sight of ships passing through the canal, perhaps heading for England, caused pangs of homesickness. Others were more concerned about the increasing number of flies and mosquitoes. One spark of excitement enlivened what was an otherwise routine fortnight when Captain Wilde's detachment at Ballah saw some Turks moving across its front. Fighting was reported at Ismailia and the 10th reinforced their pickets in case it spread. The guards were warned that parties of Indians had been cut off from their units somewhere out in the desert and might try to regain their lines by coming in at night. Whether the Egyptian interpreter anticipated that things were about to happen and feared the worst is unclear, but the man left the battalion on a three-day pass to Cairo and was never seen again.

On Sunday 2 May, Colonel Rye received orders that the East Lancashire Division was shortly to proceed to the Dardanelles. Impressed by its fitness, General Hamilton had apparently requested that the division be sent to reinforce those already on the Gallipoli Peninsula. Tents were struck and the following morning the entire battalion moved back to the African side of the canal and waited at Kantara station until trains arrived to transport it to Port Said. An extremely unpleasant night was spent bivvying on ground recently vacated by a large convoy of camels. To exacerbate their discomfort still further, the men were ordered to exchange their cotton drill for an issue of serge service dress. This immediately created speculation that their destination was not the Dardanelles but France. Amidst all the rumours and counter rumours, next morning men were allowed to wander into town. Swallow, his cousin and brother-in-law joined the throng of Lancastrians in search of refreshment. The friends teamed up with a group of convivial French *matelots* and were treated to champagne and snacks. On 5 May the whole battalion laboured at the docks from six in the morning to six in the evening and then fell in ready to embark. Each man carried full equipment, a blanket, oil sheet, emergency rations and 100 rounds of Small Arms Ammunition. While the transport section and A and B Companies embarked upon the HAVERFORD, C and D went aboard the ANSONIA. At about 1.30am on 6 May the two slipped their warps and carried the 31 officers and 850 men of the Oldham Territorials to where the war was more than eerie noises and imaginary shadows.

GALLIPOLI: THE EARLY MONTHS

IT IS NOT THE PLACE HERE to rehearse again the conception and commencement of the Gallipoli campaign. Many books have adequately covered the scheme and its mistakes of the opening weeks; the lost opportunities, the bungling in logistics and the heroism of the men of the 29th and the Royal Naval Divisions have often been recounted. Enough to say that if the plan to silence the Turkish shore batteries had worked and if the strategically essential heights of Achi Baba had been reinforced and held, Constantinople might have fallen and a blow been dealt to the Central Powers. The failure to gain the high ground and to advance inland anywhere more than a few hundred yards from the coast condemned the Allied troops to fighting with their backs to the sea and against an enemy who enjoyed the benefits of observation.

Several contemporary critics of the campaign were already denouncing its continuation. They argued that to divert more troops from the Western Front to what amounted to merely reinforcing failure was achieving nothing save the unnecessary prolongation of the war. Sufficient voices in authority however believed that with additional troops the opportunity to knock Turkey from the war remained a feasible alternative to the deadlock on the Western Front.

The Oldhamers of course knew little or nothing of the struggles being fought along the corridors of power a thousand miles away in Whitehall. What they did know was that things had not gone according to plan but, in their enthusiasm and self-confidence, decided that their arrival would soon put the campaign back on course. As Territorials they had also a reputation to maintain; Terriers had been fighting in France since October and the deeds of the London Scottish on Messines Ridge had become watch-words for pluck and doggedness. While the 10th made its way across the Aegean, bespectacled and well spoken former office clerks in the City were fighting at Ypres alongside what was left of the regular army, surprising all, save themselves, by their courage, ability and endurance. Initially little had been expected of the Territorials; now the East Lancashire Division had something to live up to.

The 10th Manchester was no different from any other of the infantry battalions in what was now known officially as the 42nd (East Lancashire) Division. Its men were considered fit and their skills adequate. Although not quite up to establishment, all of the men had been in the army for at least eight months, the greater part of which had been spent training with full equipment. The New Army divisions at home could only wonder in amazement at the benefits and luxuries enjoyed by the Territorials.

A smattering of the men, perhaps 30 Other Ranks and two officers, were veterans of the South African War. The majority of the battalion had been pre-war Territorials for at least two years, with as many as 60% having been in longer; furthermore, several of those who had only joined the Territorial Force in August were former Volunteers. Their officers were gentlemen of the higher echelon of Oldham society or the sons of such men. Imbued with a sense of duty and patriotism, mixed with a desire to experience adventure and danger, they were educated and fought for the ideals which their class cherished. It was expected that when the time came their inexperience in battle would be countered by a determination to do what was right and by a loyalty to their battalion which would supersede any thoughts of self-interest. The classicists and romantics amongst them could even picture themselves following in the wakes of the black ships of mighty Agamemnon, red-haired Menelaus and wise old Nestor. 'Golden Troy', the object of the ancients' ambitions, was but a stone's throw away across the shimmering Hellespont.

Had they been able to read the current editions of Oldham's newspapers, the Territorials might have believed the worst was already behind them. Bold headlines such as 'Turks routed', 'Turks silenced' and 'Important heights gained' boasted of early and almost complete success. On board the ANSONIA the men were hearing something nearer the truth. The ship carried return-ing wounded of the King's Own Scottish Borderers who gave the listening Oldhamers harrowing tales of how the Dublins and the Lancashire Fusiliers had been swept away by Turkish machine-gun fire as they waded ashore; they told of how the survivors were held up by submerged fields of barbed wire, of how the Turks could spot almost every movement made behind the Allied lines and of how successive waves of British troops were annihilated by Turkish fire. The men knew too that they had never practised the tricky art of disembarkation into lighters wearing full kit and while under fire. A realisation then began to sink in that they were fast approaching what was described by the King's Own Scottish Borderers as a veritable hell hole.

Life on board ship was fairly relaxed. With lights extinguished and in choppy seas the convoy wove its way between the Aegean islands. Swallow, whose priority once again seemed to be the quality of the food, thought the rations were 'rotten, everything stale ... the eggs very small and mostly bad'. Sergeant Gorbutt was a little more content than Swallow, noting in his diary that it was the first occasion since leaving Oldham that he had sheets on a bed. There was the odd company parade, constant checking and cleaning of kit, the encouraging exhortation to write their wills and endless thoughts of what was to come:

I am neither happy nor sad ... my feeling is something like that of a little boy who is about to visit the dentist and wondering what it is going to be like. To look at us you would think we were the happiest fellows alive, but somehow our mirth is very shallow for we all seem to have a tendency to laugh a great deal at the most trivial things. And now and then one might see fellows turning things over in the mind and sat quietly considering things ... Your photos have always been company and a comfort to me, but somehow I don't like to look at them now, they make me feel so sad, for they bring back memories of happier days gone past. I have them in my wallet next to my heart, and there I shall carry them until ... my task is done. (Hardman)

Once Lemnos, which was used as the Navy's principal advanced base, had fallen astern, the men could hear the distant thunder of gunfire. Lieutenant Bleakley noted that 'long before land was sighted, the roar of the guns was heard and the smell of the dead wafted out to us on the breeze as a welcome to the inferno ... a heavy pall of battle dust and smoke hung over the land like a black mantle'. The sight of so many warships firing their big guns at targets so apparently close was heartening to the men. They were impressed by the number, the noise and the ferocity of the exploding shells. An airship hung as a silent sentinel above the belching ships, and every now and then a friendly plane would swoop down amongst the flotilla of vessels to bring a cheer and a wave from the watching troops. As the ship hove to, Arthur Kirkbride marvelled at the panorama:

'We had a good view of Cape Helles and it was an awe-inspiring sight. We could see the prominence of Achi Baba and hear the crackle of small-arms fire and see the shrapnel bursting ... boat loads of wounded were rowing from one ship to another (they were) trying to find somewhere to put them. It gave one queer sensations, one minute the blood rushing through one's veins, what a glorious thing to be amongst it, the next minute cold shivers down your back wishing you were well out of it.'

At 6.30am on 9 May, C and D Companies began to disembark from the ANSONIA. No one seemed to know the whereabouts of the HAVERFORD and the other two companies but, with less difficulty than they had imagined, the platoons clambered down the scrambling nets and into the lighters commanded by young midshipmen. The occasional Turkish shell splashed in the sea around them, but all reached land without loss. Once ashore on W beach they entrenched with the evidence of recent carnage all around them. Tousled and mangled bodies were littered across the beach; others, caressed by a stained sea, floated on the gentle swell. The Oldhamers were directed to a stretch of cliff face and scrub some yards inland and told to dig. Shells fell more frequently and although none of the 10th was hit, a constant stream of wounded hurrying, shuffling or being carried past the sweating Territorials was abundant testimony to their inherent danger. At 6.30pm on 11 May, amidst rumours that the other half of the battalion had been torpedoed and drowned, C and D Companies, led by Major Bamford, marched up to the reserve trenches.

Contrary to rumours that she had been sunk, the HAVERFORD arrived safely on 13 May and began to disembark her troops. Unfortunately it proved impossible to unload the transport section. Attempts to swing the animals over the side were abandoned, so the Transport Officer, about 25 men and their assorted beasts were ordered back to Egypt. Soon after the troops landed, Private Beaumont, Major Bamford's servant, was wounded in the foot and Private Elson Warrener of Ward Street became the battalion's first man killed by enemy action. In a cheery recounting of how the other two companies finally gained dry land, Captain Sutcliffe assured his readers that 'although the Turks dropped a number of shells about us ... we never troubled about them ... For a time our chaps thought it was great fun'. 'Great fun' was far from the description several of Sutcliffe's colleagues might have used. Gorbutt became increasingly alarmed at the 'guns playing their devil's inferno all night long'; Swallow was suffering from lack of sleep, lack of water and the trauma of seeing men of a neighbouring unit dismembered by a shell. Amid the shellfire the entire division assembled on an area of ground big enough to house roughly half a battalion and awaited orders. Gorbutt came to the restrained but obvious conclusion that 'we shall lose very heavily', Swallow that 'we shall be murdered here'. Hardman looked on the bright side and thought 'if I live through this hell of flame and shell, I shall have some wonderful stories to tell'.

The first suggestion that the Oldham battalion was no longer in Egypt came to the town as a whole when a letter from Wynne dated 1 May was published in the *Standard* 17 days later. In upbeat vein, Wynne wrote that, 'I cannot give you particulars but you will probably guess our destination ... We have had 7 months of strenuous work and the weaklings have been weeded out. We only want the opportunity to prove that the Oldham lads are up to the Lancashire sample'. This was followed by a letter from a Royton man to his mother in which he cryptically announced that although she must 'guess where we are ... we are going to drive the Turks out of Europe' and a third from another Royton soldier who told his wife that 'it is rather dangerous where I am writing this ...letter we are not in Egypt or France'. By the end of May the Oldham papers had printed letters written by Rochdale men of the 42nd Division and on 2 June announced that Oldham's first soldier to be wounded in the Dardanelles was Lance Corporal Dennis Thorpe serving with the 6/Lancashire Fusiliers. Now that the secret was out and official communiqués were filtering through, printed correspondence became more regular. By June 1915 Oldham was used to hearing of the death of its sons.

Many regular soldiers and reservists had died since August of the previous year but they had belonged to a wide variety of regiments and corps. Now, as word began to get home that the town's own battalion was in an active theatre of war, a shudder of collective fear startled the town. The first reports were confusing: 'The Oldham Territorials have been in action and have suffered in the way of casualties ... Lieutenant Clegg of Grotton has been killed in action'. This was followed a day later by a report which suggested that it was not James Clegg, but his cousin James Hamer Clegg. If the authorities could not correctly report the death of an officer, what hope for the accurate reporting of other rank casualties?

Snippets of information continued to arrive but often only added to the confusion and anxiety. A sapper in the Divisional Royal Engineers wrote that he had seen a shell burst among a platoon of the Oldham Territorials killing 'five or eight of the brave fellows'. On 8 June Private Hunt's cheerful letter of 14 May reported 'we have seen some decent fighting', but apart from stating that the writer himself was now happily ensconced in a hospital bed, it gave no indication of casualties. The papers latched on to a contemporary rumour that a draft of over 100 of the 2/10th was about to be sent to reinforce the first line battalion which had suffered 'a substantial leakage in the ranks'.

Recognition that news of their activities would take time to reach Oldham was of fairly minor significance to the men themselves. Of more immediate importance was to dig some cover and stay alive. On the whole it was probably safer in the front line than when, in theory, out on rest. 'Rest' meant working and carrying parties and living in areas neatly registered by the Turkish guns. At least in the front trenches, Turkish snipers not withstanding, there was a degree of cover. Periodic torrential rainstorms created floods which swept away parapets, equipment, drowned mules and left men knee deep in water. Stands to, the energies and skill of the concealed snipers, the near continuous scream of high explosive shells and the constant buzzing of bullets all added to the strain on the novice soldiers. Three terrifying days in the front trenches did nothing to soothe the nerves of C Company.

We were all stood to when word came down the line to open rapid fire, the Turks were attacking. It was a pitch black night so we started blazing away blindly for all we were worth. We had the old pattern long Lee-Enfield rifle, no guard for your hand like the short Lee-Enfield, and the barrels soon got red-hot.

Well, what with powder and smoke and cursing and swearing when someone burnt their hand on their rifle and someone else got their rifle jammed and some yelling for more ammunition, it was merry hell for about half-an-hour. When the order was passed down to cease fire we had each fired off between 260 to 300 rounds and we decided the Turks would be piled up so when day broke we peeped cautiously over the top ... we couldn't see a single Turk. (Arthur Kirkbride)

Whit Sunday, 23 May, dawned bright and clear. Thoughts naturally turned to home, to families and to the parades of banners and bands which would celebrate the holiday among the streets of Oldham. Saturday had been a lively day. With the expectation of a Turkish attack, RSM Chittenden and the HQ staff had run the perilous gauntlet of shell and rifle fire to take up boxes of SAA to the front trenches. The attack did not materialise, and they hoped that Sunday might bring a sabbatical respite. This turned out to be wishful thinking for although the day passed reasonably quietly, orders arrived for a hazardous night-time operation. A small working party was detailed to crawl 60 yards out into No Man's Land and begin digging a new trench. With the night lit brilliantly by a full moon, the men doubted if they would return. Alf Fozzard, a single 18-year-old, volunteered to take the place of a married comrade and crawled over the parapet. Within minutes of the party's departure, the Turks spotted it and opened fire. Lieutenant Bleakley immediately ordered his 12 men to retire, but Fozzard was 'riddled' with bullets. His body and that of John Brown, one of the few non-Oldhamers in the battalion, was recovered later.

Monday was spent in cowering from Turkish shells and in attempting to repair the damage caused by another cloud-burst. Instructions arrived ordering digging parties covered by sentries again to go out at night and advance the line. Fortunately it was a cloudy night, but having witnessed the disaster of the previous attempt, optimism was not high. At the end of the night's work William Swallow, who had made a return trip into No Man's Land to collect his abandoned rifle, recorded his relief:

My God, I am still alive and not hit, but what a night we have had ... When we got back I was fool enough to go over the top

again to look for my rifle which I had left somewhere in the
excitement. It was awful, the bullets were dropping into the
ground all around me and it was marvellous how they missed
me. They were throwing star shells up and the machine guns
were rattling away. I kept crawling for a few yards and then fell
flat hugging the ground and expecting every minute to be hit
... I found my entrenching tool but my rifle was not there. I
was out in the open for about fifteen minutes but got back alright
... I would not do it again for all the rifles in the British army.

When dawn came it was realised that the new trench could be enfiladed by Turks on the opposite side of a gully. The Turks too soon appreciated the advantage and began picking off the Oldhamers. It was here that Lieutenant Jim Clegg was sniped and killed. It is perhaps not surprising that the Oldham papers were confused as to which of the cousins had been hit, but to the men of his platoon, Clegg's death came as a numbing shock. It was common for papers and men to describe their fallen officers as 'the best of men' and other such soothing platitudes, but the genuine respect in which 'Gentleman Jim' was held is clear from several reminiscences. Clegg did not die immediately but later succumbed to his wounds. He was buried 'beneath a lovely tree' with representatives of his platoon in attendance. While stretcher bearers carried Clegg to the aid post, those still alive in the trench had more pressing needs to concern them. It began to rain heavily and a flash flood swept away what little cover the men had managed to throw up as a parapet. One platoon was in an isolated trench which soon filled to overflowing. Its occupants tried making a dash for it across the top but several were hit in the process. Ernest Smalley was bowled over as he made the attempt and lay screaming for help. An officer of the 9/Manchester dashed from his trench to help Smalley, but was hit three times before reaching him. The officer managed to roll into another of the 10th's trenches and was carried away across the open by two stretcher bearers. Smalley's cries soon ceased and the men in the newly dug trench waited for the cloak of darkness to offer some release from their torment:

We were up to our knees in water all day until it got dark, and
then we were relieved by the 6/Manchesters. When we were

being relieved we had to run across the open to the old firing line, and as one of us went across, one of the 6/Manchesters ran across to take our place. We were being fired at all the time we were crossing. (Swallow)

Although relieved to be out of the front line, John Openshaw did not think the rest area was any better. On nearing scores of disfigured corpses and crowds of wounded awaiting evacuation, his first impression was that it was 'more of a slaughter house than a resting place'. Yet despite the unpleasantness of the preceding few days and the precariousness of their present position, Fred Hardman could still savour the intrinsic beauty of this ancient land. In a letter to his wife he wrote:

It is a lovely scene looking back from the trenches towards the point on the peninsula. The blue of the sky, the birds singing in the air, with the land still covered with red poppies. It makes one realise what a mockery war really is, and in the evening the scent of the wild thyme is very profuse and pleasant.

The short period since landing on the Peninsula had cost the battalion 14 killed or died of wounds and over 40 wounded. Clegg's death was followed soon afterwards by that of another young officer, Frank Griffiths. Griffiths was a former pupil of Hulme Grammar School and had served in the battalion for two years. Unlike Clegg, whose remains under the 'lovely tree' were not later identified, Griffiths has a known grave. Four other officers had also gone: Captain George Stott was in hospital with fever, Second Lieutenants Alfred Butterworth and Procktor Scott, the brother of James who was also a subaltern with the battalion, were slightly wounded, and another officer was recovering from being accidentally shot. The losses were not particularly excessive but for a battalion which had been raised together and spent eight months building *esprit* under arduous training and conditions, they were significant. The authorities had feared that Territorials, who were not considered to be as hardened and perhaps callous as regulars, would not cope well with the loss of friends, brothers and comrades. In France these fears had been proven unjustified and they were to be equally unjustified with regard to the Territorials of the 42nd Division. What was more of a threat to battalion morale was the news that the 10th was to be divided up between two regular battalions of 88 Brigade. Many Territorials who had long been suspicious of the army's loyalty to the TF feared that the battalion might be broken up in order to provide the regulars with a reservoir of trained men.

As the sceptics were shortly to discover, their suspicions proved only partially unfounded. The two regular battalions, the 2/Royal Fusiliers and 2/Hampshire, had suffered appalling losses since landing and were having men of the 4th and 5th East Lancashire and 10/Manchester temporarily attached to swell their number preparatory to making another frontal assault. Their objective was the lines of trenches lying in front of the village of Krithia. Assisted by an intense bombardment, the troops were to storm the Turkish lines, consolidate and then beat off the anticipated counter-attacks.

The attack was launched on 4 June but progress was uneven and slow. The Lancastrians swept across No Man's Land and into the enemy trenches but, during ferocious fighting throughout the following two days, the lines were forced back almost to where the assault had first begun. Losses among all the division's battalions were severe. As the 10th was attached to the 29th Division, its part in the battle received only scant mention in the 42nd Division's history.

The *Official History* also gives only the briefest resumé of the part played by the battalion. To the participants their role was worth more than a mere few sentences in an official communiqué which followed some time later. The battalion had of course already suffered fatalities and other casualties but this was the first occasion when it had made a frontal assault against heavily entrenched and defended positions. It was also the event which was to become the deepest scar on the town's communal memory. Long after other engagements had dimmed in its collective memory, Oldham remembered the fallen of Krithia.

Reports of the battle were slow in arriving. For some time after the first reports of the engagement began to drift in, the local press continued to print letters written some weeks earlier. Not surprisingly there was much confusion in the minds of the town's increasingly anxious populace. Nearly three weeks after the attack on Krithia it was still being informed of the deaths of men killed in May. There were only occasional references in the published letters that a recent and ferocious battle had caused very severe losses. Gradually a broader picture began to emerge and on 21 June the first reasonably authoritative report was printed in the *Chronicle*. One day earlier the paper had printed 29 photos of men who, it thought, had been killed in early June and on 1 July it carried the sombre headline 'Death toll of 1/10th lengthening'. By that time staff at the drill hall were posting lists of wounded men and of those reported killed or died of wounds. These lists were already ominously long and worse was to follow as more precise news filtered through to individual families. It became clear that something terrible had happened to the battalion. However, because the army did not issue collective lists of those who had been killed, the overall scale of the slaughter could only be guessed and surmised from the reports sent home by those who had survived. It would be some months before the real cost of the battle became apparent to the town as a whole.

Attempts to prepare the town for any confirmed bad news which might follow the growing number of unofficial reports were made in the local press soon after the middle of June. An *Oldham Standard* editorial warned that trench warfare was 'very sanguinary ... no one must for a moment get the impression that casualties will be otherwise than severe ... The task of forcing the Dardanelles is full of promise, but it can only be accomplished by making the greatest sacrifices'.

Many soldiers' letters had painted a similarly bloody scene of life on the Peninsula but they generally also tried to convey the impression that the correspondents were enjoying themselves and thinking little of the dangers. Letters such as these typically contain a combination of realism and reassurance to their recipients:

> *Our life at present chiefly consists of diving into the earth ... People who sit in chairs and read of it can comprehend even only an infinitesimal part of the horror ... it is hell ... Your life is never your own from one minute to another and yet through it all you are continually laughing ... (my) beard is an inch long and my face is like that of a nigger.* (Bradbury)

Similarly, 'it is really humorous to see them strolling about in a perfectly matter-of-fact fashion, with the bullets singing around their ears and shrapnel bursting overhead. I can assure you the real tussle of war is grim and gruesome'. An unknown Oldham officer reported that 'my wishes have now been gratified: I have been shelled with lyddite, shrapnel, had bombs dropped on us from aeroplanes and have been shot at by Maxims'.

While not shying away from the dreadful losses, letters referring to the attack on Krithia are generally written in a lighthearted, stiff upper lip tone. Most of them were sent by wounded men who recorded their lucky escape and the bravery of their comrades. The wounded Wilf Dunkerley wrote:

> *The roaring and the bursting of the shells was simply deafening … Despite the terrible shelling our artillery had given the Turks they were ready for us as soon as we got out of our trench and they opened a terrible rifle and machine gun fire and all the time their artillery was sending shrapnel over to us … Gradually they turned and ran'.*

James Taylor, who like Dunkerley had been evacuated to Malta, wrote that in the bayonet charge 'all human feeling was lost —the motto was 'spare no man' '. Captain Sutcliffe described the charge across No Man's Land as:

> *… a wonderful affair … all the time Turkish machine guns were knocking us about, but when we got within a reasonable distance, the Turks would not stand but turned and ran as fast as they possibly could. They did not give us the opportunity to have a hand to hand engagement with them.*

Wynne recalled that it was the first time the battalion had seen a 'pukka bombardment … the sight was truly appalling'. The troops went over 'with wonderful dash' and stormed into the enemy's fourth line. One officer called it a 'dickens of a charge', claiming the men 'went over like rabbits'. Private T. Smith called the attack a 'glorious victory' and claimed that the Allied troops captured 3,000 Turks. With the Oldhamers getting into the Turkish third line and 'taking lots of prisoners and Maxims', John Openshaw also thought 'the charge was a great success'. Sergeant Gorbutt noted that as he moved up to the advance he saw 'a lot of men crouching in trenches and the officers could not get them out. I thought this will not do at all. So I shouted, 'Come on lads, we'll show them the road'. I went over the top and the 10th lads followed and we shamed the others into it'. Fred Lawton remembered wounded and dead all over the place: 'We had to slide over them ... The charge was a treat ... the Turks ran like hell ... but it was no use, they had to surrender to us'.

An anonymous letter from one officer (almost certainly Captain Booth) also tells of hauling men out of the front line trenches. In a less than modest account, this officer, who commanded one of the two companies attached to the Royal Fusiliers, claimed that he and another captain pulled out about 50 men from the trenches and then led the charge. They swept into the enemy lines but were soon cut off and isolated. A colonel of another regiment crawled along the trench and was told by Booth that 'we could stick it, until help arrived. And we stuck it'. The following day the Royal Fusiliers' commanding officer was killed and the Turks forced the Oldhamers and Fusiliers from their captured positions:

I rallied the men and retook the trench after five hours' fighting. Next day I shot a Turk with my revolver ... I had to stand up and advance a good way under the rifle, machine gun and shell fire ... I stood up on top of the trench for nearly half an hour before getting back in ... When I stood up it was a real good mix up, with Turks only five yards away.

In the face of ferocious Turkish bombing attacks, the isolated men were forced to retreat to their original lines. It was the same story to the left where Captain L. C. Wilde took command of the Hampshires when their commanding officer was killed. The two shattered regular battalions with their Territorial detachments were compelled to give ground, retiring to their original positions.

In view of the leadership shown during those three dramatic days, another officer wrote home requesting the town give 'the fullest credence to anything (it) might hear of Captain Booth ... a hero and a born leader of men ... when he took command of a battalion of regulars, they said, "We'd follow him to hell"'. Second Lieutenant Bleakley thought he had already registered in that unwelcome place: 'The blazing gorse, the groans of the wounded, the artillery and rifle fire, the bombs and the weird cheers of our troops on the right as they made assault after assault

... made the place a veritable hell on earth'. Even an official report admitted that there were so many enemy machine guns that if a tennis ball was thrown up it would have been 'riddled with bullets'. Given this strength of opposition, 'any advance ... no matter how small, may be considered a meritorious performance'. This was in fact official confirmation of the attack's failure; but the need to maintain morale on the home front necessitated a more gentle and qualified acceptance of repulse.

A reporter from the *Oldham Standard* interviewed Captain Sutcliffe when the wounded officer returned home. Sutcliffe announced: 'Not an Oldham man stood back when the order to do their duty was given. They have proved themselves a credit to the town ... by their gallant behaviour'. An editorial capitalised upon the pride so evident in Sutcliffe's account:

> *We have no hesitation in saying there is no man, woman or child in the town who will not read it with feelings of pride and jubilation. It is a thrilling account of bravery displayed by a most efficient and highly trained body of men ... the fierce charges against almost unassailable Turkish positions make up an experience of which the men will be forever grateful. The narrative will go far to soothe the sorrow of the Oldham homes which have suffered bereavement.*

The essay appeared before the battalion's casualty list grew to an alarming length. The paper was doing its patriotic duty and accepting that however scant the official news might be, it was surely more reliable and accurate than anything emanating from either Constantinople or Berlin.

Whatever the rights or wrongs of the contemporary relationship between the army and reporters, the paper was probably going a little too far when it claimed that those who took part and survived would be 'forever grateful' for the experience. As it was the battalion's first real attack it was certainly a new and very different 'experience'; the tragedy was that such a large proportion of those who took part would not have the opportunity to reflect upon its moral value.

Although they might provide cheery reports of the attack for home consumption, it is clear that the men had known of the enormity of the task before them. The heights of Achi Baba, a heavily fortified hill which gave observation over the Allied lines and guarded the way to Constantinople, brooded to their front. Three days before the attack William Swallow had noted: 'Our guns have pounded away for hours ... when they finish ... the Turks start shelling us as if we had done them no harm at all. We shall lose a great deal of men before we take it, if we ever do take it, of which I am very doubtful'.

Similarly, while Wynne wrote home that it was 'a great honour' for the Territorials to go over side by side with the regulars, Hardman noted in his diary that it was 'an honour which nobody seems very keen about, seeing that we are all so fagged out with constant digging'. He was also unconvinced about their preparedness: 'My batman has a bag of bombs just issued to us ... Nobody knows anything about them or how to use them'. A week after the attack Hardman put on a brave face in a letter to his wife and claimed that the famous charge of the London Scottish on Messines Ridge was 'nothing to compare with ours'. He soothed his wife's anxiety by recalling: 'I was perfectly sane and cool throughout it all and I had the vision of you and my baby constantly before my eyes'.

Hardman concealed little of the truth in the privacy of his own diary. His account of 4-6 June gives a more gruesome account of the traumatic events than the one sent to Kitty :

> *As our first companies endeavoured to climb out of the trenches, the parapet was swept by withering machine gun and shrapnel fire ... back rolled the men of the first two companies, dead and dying on top of we waiting men of Z Company. In five minutes the trench was simply jammed with the maimed and dying ... Major Brandreth (2nd Royal Fusiliers) came along brandishing his revolver and ordered me and my men forward at once. The task seemed a hopeless one ... I went forward at a steady trot and, taking a glance either side of me, found that I was crossing No Man's Land alone. Many of the men who had tried to get over with me had gone down and I stood and waited as all around me in the undergrowth and brushwood seemed to be dead and dying men.*

Hardman managed to collect about a dozen men and together they battered their way with rifle butts through the uncut wire and into the Turkish trenches. Four of the 16 of Corporal George

Green's section managed to join Hardman but by the time night fell only some 60 men of the 188 of D Company remained in the Turkish lines. The counter-attacks came early next morning. Hordes of Turks throwing showers of grenades forced Hardman, Captain Owen and their diminishing number of men back into another trench. For two scorching days and with only the water they could scrounge from the bottles of the dead, the dwindling group repulsed wave after wave of ferocious Turkish attacks. For much of the time the enemy were only twenty yards away. Eventually some Inniskillings and Munsters fought their way through to the isolated Oldhamers but by that time Captain Owen was dead and Hardman commanded a mere three men. The tiny remnant began to crawl their way back across the old No Man's Land. Hardman, who had been deeply upset by the deaths of Owen, Ascroft and Emmott, noted:

> *It was a rather gruesome thing to creep and crawl ... to see lying with their faces to the ground, men, comrades, good friends, in various attitudes of agony and peace, men with whom we had trained and known so intimately through all the recent months. Now they had paid the price for 100 yards of land.*

Hardman and his three companions reached the comparative safety of their own lines and sought treatment for their relatively minor wounds. All along the line soldiers were being helped or were making their own way down to the beaches and the aid posts. The experience of Sergeant Gorbutt was probably typical. Gorbutt was hit while dressing the wounds of a comrade; using the dead as cover, he scrambled down to the beach with his arm 'looking like a bursted water tap' and found the battalion aid post. Put on to an ambulance cart and immediately immersed in a swarm of flies which took particular interest in his bloodstained tunic, he was bumped down to the beach. As he lay in agony on Y Beach a colleague informed him that his brother Fred had been killed in the attack. Four hours later, having been subjected to shell fire on and around the evacuation point, he was carried on board a ship. Having been hit in the foot, Lance Corporal Ernest Slater also spent an agonising two and a half hours lying in a trench packed with dead and wounded. An officer ordered all those who could to make their own way to the rear so Slater took the chance during a lull in the shelling and began a painful crawl and stumble of some 5000 yards.

Slater and many other wounded Oldhamers were evacuated to Malta. The initial relief of having escaped death is reflected in the letters sent from their hospital beds. Yet despite the obvious euphoria, many also contain a strong element of pathos. Amid the cool hygiene of a Malta hospital, away from the shrieking shells and unrelenting fear, there was time to reflect. Those who had experienced the maelstrom but escaped realised how fortunate they were. They had little idea of total casualties, aware only of those who had fallen near them and rumours on the battalion grapevine. James Taylor acknowledged that the battalion had 'suffered heavily', Tom Smith that 'we had paid dearly', James Mills believed 'all my pals have been killed or wounded', while Private Weston thought 'there is not many of our battalion left'. He added ruefully: 'Next time will finish the lot'. William Swallow, who had been evacuated to Alexandria just before the attack began, noted that a sergeant of his platoon told him 'our men went down like skittles ... we shall have no men left soon'.

Once the initial shock of the losses and the overall trauma began to wane, the men became more specific in their thoughts of individuals and of the part they as Territorials had played in the battle. Wilf Dunkerley noted that Charles Kershaw had had his leg amputated on a Malta-bound hospital ship while Jim Moores wrote home giving details of the wounds of other Royton men lying in hospital with him. Others, such as Weston (who recalled seeing Jack Lynn decapitated by a shell splinter) and Fred Lawton, thought that although the battle had caused such loss, the battalion did indeed have a lot for which it should be grateful. With obvious and justifiable pride, Weston wrote: 'I do not think they will call them Territorials after this. If the regulars had done as much as us in so short a time ... there would be nothing left of the Turks'. In similar vein Sergeant Barratt wrote: 'I think that we have shown that the much jeered at, so-called "Saturday afternoon soldiers" can fight ... I feel a proud man ... the charge was magnificent'. Swallow was apparently told by a regular of the Hampshires that the 'Terriers were splendid' and that 'if that was the way Terriers fought I never want to fight with the regulars again'.

This understandable pride at having cocked a snook at those who had for so long derided the Territorials was accompanied by a grim determination to get back to the battalion to finish the job. Lewis Mason admitted that he was 'sorry to hear that all my mates were killed' but that 'it can't be helped. Somebody has got to finish this dreadful war. I shall not be afraid to go back (and) I shall go with a willing heart because of my pals who have fallen'. Other men expressed a similar desire to get back at the Turks. John Smalley, a reservist retained at home in a training unit, requested a posting to the 10th so that he could avenge his brother's death. In contrast one man wrote to his former landlady in Chadderton: 'When our Captain asked us to sign for foreign service … he told us we should see life. Yes we have seen life!! I have seen more than I wanted since I came out here. Give me England. There's enough life for me'.

On the Peninsula itself, at least one of the surviving officers was clearly suffering from the effects of the attack. Not only distressed at the loss of so many of his men and particularly of two of his closest friends, Fred Hardman was also annoyed at the behaviour shown by some officers. He wrote to his wife that the local paper she had sent reported that one of the company commanders was suffering from 'shock'. Obviously furious at what he considered to be nothing short of a lie, he scrawled, 'perhaps it is as well to put it that way for the honour of the regiment, but personally I don't think any honour should be attached to him'. Hardman evidently considered that this and another officer had not held their positions during the Turkish counter-attacks. In a reference to his friend George Owen, who 'held on against awful odds and did not run away', Hardman confided to his wife 'it seems funny to make heroes of men that run away, but … keep it dark until after the war'. In another letter he expressed the hope that, 'George Owen's words will haunt him (ie the officer who had fled) forever'. At this distance it is impossible to discover what exactly had happened to make Hardman so bitter about two of his fellow officers but he was obviously a man in great mental anguish. Only 27 of his company of 180 men still remained with him, a group so small that when on parade he thought it seemed 'no bigger than a Salvation Army street corner meeting'. He was also depressed at the thought of having the battalion reinforced by what he called 'strange officers'. So few of his original friends were left that it made 'home seem farther away than ever'. His frequent thoughts of wife and child, neither of whom had he seen for ten months, combined with the shock of losing close comrades might have been enough to send Hardman into prolonged despair. When reflecting on what had happened on the shell-swept slope of Achi Baba, he used the only valve available to express his feelings.

What those words of Owen's were is unclear, but it is known that Hardman frequently received copies of the Oldham papers. An interview with the wounded Lieutenant Randal Wilde was carried in the *Oldham Chronicle* on 10 July. It was in his letter of 18 July that Hardman mentioned Owen's 'words' so it is probable it was to that interview he alluded. Wilde reported that during the Turkish counter-attack, Captain Owen had told him, 'for God's sake don't let the men retire'. That was the last time Wilde saw Owen alive.

Perhaps two officers did decide discretion was the better part of valour. The British troops were fighting in disconnected groups, short of ammunition and water and subject to intense Turkish assaults. In such circumstances it would be idealist to claim that some men would not break and make a dash for their own lines. Swallow heard that two Oldhamers had been imprisoned for five years because they had run away during an earlier attack. According to Swallow, when the section was ordered to retire, instead of seeking the safety of their old trench lines, these two men 'ran right the way back to base before they stopped'. This story was mentioned by Tom Hague in a letter to his wife. When he arrived at the battalion on a draft Hague was told that his friend HW 'has got four years for being a coward'.

Confusion in the town about what had happened to its battalion was exacerbated by printed reports which had clearly been overtaken by events. Despite the first real indication on 21 June that a major attack had been launched, three days later the *Oldham Standard* printed a letter from Colonel Rye in which the commanding officer declared that he was 'surprised that there have not been more casualties'. The letter was over four weeks old but appeared in the same edition as one from an Oldham soldier which said that his battalion had 'suffered heavily'. Two days later other letters appeared which also specifically referred to the Krithia attack. They were in juxtaposition to 17 names of wounded men and eight who had been killed or died of wounds.

All these men had died in the routine of trench warfare before the battle. However, late news must have arrived because in the same edition, another list of 98 wounded and nine dead was published. Anxious parents and loved ones scanned this long list with mixed feelings. There was still no hard official evidence to confirm that the battalion had been severely hit, but the length of the list and the recent report suggesting that a serious engagement had indeed taken place, increased anxieties. As families were becoming accustomed to the army's reluctance to supply too much information too quickly, many probably surmised that this was unlikely to be the final toll. The papers, too, realised worse news would follow and continued to print editorials designed to ease the pain when the inevitable arrived:

> For many months ... when training in Egypt, the public did not realise to the full what a crisis we are passing through, but now all is changed ... the Territorials, like other battalions have suffered terribly ... It will be gladsome news for Oldhamers when the report comes through of the fall of Constantinople but the day, we fear, is a long way off. The ground will have to be won yard by yard ... (the men) are still undaunted. A greater bravery and more enthusiasm it would be impossible to conceive.

The relatives of those 98 posted as wounded might have read this and thought how lucky they were. Astoundingly, with only three exceptions who were to die from their wounds, that list was remarkably accurate. Those men were indeed wounded rather than dead and lay in hospitals on Malta, Lemnos or in Alexandria. Another list of 36 reported wounded appeared some days later. Their relatives were not so fortunate as it transpired that 33 of those had actually been killed on 4 June. Some of the families had by then received the telegram announcing that their son or husband had been killed in action or was posted as missing. The contradiction between the reports about the fate of individuals caused false hopes and intense picketing at the drill hall. Anxious parents pressing for clarification of news were sometimes rewarded with surprising results. William Moss of Siddall Street, though twice reported dead, was eventually confirmed as wounded. More often though, the news brought dread and disappointment.

Regular lists posted at the drill hall and printed in the papers during the first weeks of July drove the impact of the battle deep into the psyche of Oldham's townsfolk. Although still far from any definitive figure, letters from the men declared that the full casualty lists would be 'an eye-opener' and 'a sorry day for Oldham'. The Council decided it had to take the lead in marking the increasingly sombre news. At a meeting on 7 July the Mayor addressed the assembled councillors and spoke of the 'grief and suffering' as well as the honour and glory recent events had caused. The meeting stood reverentially in remembrance for a few moments and this was followed by a suggestion from the Mayor that 'one day a suitable memorial might be erected to their noble memory'. The idea of a memorial gathered an initial momentum and was met with approval in the town. What shape or form it might take was discussed in only general terms, for, as the *Standard* decided, the 'time is not yet ripe'. Greater sacrifices had yet to be made.

To a town desperate for more concrete news of how devastating or otherwise the battle had been, the arrival home of Colonel Rye gave some hope of enlightenment. Rye's return aroused great interest among his commercial friends and the town as a whole. Although none had revealed the complete truth of the disaster, several wounded officers had already given their thoughts of the battle to the papers. It was not a reluctance to admit to the truth but simple ignorance; they had been evacuated before the casualty lists were complete. Rye on the other hand had remained on the Peninsula for a further three weeks. If anyone was able to give an accurate view of events, the commanding officer was surely the man. On his arrival Rye was described as 'safe and looking apparently well'. Perhaps the return voyage had allowed time for his mental and physical recuperation for when William Swallow saw the Colonel at Alexandria in early July, he recorded 'Rye looks like an old man, broken down and ill-looking'. Rye was interviewed by reporters at his Albert Mount home and gave a generally upbeat view of the battalion's fortunes. He estimated that about 40 men were killed and 203 wounded on 4 and 5 June. This is some considerable way out on the figure Rye would certainly have known to be accurate. The Colonel was in Alexandria in early July when Headquarters gave the 10th's losses as 100 killed and 452 wounded. In his interviews Rye preferred to talk of the state of the battalion before the assault rather than of the hectic violence and losses of the battle itself. He was emphatic that the 'general health is excellent' and that the provision of good quality meals worked like 'clockwork'. The men had responded to all hardships and demands in the 'best spirits' and were 'positively fearless without being indiscreet'.

Rye's interviews might have assuaged the worries of some families, but the general lack of clarity and confirmation persisted. Inhabitants of streets and mill employees would be shocked to hear of their wounded or dead neighbours and workmates but Oldham was sufficiently large for an overall view of the disaster to remain indistinct. Furthermore, when definite news of a man's death was reported in the press it was usually mentioned amongst that of other Oldham soldiers serving in a multitude of different units. This helped to disperse the impact of Krithia and delay the eventual reckoning still further.

Figures computed after the war show that six officers and 76 Other Ranks were killed between 4–6 June and another 12 men later died of wounds sustained during the battle. This brings the total fatalities to 94 men. The number of wounded is more difficult to discern. As fighting went on before and after the three days of the battle itself, it is not always clear when a man received his wound. Men wounded on 7 June might have become mixed up with those wounded earlier and who were still awaiting evacuation.

It appears that at least 320 officers and men of the battalion were wounded during this battle. They passed down the lines of communication, with the more seriously injured arriving at hospitals all over England during July. For some, it was to be only a short respite from what many soldiers believed was the inevitable. John Greenwood from Derker and Roland Whittaker of Chadderton, for example, recovered from their wounds only to be killed on the Peninsula in August.

Until locally arranged truces allowed burying parties to collect them and give them a hasty interment, the dead of early June lay out for days amid the rocks and scrub. Of the 94 officers and men who were killed or died, 75 have no known grave. Their remains might have been concentrated into the larger cemeteries after the war but could not with certainty be identified. Others simply disappeared, destroyed and pounded to dust by the constant shelling. The names of the missing are commemorated on the Helles Memorial which overlooks the area for which they fought. Among those officers whose remains were never identified were George Owen, Robert Ascroft and Tom Kirk. Owen's mother wrote to Fred Hardman expressing her intention of visiting her son's grave after the war. Hardman wrote ruefully to his wife: 'I'm afraid she will not find it, for this ground is one huge cemetery'. His prediction proved correct.

Second Lieutenant Robert Ascroft, a nephew of a former Oldham MP, had only left Charterhouse School in July 1914 and had enlisted in August. Tom Kirk was commissioned with his brother Joseph into the 10th from the 6/Manchester; Joseph returned home wounded in August and was to be killed in a motorcycling accident in February 1916. Humphrey Nevinson, the son of a rector in Market Harborough, died of wounds on board a hospital ship and was buried at sea. He had apparently told his fellow officers that he could trace his ancestry back to Robin Hood.

Many of the battalion's older and senior soldiers are also commemorated on the Helles Memorial. Sergeant Major Cyrus Dunkerley attended the burial of his brother CSM Fred, a South African veteran, whose remains were not identified after the war. Corporal Fred Hadfield, who like Fred Dunkerley was a holder of the Volunteer Long Service Medal, was at 45 one of the battalion's eldest soldiers. At the other end of the scale, James Shaw of Higginshaw Lane, was a mere 17 years. Sergeant William Nanson was another South African Volunteer, while Elijah Fitton, a moulder at Platt Brothers, had served in the Volunteers and Territorials for fifteen years. Another worker at Platt's was Sam Fallows of Kirkham Street. Fallows had spent six years in the 10th and was about to be sent home to practise his skilled trade as a tool fitter. A Turkish shell put an end to his hopes and he died of wounds on Malta.

The fate of many of the men killed during the bayonet charge remained unconfirmed for months. William Swallow enquired at the Records Office at Alexandria for news of his cousin Albert Barker. When Sergeant Wadsworth was brought into the hospital, he assured Swallow that although wounded, Barker would certainly survive. Nothing further was heard until October when Barker was officially reported to be wounded and missing. Nearly a year later it was eventually acknowledged that he had been killed at Krithia on 4 June.

The living continued to endure the ever worsening conditions on the Peninsula. The shock to morale of having seen the battalion so badly knocked about, combined with the unimaginable stench of decomposing corpses, the intensity of the summer heat, the monotonous food, the swelling hordes of flies and the resultant bouts of dysentery, plunged the survivors into despair and bitterness. In a clearly depressed state, Hardman confided to Kitty that if he had known that the battalion was to have been treated so badly, 'I should never have left you'. Only five original officers remained and he was on his fifth batman. In grim acknowledgment that their chances of remaining alive for much longer were slim, he and Lieutenant Bleakley gloomily witnessed each other's wills. The arrival of Rye's replacement did little to alleviate the depression. Colonel Robinson, late of the Punjab Regiment, seemed a 'faddy old gentleman' and delivered daily strafes to his apparently incompetent and ill-disciplined Territorial officers. Hardman thought that whatever Robinson 'knew of black troops, he certainly has a lot to learn about the British Territorial'. To add to the difficulties, neither Robinson nor his Punjabi servant Kareem could apparently understand the Oldham dialect spoken by most of the men.

Although in a more comfortable billet, William Swallow was equally despondent. At the hospital in Alexandria where he was still recovering from damaged feet, Swallow eagerly asked recent arrivals for news of individuals in the battalion. He heard conflicting stories of the battalion's strength: 402 one day, and 100 the next. Dismayed at the arrival of scores of broken comrades caked in blood and dysentery, Swallow exploded:

> *We have been treated by most of our officers as though we were something inferior to their house dogs, and then at the end of it all we are shot down and our lives given with about as much consideration as a butcher has for the sheep he slaughters. Really one would not care so much about taking the risks if we had*

the consolation of knowing that we had been treated with a little respect while training ... instead of being treated like citizen soldiers would naturally be expected to be treated, we have not had half the consideration that the officers show to their pet monkey ... We have been treated like dogs instead of men.

Many Oldhamers struggling for existence among the trenches and gullies of the searing Peninsula probably held similar sentiments to those of Swallow. Strong rumours abounded that the division was about to be withdrawn; the other East Lancashire battalions had suffered similar casualties to the 10th and it was widely believed that they would all be withdrawn to Egypt for rebuilding. These hopes were dashed when it was confirmed that reinforcements from the second-line units were about to arrive. As Hardman morosely observed: 'Our division has been treated badly, but I suppose nothing will be done until we are wiped out'.

REINFORCEMENTS AND EVACUATION

FORTUNATELY, FRED HARDMAN'S GLOOMY PREDICTION proved only partially correct. The men of the East Lancashire Division were convinced that when its individual units ran out of men they would be disbanded and the division eliminated from the order of battle. However, when the War Office had allowed the creation of second line Territorial units in September 1914 it had been with an eye to using these battalions to provide reinforcements to the first line. The decision to group the second line units into daughter divisions of the first meant that yet another battalion would have to be raised to provide drafts for both the first and second line. The third line training battalions were raised in October 1914 but it was to the 2/10th rather than the 3/10th Manchester that the survivors of Krithia and after looked for reinforcements. They knew of the shortages of equipment and accommodation experienced by their townsfolk in the 2/10th and the competition it faced for men and materials from the New Army battalions. As yet of course, there was no guarantee that the politicians and the War Office would be prepared to reinforce what was becoming on the Peninsula an expensive failure; the political and resource demands of the Western Front might well prove overwhelming. Even the most confident of the 1/10th knew that if reinforcements were eventually to arrive, their training and experience would do little to prepare them for the calamity that had befallen the British and French on Gallipoli.

The enthusiasm with which the young men of Oldham enlisted in the new battalion reflected the scenes in Rifle Street of a month earlier. Queues formed at the drill hall and included those who had failed to get into the first line and men who had since been inspired to attest. With nearly 800 enlistments in three hectic September days the battalion was up to establishment within a week. Motives for enlisting were the same as those which had driven their comrades in August: patriotism, duty, revenge for German atrocities, the great adventure and, by no means the least important, civic pride. Colonel Paterson, who had commanded the 10th until 1913, was appointed to command the new battalion. The problem was knowing what to do with 1,000 enthusiastic volunteers. They paraded daily at the drill hall and on Oldham

Edge and went on endless marches across the local moors. A liberal ration of humour and tolerance was essential for although the men might believe they were becoming soldiers they certainly did not look like them. The War Office and Territorial Force County Associations could not cope with the explosion in the size of the army and it would be months before the mills and factories of the nation could provide all units with the necessities of army life.

Under the eyes of watching townsfolk, the battalion drilled and manoeuvred for seven weeks. On 13 November, with news of the titanic struggle then being fought at Ypres emblazoned across the press and with the town buzzing over the attempt to raise its own Pals battalion, the 2/10th entrained for Southport. Hundreds of relatives and well-wishers cheered as the men, in what were now very tatty civilian clothes, marched in as soldierly a manner as their short training allowed, to Clegg Street goods yard. The Mayor sent them on their way with a ringing endorsement of their patriotism:

> You are brave men whose hearts are beating fast with the prospect of being able to do your share ... You must crush this tyrant and avenge the outrages on the people of Belgium. You have every justification to fight ... the cause of right, and for liberty and justice, for your own homes and the defence of all that is near and dear to you.

When news of the departure reached the 1st Battalion in Egypt, it prompted Fred Hardman to fire off an indignant letter to his father:

> The Mayor's speech ... has caused great amusement here. He is pathetic, and if they are going to return as 'Oldham's great heroes', what about us? He seems to forget that we are Oldham's 1st Battalion, but perhaps it is because we stole away in the middle of the night that he has forgotten we exist ... We shall have struck our blow for England and humanity before they enter the arena and come in to fill the gaps.

Among the many young men who marched with such confidence and pride to the station were 14 members of Oldham Rugby League Club, Wilf Cook from Springhead, Corporal Dean, whose son Charles was to be killed in June, Jack Street, a young 17-year-old from Lees Road, Albert Turner who was to die from what was recorded as 'shock' and 'disease' less than a year later and Sergeant Tom Gardner who was to die in the hand-to-hand fighting in the Vineyard in August. The officers who marched at the head of the companies and platoons were, like the men they commanded, largely from Oldham. One exception to this was Lieutenant Harold Spielman, son of Sir Isidore and Lady Spielman of London.

Like so many young men from a privileged background, Spielman had enjoyed the advantages of an education at Clifton School and Cambridge. In the balmy summer of 1914, Spielman wrote affectionately and appreciatively to his parents:

I think it unlikely that I shall be able to enjoy life as I enjoy it now, even if I have the leisure and means to do so. Can I ever again spend such evenings and grow merry with a dozen other men on cheap port and mediocre Moselle? Will the games be the same? The tennis parties? The picnics on the river? The dances? The motor drives to … Norwich or Ely? And to you for giving me these three years I am eternally grateful.

Spielman came from a very different background to the men in his platoon. The gruelling cycle of unemployment, poor housing and diet, the long hours of unhealthy work in stifling mills and the ever present danger of deadly diseases ensured a huge divide between Spielman and Jack Street. Nevertheless, the volunteers of 1914 had a unity of purpose and a common drive. They were determined to make the most of their circumstances and prepare themselves for overseas service.

At Southport the men spent much of their time drilling on the sand and digging trenches. They adopted donkeys as mascots, lived comfortably with families in local houses and eventually acquired the constituent parts of a uniform and equipment. By May all men were reported to possess a rifle, albeit an obsolete single shot pattern. That same month, while their friends, brothers and sons were beginning their period on the Peninsula, the 2/10th moved to Cuckfield in Sussex. Sergeant Parkinson described it as a 'charming village', but Jack Street was disappointed with the accommodation. His company's first home was the local workhouse, 'not a fine place to be in'. The men performed some musketry practice but most of the time was still spent in drill and route marches. This was not particularly onerous as the weather was fine and the Sussex lanes appealing. By early June rumours of a draft to the 1st Battalion were in widespread circulation. It was too early for the news of Krithia to have reached home, but word of substantial losses since the 10th's landing excited the men of the 2/10th and began mass speculation on who and how many might be sent.

A move was made, but only to Pease Pottage a small village on the Mid-Sussex ridge. Here things deteriorated. Instead of billets in houses or schools, accommodation was now in tents and food was neither as plentiful nor edible. Many began to believe with some fervency that if a draft were to go, life on Gallipoli might not be as bad as life at Pease Pottage. The rumours became fact and during July two drafts amounting to over 300 men left Sussex for Gallipoli.

Harold Spielman took the first draft of over 200 men. It embarked on the ss IONIAN on 3 July, sailed uneventfully through the Bay of Biscay, passed Gibraltar in darkness and arrived at Malta on 12 July. The party was not allowed ashore but the men were free to gaze at the awesome collection of French and British warships crowding the harbour against the magnificent backdrop of the Templars' forts.

The IONIAN ploughed on to Alexandria and then spent five days moored alongside the quay. Lying next to the IONIAN was the ASTURIAS, one of the convoy which had originally taken the East Lancashire Division to Egypt. William Swallow, whose feet had not sufficiently healed to allow his return to the battalion, had just embarked upon the ASTURIAS and was looking forward to the trip home. On hearing a hail of, 'Anyone there from the 10/Manchesters?', Swallow saw an old friend, Sergeant Alf Hopley, shouting from the IONIAN. Hopley nipped off his vessel without permission and enjoyed a short reunion with Swallow before returning aboard. George Kirkham, who had formerly acted as Second Lieutenant Emmott's orderly, also observed the draft. He considered, 'They'll soon get accustomed to change ... at any rate they have a good chance for I do not expect they will see their home town again until it's all over'.

The IONIAN slipped its moorings and on 22 July, three weeks after leaving Southampton, the draft landed on the Peninsula. As it disembarked Turkish shells began to fall on and around the semi-ordered chaos that was Gully Beach. Wounded men awaiting evacuation lay on stretchers, stores piled high under the cliffs, ration parties came and went and burial parties dug graves for the heaps of corpses piled on the beach. Jack Street's first impression was of the evil stench and decay of the area. He disembarked and later recorded the 'rather rough time which I do not wish to go through again'. The reinforcements were joining a battalion whose effective strength was down to eight officers and 200 Other Ranks. It was a battalion enormously reduced in strength, but with a strangely resilient morale.

The day before the draft landed, a large working party had been ordered to dig a communication trench. The Turks spotted the men and two were killed and seven wounded before they could take cover. Fred Hardman thought: 'the genius who had the bright idea of carrying out this work in daylight ought certainly to be decorated'. Nevertheless, Sergeant Walter Eastwood, while bemoaning the lack of leave and rest, claimed to be still looking forward to making another bayonet charge on the Turkish lines. Both he and Harold Tarbuck hoped that the arrival of more men might allow those originals who still remained some rest. Tarbuck thought: 'The hardest thing to get on the Peninsula is sleep because during the day one is ... digging and at night all have to stand to in case of attack'.

Harold Spielman, enjoying the first flush of active service, was full of confidence. Perhaps ignorant of the number of times it had been attacked and the hundreds of decomposing bodies strewn around its trenches, he believed the heights of Achi Baba 'will fall soon'. Initially surprised at how 'extraordinarily callous everybody is about it all' he soon discovered the callousness was not only infectious but also essential. He was astounded at the 'wonderful spirit and determination' shown by the Territorials, which he ascribed to the better food than he and his draft had consumed at Pease Pottage. After four days on the rocks, he decided that the Peninsula was 'neither heaven, nor earth, nor hell, but a mixture of all ... These few days have made a fatalist of me ... I am a perfect savage living in a hole'.

Wilf Cook also wrote home a few days after his arrival and, like Spielman, concluded good personal hygiene was something of an idealistic ambition:

We have been in the firing line for three days, and it has been exciting I can tell you! We had three bombardments in twelve hours yesterday ... You will be a bit surprised to hear that I have had only one wash and one shave in eleven days, but we have more important work on hand than mere ablutions, so we do not bother. I have only been here three weeks, but it has taught me that reading about war and taking part in it are different things altogether. I have seen things here that I would never have thought about – fine, strapping fellows, smashed and battered to pieces. It is awful. It is not war, but murder absolutely. What we see is all in the day's work, and it is forgotten the next day.

The conditions which greeted the new arrivals are well described in the divisional history:

Dysentery and jaundice were rampant, and an epidemic of septic sores ran through the division ... There had been no break in the hot, dry weather. Many of the wells had gradually become defiled, others had run dry, and this no doubt contributed greatly to the amount of sickness. The insanitary conditions inseparable from the type of warfare waged in so confined and exposed a space, the continuous strain exacted from all, the lack of sleep, the tropical heat, the monotonous and unsuitable food, the lice, and above all the plague of flies, with which no sanitary measures and precautions could cope, all were in their degree responsible for the deplorable results. The country was one huge graveyard in which hundreds of corpses of friends and foes lay unburied, and the air was heavy with the stench. Flies clustered in noisome masses on everything that attracted them, on the food and in the mess tins as these were carried to one's mouth, on sores, on faces and hands – blue and green monsters too lazy to fly or crawl away, and to kill fifty was but to invite five thousand to attend the funeral.

This description of the living conditions endured by the troops is reiterated in many of their letters. Private Bully of Failsworth thought the 'flies are the biggest pest ... and worse than the Turks ... the latter give us some peace now and again, the flies do not'. When one man proudly displayed a nest of the vermin inside the camphor bag slung around his neck, the authorities accepted that the use of these supposed prophylactics was futile. John Booth of Royton wrote of the 'hundreds of dead all over the place' and somewhat optimistically believed that his relatives would be able to 'imagine what it is like to wake up next to dead bodies that have been lying there for weeks'. Private Craven of Glodwick described it as 'murder here. They are laid down in heaps all over ... we had to walk over dead and wounded Oldham lads on our way out of the trenches'.

Thomas Hague of Dawson Street was one of the second draft which arrived in mid-August. The group had left Pease Pottage only one day after embarkation orders arrived. Those selected were not given any opportunity of furlough, a consequence, according to a clearly disappointed Hague, of the number of men from the first draft who had overstayed their embarkation leave. Hague posted a letter to his wife announcing his departure but, as he had not yet been paid, he could not stamp it. Three weeks later the trooper docked at Alexandria where the reinforcements saw some of their comrades of the first draft in the process of being unloaded from a hospital ship. Within a week Hague and his companions were in what he succinctly described as a 'hell hole'.

The natural initial confidence and enthusiasm of the new arrivals was not matched by Fred Hardman. Having looked over the first of the reinforcements from the 2/10th, he wrote to Kitty: 'The new draft seem to have practically no knowledge of musketry, some of them have never seen a service rifle and as a result, it is highly dangerous to be in their vicinity when they get one in their hands'. Wynne also recalled that the draft was taught how to load and fire their weapons within yards of the Turkish trenches.

Adequately trained or not, the newcomers had to take their chance and do their turn of duty in the front lines. Almost immediately many became victims of diarrhoea. Given the environment in which they lived and fought this was both unfortunate and uncomfortable. The symptoms varied from a slight discharge to a persistent passage of slime and blood. The continual drain or disability of men added to the difficulties of the still extremely understrength battalion and it lost a further nine dead and over 50 wounded when in reserve for a 'demonstration' to cover the Suvla landings further up the coast. Among those killed were Sergeant Frank Bowden of Primrose Bank and Sergeant Tom Gardner. Gardner was one of the new arrivals from the 2/10th and died close to Bowden as the pair carried water cans to the front trenches.

The following week was one of routine trench warfare. This allowed a further period of relatively peaceful acclimatisation for the men of the 2/10th but large numbers of them, as well as several of the older hands who according to the Medical Officer were showing signs of strain and 'soldier's heart', were evacuated to the hospitals on Lemnos, Mundros and further afield. On 11 August Harold Spielman wrote what was destined to be his last letter. Much of his earlier optimism had faded and the responsibility of command allowed him little time for leisure or reflection. He assured his parents he was well and that he was looking forward to a wash and a good night's sleep. Two days later he and another 17 men of the Oldham battalion were dead.

Other units of the East Lancashire Division had taken the area known as the Vineyard as part of the diversion to lure Turkish troops away from the Suvla landings. Leaving piles of corpses after every attempt, time and time again the Turks hurled themselves against the newly captured British positions. John Masefield described it as 'not a battle in the military text book sense ... It was a week-long cursing and killing scrimmage'. One of the 2/10th draft who went out with Spielman survived the fighting and described the manner of his officer's death:

We fired as fast as we could load; so did the Turks who got in a trench in front of us and bombed our men out. We sent bombing parties up each side, and both sides were throwing bombs for hours on end. Then, about one o'clock in the morning ... 50 of us under Captain Spielman ... rushed the trench which our men had left earlier on. Unfortunately we were enfiladed and driven back ... Captain Spielman had been killed.

According to Lieutenant Joe Boyd, another who had come from the 2/10th, the Turks stripped Spielman of his boots and equipment. His body was recovered some time after and taken down to Pink Farm Cemetery. Officers of the 10th gathered around his grave where, in the absence of a rabbi, an Anglican padre said some appropriate words. Of the other 17 Oldhamers who died during the night of 13-14 August, only three have a known grave. Victor Hadfield, another of Spielman's draft, and Roland Whitaker from Chadderton, who had only recently recovered from his wounds of 4 June, were buried in Redoubt Cemetery. Gilbert Crawshaw, a platemoulder at Asa Lees, died of wounds at an aid post and was buried in Lancashire Landing Cemetery. Wilf Cook from Springhead, who from the IONIAN's decks had apparently achieved his life's ambition of seeing the Eddystone Lighthouse, lies in an unmarked or unknown grave.

In recognition of the mauling the battalion had undergone in the Vineyard, the authorities decided that the 10th and other units of the 42nd Division could now be allowed a period of rest. On 17 August the Oldhamers made their weary way back to the beach area and into dugouts only just vacated by the 52nd Division. Like most of its division the 10th had been continuously engaged for three months. In the compact combat zone complete rest was an impossibility; troops not in the front lines were invariably required to provide digging and carrying parties. During periodic lulls the specialists undertook skills training and on 29 August the whole battalion, or what was left of it, assembled for a church parade. By that time the battalion had once again spent a tour of duty in the line; the supposed period of rest had lasted for just four days. This was followed by five successive seven-day tours spent alternately at Fusilier Bluff and Fifth Avenue. With the Turkish trenches in places only ten yards away, nerves remained taut.

Trench tours were dangerous and debilitating, but for the Oldhamers the period of set-piece battles was over. With the Turks on the higher ground and the Allies penned in with their backs to the sea, the campaign had reached stalemate. Positions were so entrenched that any attempt to dislodge the enemy did little except further add to the number of corpses scattered around and between the lines. Morale amongst the Allied troops was low and the strategic position was hopeless. However, for the time being there appeared to be little alternative to hanging on and enduring the hardships.

Finding little solace in the companionship of newly arrived officers and despite Kitty's frequent and loving letters from home, Fred Hardman remained despondent:

My own battalion is gone and now I have to struggle on with half-trained men whose whole time seems to have been spent in parading the streets airing their uniforms. I didn't think much of this batch of officers. There is only one fellow from Oldham. The rest were attached at Southport and have apparently come out because they were too ashamed of being continually asked when they were going to do something.

In a battalion which bore little resemblance to the one which had left Egypt three months earlier, Hardman was feeling increasingly isolated. By 17 August, of the 29 officers who had landed on the Peninsula, 11 were at home or on their way there, eight were killed, one was missing, two had been evacuated sick and three were wounded. The following day the Adjutant, Major O'Kelly, 'went absolutely mad, and was taken away'. When Lieutenant Wilkinson and Captain Wilde temporarily went away sick in early September, Hardman became the only surviving original officer.

It is difficult to be precise about the numbers of original Other Ranks who had been wounded or evacuated sick. It is probable that between 80–85% of those who were not dead had been off the Peninsula with wounds or sickness during the three months. The weekly average of those who were not fit for duty during August and September was 19%. This was severe enough but it grew worse and by the third week in October effective strength amounted to a mere seven officers and about 180 Other Ranks. Besides the commonplace diarrhoea and dysentery, occurrences of jaundice and dyspepsia showed alarming increases. The Medical Officer, Dr Baird, ascribed the jaundice to dyspepsia caused by the monotonous diet or to chills and the variable weather. Those who were capable of work often manned the front line, constructed barricades, provided carrying parties or performed normal trench maintenance. As mine warfare had become a regular feature of life and death on the Peninsula, others were employed in tunnelling shafts and galleries. Moments of light relief, such as the five rounds *feu de joie* to celebrate the allegedly good news from the Battle of Loos, were few and far between. One of the campaign's few positive aspects was bringing the supremacy of the Turkish snipers to an end. It had been a long and difficult battle but the Allies had learnt much from the Turks' skills of concealment. Putting this bloody education to good purpose, they were able to turn the tables on their adversaries.

There was little else to be cheery about. The monotonous but deadly routine of trench warfare continued into the autumn months. Several men died of disease and of wounds during September, but only one man was killed outright. Having spent a week in hospital with diarrhoea, Thomas Hague returned to the trenches and was killed shortly after. Although the number of fatalities was much reduced, the drain of men became so acute that several of the 9/Manchester were attached to the battalion to make it up to something approaching viable numbers.

October saw the arrival of a handful of new officers, two from the General Service list and three from the 9/South Lancashire. Although Wynne thought these young men proved to be 'most valuable officers', a later draft of eight young second lieutenants from the second line battalion was greeted with greater enthusiasm.

One of these subalterns was Selwyn Rowbotham. This young officer, the son of Saddleworth District Council's Chief Clerk, was destined to serve with the battalion for the rest of the war and eventually became its commanding officer. These officers arrived without an accompanying draft of Other Ranks but one hundred men, along with another two subalterns, did appear at battalion headquarters towards the end of the month. These men were the first draft to be sent from the third line battalion, then stationed at Codford. They were men who had enlisted from October or November 1914 onwards and, like their counterparts in the 2/10th, had initially suffered from acute shortages of equipment. The new arrivals were described as being 'not of really bad physique' and their training and discipline was assessed as 'good'. Given the extremely low strength of the battalion only days after their arrival, it seems likely that many of these men went sick within a very short period of time.

The end of the period of set-piece slaughter allowed more time for mine warfare and improvisation. The battalion was often called upon to assist the Royal Engineers and Pioneers of the neighbouring division to tunnel towards the Turkish trenches. In mid–October three Oldhamers and several men of other units were buried in a gallery when the Turks blew a camouflet. Tom Knott was discovered close to the tunnel entrance but when dug out was found to be dead. Privates Talbot and O'Connor, along with the others who survived the initial explosion, managed to dig themselves out of the collapsed gallery. On hearing of their good fortune the corps commander wired his congratulations to the two Territorials on their safe return to the battalion.

The possibility of standing above an enemy mine when it exploded did nothing to help morale on either side. Light relief could at times be manufactured by holding sniping contests (complete with score cards) across No Man's Land and by various gadgets designed to make the enemy's life a little more uncomfortable. One of the favourite pastimes in the trenches was to attempt to knock down Turkish wire barricades by catapulting grenades from improvised ballistas. As they held the higher ground, efforts to divert streams into enemy trenches was usually far more successful for the Turks than the British. Although bloody and serious, the fighting was generally done according to the rules of war; the Oldhamers developed a healthy respect for the hardiness and endurance of 'Johnny Turk'.

Any British wounded left in Turkish trenches were well treated by their captors and when he offered to surrender the Turk rarely employed any trickery or deception. They were largely simple peasants with an honourable code of soldierly conduct. Among others, Sergeant William Read from London Road, wrote home of how the Turks fought 'cleanly' and 'played the game'. In contrast, the national and local press thundered about the duplicity and dishonourable behaviour of the Germans on the Western Front. To a nation brought up on the idea that anyone with anything other than a pure white skin was by definition untrustworthy, this was a difficult concept to grasp.

The strain of active service and the deteriorating weather finally put paid to Fred Hardman's physical resolution. In October, Dr Baird sent him to Lemnos suffering from jaundice. After a stay in a hospital on the island he boarded the AQUITANIA and was carried home to England. Fifteen months after he had left, Hardman arrived back at his Queen's Road house to remake acquaintance with his wife and child. He remained in the UK for over 12 months, eventually rejoining the battalion as it wandered about the Egyptian desert.

In early November, torrential rain turned the Gallipoli gullies to seas of gushing mud. There had been little or no preparation for winter quarters and the men suffered accordingly. A tardy start was made to construct more substantial quarters but efforts were handicapped by a lack of roofing material. According to Wynne the construction of the Staff's winter quarters took precedence over those of the men but, by the end of November some inadequate supplies of winter clothing appeared. The men, many of whom were suffering from frostbite and exposure, were supposed to draw comfort from the army commander's message in which he assured his troops the Turks were even worse off. He was 'glad our boys are so hearty' and was confident in their ability to show that 'a winter campaign against British troops is bound to end in defeat'.

There are no recorded comments on whether the Oldhamers took any solace from this missive. No doubt it was well meant, but to a freezing soldier still in the remnant of his summer uniform, it was undoubtedly dismissed as simply an example of the Staff's inability to grasp the realities of life in the front line. In fact, the Staff and their political masters at home were perhaps more aware of the reality than the troops gave them credit for. The campaign had failed to achieve any of its principal objectives and had resulted in a wastage of lives and of resources which could have been used more profitably elsewhere. Moves were in train to withdraw the remains of the proud battalions which had fought and suffered so much but which had achieved so little.

Until the withdrawal was made, Oldhamers continued to die. Fortunately, the fatality list for November was the lowest of any month since the battalion landed: Sergeant Harry Hinchcliffe of Lees was killed in the middle of the month and a few days later Fred Jones died when a British grenade exploded in his trench. There might have been only two deaths and eight wounded, but no fewer than nine officers and 66 men were shipped out to hospital on Lemnos or further afield. Despite the arrival of the draft from the 3/10th in October, by the end of the month battalion strength was down to 387. There are no accurate figures for the numbers of wounded and sick evacuated during December although incidental references can account for at least 35. This cannot be the complete total for by the time of the withdrawal, battalion strength was once again below 200. What is certain is that during the month three men were killed and another three died of wounds. John Brierley of Burnley Lane, Chadderton, was a former Volunteer but had not re-enlisted in the 10th when it became a Territorial Force unit. He eventually joined the 3/10th in February 1915 and was killed on 9 December. Brierley was buried in Pink Farm Cemetery, whereas Wilson Pickles, an 18 year-old postman from Werneth, was carried down to an aid post on the beach and later buried in the Lancashire Landing Cemetery. Harry Morgan of St Stephen's Street is the only one of the five December fatalities not to have a known grave. He died of wounds on board a hospital ship and was buried at sea.

London and Paris decided that the Allies should cut their losses and withdraw with as much dignity as could be mustered. The tactical situation had long been hopeless and there were new theatres of war opening up which, it was hoped, might prove more successful. The national and local press were now more interested in events developing elsewhere, coverage of a static war in a far away place having lost much of its original appeal. All that remained was to organise the evacuation in a way that would keep casualties and humiliation to a minimum. The method employed proved to be remarkably successful and caused many observers to wonder why the original landings could not have been planned and executed with such adroitness.

The first evacuations began at Suvla and Anzac on 10 December. On 19 December the 10th, still perched on its rocky cliff near Fusilier Bluff, was ordered to make a 'demonstration'. The idea of the display was to cover the final withdrawal further north. With the Turks behaving in a quietly sociable manner a dreary Christmas was spent in the trenches. Fury, however, burst not from the enemy but from the mouth of Colonel Robinson. Robinson exploded when informed that the supply of cigarettes he had acquired for the men had disappeared from the safe-keeping of the Quartermaster. The culprits were seemingly never apprehended. A few days later it was the Oldhamers' turn to trek down to the beach for the final time; the 42nd Division being replaced in the line by the 13th. The Western Division and the long-suffering 29th were to hold the line for another week. They too were then withdrawn and the Peninsula once again lay entirely in Turkish hands.

It was with mixed feelings that the Oldhamers and their divisional comrades left the familiar gullies, ravines and trenches. The few members of the battalion who had remained with it during its entire stay had suffered disease, shelling, mining, flies, monotonous diet and constant debilitating strain. In November and December, frostbite, blizzards and mud-filled trenches added to the discomfort. They were withdrawing knowing that strategically the mission had been a bloody failure. Their endurance, bravery and fortitude had in the end accounted for very little.

The military muddle, personal antagonisms, failures in Allied co-operation, bad luck and a dogged and honourable defence by a respected foe, had sealed the expedition's fate. As they trudged down to Y Beach on feet painful from prolonged immersion in water-filled trenches, the Oldhamers had little time to reflect on what had been achieved. Their main concern was to escape the Peninsula before the Turks realised what was happening. To have survived so long only to be killed or maimed at the last moment would have seemed harsh justice. The files of men wound their way once more down Gully Ravine; shells followed them all the way and in places the gully was blocked by mud, rocks and transport carts. Enemy searchlights swept the open plateau over which the men had to cross. Burdened by packs and handicapped by physical discomforts, the troops made their way across as fast as their personal circumstances permitted. The beach was not a safe haven as enemy shells regularly bracketed the area, throwing stores, men and animals into the air and the swelling sea. A collection of lighters was drawn up on the beach and on a rough December night the men cursed and slipped as they scrambled aboard. As they hove to alongside the darkened mass of the ROBIN REDBREAST, the difficulty of embarking became horrifyingly apparent. Encumbered with kit and enveloped in what one officer described as a 'mood of sullenness', the men hurled themselves from the bucking lighter through a hole in the side of the larger vessel. Naval arms grabbed them and threw them unceremoniously inside. When embarkation was complete 180 men of the Oldham

Territorials, all that remained of the 850 originals and nearly 500 reinforcements, turned their backs on the rocky outcrop and the bones of their fallen comrades.

⋯⋯

RETURN TO THE DESERT

CARRYING THE REMNANTS of once full battalions, the ROBIN REDBREAST chugged into Mundros harbour and discharged its weary cargo of sullen Oldhamers and Mancunians. A few days among the field hospitals and tented accommodation allowed the troops time to shave, clean up and sort their equipment. The officers generally let the men get on with the job themselves; as despondent as their men, they kept the chivvying to a minimum. The occasional football match was organised, but most of the men seemed to spend the period lost in their own thoughts and reflections on what might have been. Those who saw newspapers from home learned that the inquisitions into the Gallipoli fiasco were already underway; criticisms of the original plan and of the subsequent operations were being openly aired in Parliament and the press. The controversy offered little comfort to the survivors for they were more concerned with what might come next. There was the possibility of France and, with luck, home leave. All they could do for the moment was to go through the motions of recovery and await authority's decision.

On 11 January an advance party of 50 men under Lieutenant Truman left Mundros for Egypt. On 14 January the rest of the battalion embarked upon the ARCADIAN and, after a stormy crossing, reached Alexandria three days later. For the few men still with the 10th who had left on the HAVERFORD eight months earlier, it was almost like coming home. The battalion moved into a camp near the pyramids and once again began to look like soldiers. New uniforms and equipment were issued, companies were reorganised and a general period of smartening up followed. Lieutenant-Colonel Robinson returned from a few days local leave and closely supervised the improving appearance of the men. Officers became more assertive and the NCOs louder. Within a few days the still very understrength battalion was deemed fit enough to travel. It climbed aboard open railway trucks and prepared for another foray into the desert.

The journey was, like so many experienced by men during the war, awful. It lasted for only two days, but during that time the men were subjected to cramped accommodation, rations of biscuits and bully and the broiling heat. When the train arrived in the middle of nowhere, the troops almost fell from the trucks to stretch their aching limbs. Shaluf, just to the south of the Great Bitter Lakes, was little more than a couple of shanties alongside the railway. The Oldhamers and the rest of the 42nd Division were greeted with a view of nothing but sand in all directions. Tents were erected and some sort of military order brought to this isolated patch of desert. The men were given lectures on 'Flies, and how to deal with them' and issued with pith helmets. The latter were useful, but there was little that could be done to lessen the impact of the millions of insects which infested the camp.

The men were soon put to work digging. The General Staff believed that the Turks would make another attempt on the canal, probably in the area between Suez and the Bitter Lakes. The 10th spent nearly two months east of the canal digging and wiring defensive positions known as Ashton and Oldham Posts. Although the work was hard and exhausting and the sun unrelenting, fatalities were very rare: Herbert Bowes of Crompton Street, who had earlier been evacuated from Gallipoli, died of pneumonia in a base hospital and Joe Miller, formerly of the King's Own Yorkshire Light Infantry, died from 'enteric' at Suez. The unfortunate Joseph Tyson of Horsedge Street was crushed or suffocated when a wall of sandbags collapsed upon him. A Court of Enquiry decided that he had been 'accidentally killed' and drew attention to the dangers that life miles away from the enemy posed. An unknown but certainly substantial number of men was admitted to hospital suffering from disease or the effects of the sun. Private Dearden for example wandered off into the desert and when discovered by a search party was found to have lost his memory.

Joe Miller of Sheffield was the first man of a draft of KOYLI to die while serving with the Oldham battalion. Over 100 men from South Yorkshire, reputedly from the regiment's 1st and 2nd Battalions, arrived for duty with the 10/Manchester during March. At first they were not particularly welcomed because, as regular soldiers, they apparently 'assumed a rather superior air towards the Territorials'; it took some considerable time before they settled down and became accepted and integrated members of the battalion. The KOYLI intake was just one of several drafts of officers and Other Ranks which arrived during February and March. Although the battalion had suffered grievous losses during the Gallipoli campaign and, despite the arrival of the South Yorkshire men, it remained very much a battalion of Oldhamers. Since leaving England in September 1914 the unit had lost 43 officers and 1,136 men. Of those, 237 men and 14 officers had been killed or died of wounds or disease. In all a total of 79 officers and almost 2,000 men had served with the unit but by April 1916 only two officers and 67 men had served continuously. Within this very low figure were one officer and 30 Other Ranks of the transport section who, although retained on battalion strength, had never actually landed on Gallipoli. Another seven officers and 175 men had returned to the battalion having spent some time in hospital either at home or in the Mediterranean theatre. Now working in the heat of the Egyptian spring the battalion contained a mixture of men inexperienced in actual warfare and of those who had spent at least some time in the inferno of Gallipoli. Among the other drafts was a small group of men from the 3/Manchester, a reserve battalion stationed on the Lincolnshire coast, and a substantial number from the 10th's own training battalion, the 3/10th Manchester. These men had come from the depths of a British winter where, according to Jack Street, they had been 'up to the neck in mud', to the heat of the Sinai desert. They had joined a battalion which now comprised only eight officers and 215 men of the original 1st Battalion. The remainder of the 28 officers and 592 Other Ranks had come from the 2/10th, 3/10th or from other regiments.

In early April the 42nd Division handed over its defences east of the canal and moved south to Suez. The town was a pleasant break from the never ending vista of sand and scrub, but the newly erected camp which was to become the home of the 10th was far from salubrious. Despite active concern for his men's welfare, Lieutenant-Colonel Robinson's efforts to improve the conditions amounted to little. They shared their encampment with the by now traditional myriads of flies and a seemingly almost equal number of small boys. As the heat prevented work other than in the early morning and evening, long, monotonous and uncomfortable hours were spent inside their cramped tents. Relief came with the sporadic issue of leave passes. Officers were enrolled as members of Port Tewfik Club, in whose confines cool drinks and civilised conversation could be found. A substantial number of French and British civilians remained in the town, living in well appointed houses on broad, cool boulevards. The ordinary Tommy was not invited to such exclusive environs, but he could still gaze in appreciation at European women promenading in loose, fashionable clothes. By contrast, although it was periodically deloused by the army, his incongruous, coarse, ill fitting drill uniform was, within hours, again covered in sand and sweat.

Despite the heat, the army still required the men to train. Practice attacks, drill and saluting competitions were held under the watchful and critical eyes of the staff. In June conditions in the camp deteriorated so much that all tents were struck for two hours to ventilate the site. It was with some optimism that the men began to hear rumours of a move, possibly to India. However, these were superseded by more persistent rumours that the Turks were again advancing towards the canal. Ordered to move at short notice, the battalion was soon on its way north to El Ferdan. If the men had dreams of improved facilities, their fantasies were rudely shattered. After much confusion and argument about who they were and where they were supposed to be, the 10th occupied a camp recently evacuated by the 8/Duke of Wellington's. The 'Dukies', who like the Oldhamers were veterans of Gallipoli, were on their way to France. Perhaps assuming that they would be far enough away to ignore any criticism, they had left the camp in an awful state; half-buried rubbish had already been discovered by an advance guard of a million flies. When this multitude was reinforced by its relatives, the Oldhamers reflected upon Port Tewfik with almost fond memories.

There was, however, little time for reflection. On 16 July the battalion was told to stand by for another move. The initial rumour of a trip to the coast was soon dashed when half the battalion hastily entrained and disappeared east. Stories of Turkish and British cavalry clashes in the desert and of a strong enemy force approaching the canal swept through the companies. As the train crawled on across the wastes, the suspicious soldiers of the 10th were informed that they had now been attached to the 7/Royal Scots of the 52nd Division. By the time it detrained at Romani, and never having set eyes on the Royal Scots, the half battalion was once again a discrete unit. The rest of 126 Brigade also arrived and headed off into the desert. As they tried to piece together the scattered intelligence coming from cavalry patrols and down the wires, something like panic spread among the staff of VIII Corps. It was estimated that a division of Turks, supplemented by German officers, artillery and machine-gunners, had crossed the desert in a remarkable feat of rapid marching and was about to descend upon the British positions. Having toured the defences allocated to the 10th, Lieutenant-Colonel Robinson arrived back at his HQ with a worried face. At a conference of battalion officers he warned them to 'Save your ammunition... and give them the bayonet'. He concluded the meeting by cheerily observing 'I don't suppose any of us will be alive in the morning. Good night'. Guards were posted in advance of the defences, working parties wired and dug, and those off duty grabbed what little sleep their imaginative minds permitted them.

Next morning gunfire was heard to the east and British wounded passing through the 10th's lines reported the enemy to be only five miles away. At this news, the Egyptian camel drivers panicked and fled. Sweating under the scorching sun, the Oldhamers stared to their front. Their only protection from the ferocious heat was to tie two blankets together and prop them up with poles over their sand scrapes. Tension mounted during the day as the rumble of gunfire continued to echo across the wilderness. Then, seemingly without reason, the battalion was ordered to fall in and march off. The next few days were spent in a bewildering series of marches and counter-marches, all of which, according to the participants, defied any sort of logic or reason. The 10th wandered about the desert and on one occasion, entrained. When it arrived, with no rations or tents, at an indefinable spot in the desert, a Staff Captain announced that the battalion should have been sent elsewhere. Five minutes later, the Oldhamers were once again on board the train.

Having spent several weeks away from the battalion working as a clerk at Port Tewfik, Jack Street had only recently rejoined the unit. Fed up with the apparent senselessness of contradictory orders, Street confided to his diary his regret at having rejoined this 'ragtime mob'. Fortunately for Street and his comrades, order was about to be restored. During one of its frequent pauses for further instructions, the battalion witnessed the arrival of some German and Turkish prisoners. There was a good deal of fraternisation between the Oldhamers and the Turks, many of whom tapped medal ribbons on their tunics and mouthed 'Gallipoli'. Water was already in short supply but the Turks were in a bad way. Clearly undernourished and looking very bedraggled, their tongues were swollen for want of water. Canteens were passed around and some cheery banter followed. The German prisoners were less friendly. Sergeant Maurice Bradbury recalled they were aloof and sullen and 'drew themselves haughtily away from their fellow captives'. Rumours of atrocities committed by German machine-gunners had reached the camp and several Australian troops climbed aboard the Germans' trucks and told them in plain Anglo-Saxon what they thought of them. The more reserved Oldhamers contented themselves with cutting buttons as souvenirs from the Germans' tunics.

The desert battle was not yet over and the 10th was soon on its way again, this time a few miles nearer the coast at Pelusium. It was once more given a supporting role, digging defences and covering the railway. By 4 August the crisis was over. The Turks had been decisively beaten at Romani and their advance on the canal stopped. Other units of the 42nd Division would remain engaged for the following few days but the 10th could afford to relax and have a rest. The three days at Pelusium were spent in playing football, bathing and reorganising. The officers even managed to get a boat transported by rail from Port Said and enjoyed themselves pottering about on the canal. There was also the long delayed presentation of medals to those men who had played in and won the divisional football cup at Gallipoli. The match had been interrupted several times when shells fell near to the 'pitch' but the Oldhamers had triumphed. Two members of the team, Lance Corporals Ogden and Kirkman were on Cyprus, presumably still recovering from wounds or disease and another member was based at the Kantara railhead; their medals were sent on but the remainder of the team had theirs presented at a battalion parade during the cool of a Pelusium evening.

The army was determined to take advantage of its Romani victory but for some sections of the 10th the next few days were spent in clearing the dead from the battlefield. While refitting among the ancient ruins of Pelusium the remainder of the battalion was supplied with 100 camels and about 40 native drivers. An unfortunate subaltern, who attracted around him a motley collection of assistants who either claimed or were told they had a knowledge of working animals, was appointed to command the new recruits. Getting to know these often truculent and awkward animals proved difficult. Eventually a rapport of sorts was established and in the weeks to come the camel section was to become a particularly important part of the battalion. The division was reformed into a series of mobile columns and was to spend much of the next three months guarding the railway and water lines under construction towards El Arish. The division alternated with the 52nd in this boring and repetitive, albeit essential, task. The army was gearing itself up for a march across northern Sinai but before any serious campaign could be staged, the rear areas had first to be expanded and future water supply secured. New wharves were being built along the canal and a variety of vessels docked alongside to unload the multitude of stores and equipment required by the troops. Hospitals, casualty clearing stations and field ambulances pitched camp along a railway which was being laid at the phenomenal rate of up to one mile a day. Parties of Royal Engineers set off into the wastes to drill for water and plot the new bore holes. When discovered, the water was brackish and largely unfit for human consumption. Captain Bleakley, who had rejoined the 10th after the evacuation from Gallipoli, noted that even the animals refused to touch the water until thirst finally compelled them to drink it. Water from the extending pipeline was supplemented by that brought by camels. Each animal carried two metal tanks containing twelve gallons. Yet despite these efforts there was never enough water for the troops and animals. Often having to exist on as little as one litre per day, men of the 10th were described as bearing a remarkable resemblance to 'South Sea cannibals'.

The land across which the Oldhamers marched and guarded alternated between energy-sapping ankle deep sand and rocky hills rising to 300 feet. The sand was sculpted by the wind into curves and crests of beauty and delicacy. In sheltered hollows where the water lay not too far below the surface, dates and watermelons were in plentiful supply; birds with magnificent plumage were often seen in the trees and beautiful wild flowers adorned these small 'hods'. Jack Street was less impressed by the drill and marching considered necessary by the officers during quiet times. He was almost happy in September to fall victim to malaria and to spend a month in Cairo's Citadel. Sand storms were another problem. Anything not anchored was hurled across the encampment, tents flapped and shuddered in the torment and sand penetrated everywhere. It made its persistent way into food, clothing, blankets and mouths; breathing became difficult and eyes smarted under the barrage of tiny storm-driven particles. Cholera was known to exist within the Turkish army and as the enemy retreated they left thousands of unburied dead in their wake. The sand storms carried the smell of the rotting dead and of foul camel lines across to the British troops. There was little the men could do except endure it and hope that relative peace would soon be restored.

During the day the sun beat down with merciless heat. In addition to the problem of possible dehydration, the troops suffered from the terrain. Several attempts were made to improvise a better form of boot for desert marching. A variation of wide-soled snow shoes was tried but the best answer came with the construction of a wire netting road laid on top of a bed of scrub collected by the Egyptian Labour Corps. Other sections of the march took the 10th across a salt pan whose stunning brightness threatened to blind the weary travellers. To test the nerve and surefootedness of the men and their plodding camels, the route sometimes lay between almost sheer drops of precipitous sand dunes.

There were also some lighter and more enjoyable times. The battalion acquired a goat (immediately christened Abdul) as mascot from a group of Bedouins and there were nights around camp fires where men sang and turned their thoughts homeward. The night canopy of glittering stars thrilled the romantics among them but the hours of darkness could be bitterly cold. All heavy baggage, including greatcoats, had been left at Pelusium and it was some weeks before they were brought up. Blankets and newspapers had to suffice as protection against the sudden nightly drop in temperature and the mornings' heavy dew. A strange disease with characteristics similar to cholera claimed a number from the column and influenza was also responsible for a steady stream of men disappearing down the lines of communication. Enemy aircraft nightly flew over the railway and supply dumps, killing five men of the 10th in November. The dead were originally buried alongside the railway but were reinterred at Kantara after the war. Shortly before Christmas the lines of communication were sufficiently secure and bulging with men and equipment for the army to make an attack on El Arish. The Turks however, electing not to stand and fight, abandoned their considerable defences and continued their retreat towards Palestine. Once again, having heard only the rumble of distant gunfire, the 10th was warned for a move back towards the canal. Padre Raymond was apparently the only man disappointed to learn that the Oldhamers would not pursue the Turk into the Holy Land.

At the beginning of December the battalion welcomed back one of its old familiar faces. Fred Hardman had spent a very uncomfortable three weeks on a ship carrying him and a draft of officers and men from England to Egypt. He had served for almost a year with the 3/10th and had witnessed the departure of many drafts to France for service with battalions of other regiments. Against the odds, Major Bamford had managed to get Hardman sent out to rejoin his old battalion. According to Hardman, accommodation on board the trooper was exceptionally cramped, the other officers lifeless and listless, deckchairs in short supply, the food rotten, the concerts boringly repetitive and the ship's library soon exhausted. To add to the discomfort, the ship had drifted in a Channel storm for five hours with her boilers flooded, the pumps broken and all the lifeboats smashed to matchwood. With the ship broadside on to towering waves and expecting any minute to be pounded on to the rocks off Brest, the captain managed to regain control of the vessel. Ten officers with broken bones later disembarked at Gibraltar for hospital treatment. Hardman had plenty of time to brood over his misfortunes and whenever the ship put into a harbour, dispatched increasingly sentimental letters to Kitty and his son. Things did not improve much when he joined the battalion. He was appointed to command A Company and, although he was delighted to have Chic Taylor as his second in command and a full complement of four subalterns (two of whom, Hassall and Cooper, he knew of old), the monotony of desert life soon affected his spirits. Days spent trudging across the unrelenting sand and nights spent huddled in cold bivvies reminded him of the days of torture when the battalion first went out to Egypt. He came up with what he called a new definition of misery: 'Freezing on a damp desert'.

Hardman brightened up a little as Christmas approached. He was hugely impressed by the Australian cavalry screening the advancing infantry and by the number of men and guns advancing upon El Arish. Like many others he recorded the entry of British forces to the town as a 'fiasco' (the Turks having already fled) and hoped that the column might halt for Christmas festivities. Reports of how the Oldhamers spent their third Christmas of the war vary. Lieutenant Wynne remembered that 'enormous' quantities of special fare were brought up by railway from Kantara and the battalion's camels were fully employed in carrying them on to the battalion. Bundles and parcels of delicacies and plum puddings from home, washed down with barrels of beer made, recalled Wynne, for a remarkable and memorable holiday. Sergeant Bradbury remembered it differently:

> *Christmas existed in name only. It was impossible to get up anything extra in the way of drink or eatables, and by an unpleasant coincidence, strangely characteristic of the British Army, bully beef and biscuits were the issue for 25 December … Imaginative men were left to draw mental pictures of turkeys and geese and other Christmas luxuries. A little beer did come from somewhere, but it was too pathetically small a quantity to rouse a Christmasy feeling.*

New Year passed with a bitter, drenching wind and the battalion continued with its routine work of manning guard posts along the railway. Midway through January the battalion again marched into El Arish. It just had time to pitch its tents when the already howling wind developed into the full-blown *Kampseen*. Three miserable days were spent cramped into tents enveloped in an impenetrable fog of sand. To add yet more unpleasantness, the sand originated from an area where thousands of camels had been coralled for a considerable period.

It was during this time at El Arish that the entire 42nd Division became submerged in gossip and speculation about a move to France. These were reinforced by occasional, more tangible signs of a shift to another theatre: men who had been attached to other units for clerical duty rejoined and three of the 10th's miscreants, Privates Boocock, Taylor and Arundale, returned from a military prison under a suspended sentence. On 31 January, five officers and 21 Other Ranks were sent away to Port Said as an advance embarkation party and six days later the entire battalion struck camp and climbed aboard a collection of open trucks for the rail journey to Kantara.

A two-day march along a tarmac road to Moascar followed. To feet that had spent months marching across soft sand, this proved testing and painful. It was consequently a rather ragged battalion which limped into the town. It was here that the long held suspicion of a move was finally confirmed; rifles were handed in and serge clothing drawn. The next three weeks were spent in a flurry of reorganisation and re-equipping. The divisional historian believed that the 'prospect of a change from the sand, the glaring sun, the discomfort of intense heat, the monotony and isolation of the desert, was hailed with joy by the majority'. The prospect of home leave was certainly a tempting lure, but there must have been many among the battalion who shared similar doubts to those of Maurice Bradbury. As the train carrying the battalion headed north to Alexandria, Bradbury believed there were 'not a few who were sorry to leave that country of colour and sunshine'. Wynne remembered that the hardship and discomforts experienced in the desert were compensated by the 'freedom from the irksome conventions of civilisation, the unrestricted movement across hill and dale, the glorious sunrises and sunsets (and) the awesomely beautiful nights'.

Despite the arrival of a draft in late October, the battalion's composition had remained fairly constant since April. Only eight men had been killed or died since the unit returned from Gallipoli although a ninth, Elias Holmes from Hollinwood, apparently fell from the train and was killed as it approached Alexandria. An unknown number had spent some time in hospital suffering from one or more of the diseases so prevalent in the desert zones and several were still in hospital or a convalescent camp when the battalion set sail for France. The accumulated losses since September 1914 meant that there were few men left of the battalion which had sailed into Alexandria with such optimism 16 months before. According to Bradbury, the remaining originals were:

... sadder and wiser soldiers, men who had found that fighting was a bitter, merciless game, but ... there was at least the memory of brilliant sunshine and Eastern sunsets ... Men knew there could be little romance in water-logged trenches in Flanders, where battlefields were nearly two years old, where shells dropped where they had been dropping since the fateful days of August.

New terrains and new enemies

As they steamed across the mediterranean, the mood among the men of the 42nd Division was somewhat mixed. Now familiar with the demands and reality of war, they knew there was nothing left of the imagined glory or romance which had initially caused them to enlist. Furthermore, they knew that the Western Front with all its attendant horrors would be more likely to maim or kill them than had been the Turk or Sinai. The climate too would be a shock to those men who had spent over two years in the sun. On the other hand, there was the prospect of home leave. The smoking chimneys and grimy streets of Oldham might not be one of the world's most beautiful images, but for those originals still alive and now sailing eastwards, they were still home.

German submarines were known to be prowling the Mediterranean so the convoy followed a zig-zag course towards Malta. Many of the troops who had been wounded or who had fallen victim to disease on Gallipoli had convalesced on the island. To them the squat fortifications of Valetta no doubt revived memories of pain and discomfort but also of rest and nurses in crisp uniforms. Unfortunately, a few officers only were allowed the opportunity to land and stretch their legs on its ancient streets. Twenty-four hours after anchoring in Grand Harbour, the HUNTSPILL was again on her way. Following lookouts' reports of a torpedo track passing astern of another trooper, a feint was made to pass south of Sicily. During the darkness of a spring night the convoy changed course and slipped through the Straits of Messina and hugged the Italian coast. On 6 March the HUNTSPILL and its cargo of Oldhamers tied up alongside a Marseille wharf.

At first sight the men were not too concerned about the condition of the train drawn up on the harbour siding. The sun was shining and the men were glad to be off the ship. The journey had been cramped and daily PT parades had done little to relieve the monotony. The train consisted of a strange conglomeration of carriages and wagons, the majority of which possessed no windows or doors and only the rudiments of a roof. As they were about to climb aboard, a severe storm swept in from the sea drenching the men with a penetrating, chilling rain. They embarked still soaked, crammed themselves into the allotted spaces and began a journey which, as the train rattled and jerked its way northward, grew increasingly desperate.

The rain changed to a blanketing and depressing snow. Whipped by a howling wind, it whistled through the unglazed wagons to settle on their huddled and numbed occupants. When the men's already wet clothes froze, their misery seemed complete. Several times the train shuddered and clattered to a halt but the men were not allowed to stretch their legs. Station masters and French RTOs reported frozen pipes, so hot drinks were unavailable. When the opportunity presented itself officers dashed off to plunder local cafés for coffee and cognac and troops could sometimes obtain boiling water from sympathetic engine drivers. When one party of officers returned late from a foray causing the train to be delayed, Colonel Robinson erupted into one of his legendary wraths. With leaping monocle adding to the terrifying thunder emanating from his furious mouth, Robinson tore into Padre Raymond. The unfortunate cleric, whom Robinson blamed for the delay, quaked under the onslaught and was threatened with arrest. Not dissuaded by the padre's experience, a few hours later another party of officers made a break for a track-side estaminet. This time the train did not wait and the three officers were forced to jump several open goods trains until, more dead than alive, they finally caught up with the battalion. All three underwent what one called a 'volley of hate' from the puce colonel. After sixty interminable and indescribably uncomfortable hours, the battalion detrained at Pont Remy near Amiens. Dozens of men suffering from bronchitis and near to collapse from exposure reported sick.

Those still standing fell in and marched seven miles in a snow storm to the village of Huppy whose slumbering inhabitants showed no inclination to open their barns to yet another battalion of British troops. Eventually, and after a combination of both bullying and cajoling, the farmers allowed access to their outbuildings. The weary, chilled and hungry troops collapsed into the less than fresh straw of Huppy's cowsheds and barns. Sleep, hot food and a warming of relationships between the Oldhamers and the daughters of their French hosts worked wonders for morale. It improved further when home leave opened soon after. The difficulties of having served in the East are illustrated by the fact that in one company 35 men had not been home since September 1914. Hardman's batman, for example, had eight children; while he was serving abroad the man's wife had died and his children had since been living with his elderly mother.

The three weeks spent at Huppy were busy and innovative. The battalion was issued with the short Lee-Enfield rifle (a better weapon than the version they had used in Gallipoli and Egypt), steel helmets and box respirators. These were novel and caused some amusement to the troops. So too was the digging of cruciform posts and battalion training in what were described as 'new tactics'. These involved lectures by several officers of the advance party who had already spent some days in the front line and schemes in which men practised deployment in a variety of formations. Other activities included digging trenches then filling them in, and laying and regathering copious amounts of barbed wire. Route marches along mud-covered lanes and across sodden fields were supposed to harden the men's feet; instead, the battalion's first cases of trench foot were reported. Other men continued to fall victim to the weather, septic sores and the food. There were constant complaints about the quantity and quality of the rations, the blame being placed squarely at the door of the new divisional train. The train was comprised largely of ex-regulars – old sweats well skilled in the art of ensuring their comfort came before that of the men they served. Scornful of their new Territorial comrades, these wily individuals contrived to keep the rations poor. The state of the division was such that one officer of the 10th remarked 'scarcely an officer or man in the division was fit. But the High Command, having blundered, decided to kill or cure'.

One man who did leave the battalion, and all knew it was for good, was Colonel Robinson. Too old and possibly too inflexible for the demands of the Western Front, he went on home leave and did not return. With his Punjabi servant and monocle, Robinson was too much of an anachronism. From the outset his regular Indian Army manner did not sit well with Lancashire Territorials but, in time, the troops did appear to warm to him and appreciated what had developed into a barely concealed hostility between Robinson, fighting on behalf of his men, and several of the divisional staff.

In common with the Territorial Force as a whole, the troops were issued with new numbers and ID discs. They swapped their old four-digit number for a new six-figure one, the first three digits of which indicated to which battalion of the Manchester Regiment they belonged. Armed with their new numbers, rifles, helmets and the thousand other accoutrements of war, yet still far from acclimatised, the battalion entered what they soon witnessed to be the war zone.

In mid-April the Oldhamers marched across the area largely devastated by the Germans as they had withdrawn towards their new defensive system known to the Allies as the Hindenburg Line. The carnage on the Somme between July 1916 and February 1917 convinced the German High Command it needed to shorten its line, thereby saving a significant number of divisions. The Hindenburg Line was begun as early as September 1916 but it was only in February 1917 that the Kaiser authorised a withdrawal to begin. Troops and forced labour had been hard at work wrecking anything that could be wrecked. Woods and orchards were cut down, villages and hamlets destroyed and roads cratered. The pursuing Allies were advancing through a wilderness, across which they had to transport men and material and repair communications. To add to the hardships, troops found little shelter in the ruined buildings and what few shelters did remain were found to be booby-trapped or had delayed-action mines ticking away. It was into this zone of desolation, in the midst of one of the coldest winters for decades, that the Oldhamers came.

The battalion trekked across the flooded Somme Valley and eventually into the ancient town of Péronne. Wynne was particularly appalled by its wanton destruction:

In pre-war days wealthy merchants from Amiens and Paris had retired to Péronne and had built splendid houses overlooking the river. The British troops, at the special request of the French Government, had refrained from shelling the town during the German occupation, but the enemy when driven out had no mercy, and his gunners had levelled to the ground some of the finest houses to be found in this part of France.

An equally disturbed Hardman wrote to his father:

The sights we see around us condemn (the Germans) to extreme perdition and though an Englishman is not given to hating, it would be a great sin if the Bosch were not classed as swine by Englishmen for many generations to come.

From Péronne the battalion marched another three miles to Buire. Only a small village at the best of times, the cottages had been razed and the roads cratered. The battalion spent long arduous hours in the numbing cold attempting to put the road between the village and nearby Longavesnes into good repair. When their shift was over, the men sought what little shelter a few flaps of canvas or sheets of corrugated iron could offer. Some officers were daily going forward and entering the trenches and shell holes held near Epéhy by their fellow Territorials of the North Midland Division. Others were going in the opposite direction to attend courses and lectures in the rear areas. On return to the battalion they had to spread the message to their companies and platoons. Several of the lecturers at these Army Schools had become legends throughout the BEF. Lieutenant-Colonel Campbell in particular, was renowned for his enthusiastic and blood-curdling talk on the 'spirit of the bayonet'. Hardman came back from one such visit and wrote of 'drinking blood'; he next had to instil in his company the same fervour as Campbell had inspired in him.

That proved difficult. The weather remained foul and the work heavy and uninteresting. When the battalion moved into the ruined shell of Longavesnes things did not improve. Accommodation was again largely non-existent. Some officers managed to secure a vague protection by inhabiting a former chicken run while others enjoyed the dubious luxury of a cow byre. Most of the men simply hacked a hole in the frozen ground and draped a ground sheet across the top. It was in this soul-destroying place that the battalion suffered its first fatality since leaving Egypt. Captain Leonard Baird, commonly known as 'Dicky', was sitting some 100m away from a stone gate post when it suddenly exploded. A delayed action fuse planted beneath the post by the retreating Germans blew the masonry to smithereens, broadcasting lumps of stone in all directions. One piece struck Baird on the head and he died about one hour later. Earlier in the day he had joked with the RQMS about the dangers of booby-traps. 'If you hear a mine going up and somebody being killed' he said, 'it will be me'.

Having served continuously as Battalion Medical Officer from before the war, Baird, through his dedication and skill, had saved many lives on Gallipoli and in Egypt. He was buried in Longavesnes the following day and was posthumously awarded a Military Cross for his work on Gallipoli.

Four days later the battalion lost two more men. The companies had moved into the line near Peiziere, taking over for the first time in France responsibility for their own sector. Battalions either side of them made local attacks and in the retaliatory barrage Private John McNulty was killed and Private James Arundel mortally wounded. When the shelling extended to the transport lines the battalion's animals, which like the men had suffered wretchedly from the change in climate, broke lose from their tethers and fled in terror. Having become hopelessly entangled in barbed wire they were all eventually rounded up.

The battalion and division soon settled into a routine of trench life. The Gallipoli veterans immediately realised the difference between trench warfare on the Peninsula and that of the Western Front. Here, as No Man's Land was usually substantially wider than on Gallipoli, patrols were sent out nightly to inspect enemy wire and sap heads. By late April the weather had begun to improve and the German withdrawal to the Hindenburg Line was complete. The 42nd Division, like many other divisions up and down the line, spent much of its time consolidating the new positions; shell holes were connected to form front and support systems with communication trenches running between them. The Germans had built their zone of defence with extreme care; the main and support trenches were on reverse slopes and the outpost line commanded observation over the British positions. The 10th continued to improve the trenches, dig cruciform posts and lay wire. When the battalion moved two miles south to the Lempire sector, German observation made daylight communication between Battalion HQ and the front posts impossible. This sector included what had already become the rapidly disintegrating and notoriously bloody acre known as Gillemont Farm. Before it eventually achieved its objective the 48th Division suffered heavy casualties during several attempts to take the pulverised farm. Edwin Vaughan, an officer of the 8/Warwickshire, later recalled that soon after handing over the captured farm to the 10th, a

German counter-attack retook it. Vaughan's battalion was sent back up to regain it and on the way to its assembly positions passed some of the 10th. Annoyed at having to risk their lives again through what they perceived to be the faults of others, the Warwicks suggested the Oldhamers should 'make way for real soldiers'. According to Vaughan, several fist fights erupted before officers of both battalions restored order. There is no mention of the incident in any of the 10th's records and Vaughan's accuracy and chronology are sometimes in doubt. However, another example of the East Lancashire Division's inexperience occurred when a battalion of the King's Royal Rifle Corps relieved the 8/Lancashire Fusiliers in the Villers-Plouich trenches. Shortly after the relief the Germans raided one of the posts and captured a rifleman. The KRRC made enquiries of the departed Fusiliers as to how the Lancastrians had failed to report that the wire in front of the post had been cut, by hand, some time before the Rifles had taken over.

What is known for certain about the 10th's occupation of Gillemont Farm is that it was extremely uncomfortable. The approaches to the front posts were knee-deep in mud and the disputed area was regularly shelled and trench-mortared. In early May, A Company was holding the front positions when the Germans made a determined attack on the shells of the out-buildings. Weighed down with inch-thick mud on their uniform and equipment, A Company counter-attacked and drove the Germans back to their own lines. Its success, at the cost of only one dead and six wounded, prompted a congratulatory telegram from the brigadier.

Accommodation for those not in the line was equally poor. Peiziere did have some reasonably intact buildings but, surmised to be booby-trapped, they were placed out of bounds. Two companies of Lancashire Fusiliers in nearby Malassise Farm had suffered grievously when a delayed-action device blew up a barn. Undeterred by this deadly warning, some officers of the 10th decided to throw caution to the winds and occupied a reasonably roofed house in Peiziere. One young subaltern, a little more circumspect than his colleagues, decided to investigate the building and discovered a quantity of high explosive taped neatly to one of the rafters. The place was evacuated and the next day a shell landed squarely upon it. The house disappeared in an eruption of brick dust and roofing tiles.

In mid-May the battalion was relieved in the Lempire sector by the 3/Hussars and the Oxfordshire Hussars of 4 Cavalry Brigade. Although the 10th warned the Hussars about approaching the front positions in daylight, several of their officers made the attempt and suffered as a consequence. One of the Oxfords who lost his life fighting for Gillemont Farm was the father of James Bond's creator and MP for South Oxon, Valentine Fleming.

In June the battalion shifted a little north to take over trenches in Havrincourt Wood. By this time the battalion was commanded by Lieutenant-Colonel Lewis of the Devonshire Regiment. Major Booth, who had been in temporary command since his return from hospital, was consequently transferred to a Territorial battalion of the 59th Division. Men who had gone off to hospital soon after the battalion's arrival in France were also returning. Jack Street, who in April had departed with a septic hand and leg, rejoined the battalion during its tour in Havrincourt Wood. He wrote of it being a 'treat to be beneath green trees and to hear the birds singing'. Street returned just in time to receive a new issue of clothing. Divisional baths had been constructed at Ytres and men who had not had their clothes off for almost four weeks now had the opportunity to divest themselves, albeit briefly, of their louse-ridden underclothes and shirts. New boots had also arrived to re-equip the battalion. The pairs issued as it left Alexandria were no doubt suited to the desert sand but when exposed to European mud, disintegrated in an alarmingly short time.

Havrincourt Wood was indeed a welcome relief after the mud of Lempire and Gillemont Farm. It had not suffered the fate of so many woods and copses during the German retreat and in early May the trees were sprouting leaves and the flowers were in full bloom. Birds flew above the heads of weary soldiers and reminded them of happier days. For, although it had not long been in the line, the 10th's introduction to trench warfare on the Western Front had been testing. Despite the almost constant chatter of machine guns and the regular artillery exchanges, Havrincourt Wood did offer the opportunity for men to rebuild their spirits. Accommodation was again inadequate yet (apart from a storm on 21 May which turned trenches into foaming rivers and roads into quagmires), the weather was beautiful. Little occurred to threaten the almost idyllic existence. Patrols went out nightly, occasionally encountering enemy patrols or working parties, but usually returned from No Man's Land without incident a couple of hours later. Lieutenant Lee regularly led groups to investigate the enemy wire and a chalk pit lying in No Man's Land. During one such excursion he and Lieutenant Whittaker were both wounded. Whittaker had just returned from an interview for a post with the Intelligence Department at GHQ while Lee was one of the battalion's original officers and had served on Gallipoli. At the end of June the battalion was relieved and moved to a camp in Ytres. There was a short time to smarten up and bathe before working parties were warned for duty. These could involve carrying rations and engineering stores to the front, wiring, road-making, unloading artillery ammunition, making horse-standings and digging communication trenches. On the night of 6 June one such party came under sustained shell fire. Six men were killed, two died of wounds a few hours later and about 20 were wounded. Lance Corporal Thomas Claber, whose father had been killed with the battalion on Gallipoli, and Charles Howard of Hathershaw Street were buried by orderlies at a casualty clearing station at Péronne. The six killed outright were carried back to Green Jacket Ridge and buried in a little cemetery at Neuville-Bourjonval. After the war the parents of Sergeant Farrar Stansfield of Royton and William Boyd of Tunnel Street decided against having a cross carved upon their sons' headstones. Both have a simple inscription paid for by their families. Stansfield has: 'He was a good son' and Boyd: 'He gave his richest gift, his life'.

Throughout June, officers and men continued to depart on courses. Having attended a signalling course at the divisional school, Jack Street returned to the battalion to discover that four of his closest friends had been killed: Harry Highton, Tom Beaumont, George Holt and Tommy Dyson were all killed on the same day. Another man, George Taylor, had also fallen victim to the same spate of German shelling on the wood. Of the five killed only Taylor's and Dyson's bodies were identified after the war and have a known grave. Like Street, both Beaumont and Dyson had been original members of the 2/10th and had served on Gallipoli.

Several awards were given during this period in the Havrincourt sector. Captain Baird's posthumous Military Cross was confirmed, Major Wilde was awarded a DSO and three men were awarded the Military Medal for the daylight capture of four Germans. Spotting a casual German sentry, Sergeant J. Sugden and Privates Cook and Macnamara crawled through the long grass of No Man's Land and in perfect German called upon the snoozing sentry to surrender. Three of his companions were also persuaded to emerge from their dug out and the party made its way back towards the British lines. These four unfortunate Germans are thought to have been the first prisoners captured by the 42nd Division. Sugden, who apparently had the 'heart of a lion and the soul of a poet', had enjoyed an interesting past. While working for Krupps, the German armaments firm, he was reported to have been arrested and deported as a spy. He was again arrested in Amsterdam and put on a ship to Hull. Falling in with some Hungarian gypsies he eventually ended up in South America. He was later commissioned and survived the war. One of his companions, Private Macnamara, also survived the war only to be killed when he fell 90 feet from an Ashton mill chimney in May 1919.

At long last the men began to enjoy an improvement in the quality and quantity of their rations. Although it remained uninspired and monotonous, there was some variety. Rissoles made a change from bully beef and parcels from home began to arrive with more regularity. Families of many men had enough difficulty feeding themselves and were often unable to send luxuries to their menfolk in the trenches. In order to ensure that all troops might receive the occasional surprise from home, Comfort Groups in Oldham's schools, mills and offices collected and despatched food, cigarettes and socks.

Besides the usual activities of football and other sports, men out on rest were attracted by another pastime. Not content with spending so many of their so-called 'rest' periods employed as navvies, men of the 42nd Division could often be observed hacking away at the gardens of ruined cottages behind the line. The craze had begun after several idle Oldhamers had watched a French civilian and gendarme enter the battalion's rest area. Accompanied by a British officer, the civilian had commenced to dig a hole in what had been his back yard. To the amazement of a growing band of interested onlookers, the hole yielded a hoard of gold coins buried in 1914. Within hours every garden in the vicinity was covered by swarms of shirt-sleeved British troops digging earnestly for what they believed would be their passport to riches.

In late June, 20 Other Ranks under the command of Second Lieutenant Holt began serious training on how to conduct a raid. These events were becoming increasingly common along the front, their object being to enter the enemy trenches and grab a live prisoner. He would then be dragged, pulled or otherwise persuaded to return with the raiders and undergo interrogation. Information could be gathered on the man's unit and even, judging from his equipment and rations, how deeply the naval blockade on Germany was biting. Given the often high casualty rate and the frequency with which they went wrong, raids were generally hated by those ordered to conduct one. The normal procedure was to cross No Man's Land under cover of a box barrage and smoke, the enemy wire having had gaps blown in it by trench mortars or Bangalore torpedoes. The raiders, carrying an assortment of mediaeval and modern weapons, were then supposed to dash in, capture a prisoner and get out before the enemy recovered from the initial shock. We can probably assume that Holt and his men were not particularly down-hearted to learn some time before the raid's scheduled day that the battalion and the division were being pulled out of the line.

On 11 July the 10th marched into the pile of rubble that had once constituted the village of Courcelles-le-Comte. The new abode lay in the devastated zone west of the main Bapaume-Arras road. The sparse accommodation was reported to be 'indescribably filthy' so the men, already caked in mud and with uniforms tattered and shabby, were put to work to make what improvements they could. A bathing parade and change of underclothes helped to restore spirits and the men did what they could with their boots, puttees and tunics. Although Courcelles was in ruin, it was far enough behind the line to prevent harassment from all save the largest calibre of enemy shells. Six weeks were spent there and, with hard work and a drying ground, conditions were made reasonably habitable. There was little to do except train and work. Civilians had not been permitted to re-enter the zone so there were no estaminets where troops could spend some of their meagre pay on egg and chips. A Church Army canteen did offer some solace but there were no chance encounters with French mesdemoiselles capable of taking the edge off the monotony. Much of the training concentrated on attacking and subduing concrete pill boxes and consisted of sectional, platoon, company, battalion and eventually brigade schemes. One day Sergeant Bryant of the Welsh Guards arrived to give the battalion the benefit of his expertise on the parade ground. He first put the warrant officers and sergeants through their paces and then for an hour directed his marginally more polite invective towards the subalterns. As his finale, the entire battalion had the pleasure of enduring 60 minutes under his watchful eye and colourfully convincing language.

Other methods of fostering *esprit* included sport and inter-unit competitions. In the brigade 'turn out' competition the 10th won first prize for the appearance of its transport limbers but received the wooden spoon in the officers' chargers competition. There was also the welcome news that the Oldham Comrades Battalion, Pioneers to the 7th Division, was working at Ervillers only four miles away. Old friendships were renewed during inter-battalion football matches and smoking concerts. The Comrades had endured a torrid time during the Battle of Bullecourt and were expecting, as indeed was the 10th, shortly to move north to take their turn in the slaughter then in progress east of Ypres. The 42nd had been fortunate not to have been involved in the Battle of Arras; only the most supreme of optimists would believe that it could escape involvement in the summer's principal offensive.

Time at Courcelles passed swiftly. Troops listened to lectures on field engineering, wiring and gas drill and, as a sign of the times, there were exercises in co-operation with contact aircraft. A good deal of time and effort was expended in removing fields of old German wire. This was in anticipation of civilians returning but, as events seven months later were to prove, the battalion could well have done with the wire still in place. The positive aspect to emerge from this period was demonstrated in March 1918 when, as the 10th fought to contain the German advance, many of its officers and men were familiar with the lie and nature of the land.

The stay at Courcelles certainly improved the spirits of the battalion. At least one draft of 37 men arrived from the Reserve Battalion then in training at Hunmanby but, as so many of its members had predicted, the division moved north. A two-day march across the old Somme battlefield brought the 10th to Forceville, 12 miles north-east of Amiens; there it entrained for yet another of those seemingly interminable journeys on French railways. With the men cramped into horse boxes, the train shuddered, crawled and snorted its way to Proven. A march to Watou took it to a camp of flapping canvas and a few days of more intensive training on how to storm concrete emplacements. If there had remained any uncertainty as to where the battalion's next tour would be, the incessant roar of the guns, the soaring night-time flares and the constant movement of ambulances and limbers, convinced the doubters that it would be in the crucible of the Salient.

The division's apprehension was well placed. On 31 July British divisions had attacked towards the Passchendaele Ridge and had met with only patchy success. With the drainage ditches which criss-crossed the low-lying land long since destroyed by concentrated artillery fire, the battlefield east of Ypres had degenerated into a quagmire. Some advance towards the marginally higher ground had been made but at tremendous cost. Men, tanks and guns disappeared into the stinking, fetid mud that clogged weapons and destroyed the souls of men. Already, various positions had become almost household names: Hell Fire Corner, Shrapnel Corner and the Menin Road conjured up images of death, mutilation, incessant shelling, ineluctable mud and an endless procession of wounded. Corpses dating from the First and Second Battles of Ypres were daily thrown up and reburied by the constant barrages and bombardments. Movement above ground in daylight was courting disaster and at night working and ration parties ran the likelihood of slipping from the trench board tracks to drown unnoticed in the slime of adjoining shell holes. Guns sank to their muzzles and limbers and horses were blown to oblivion by salvos of well placed shells. It was an area where men existed, endured and prayed for relief. To add to the misery, Allied attacks were usually presaged by downpours of numbing rain. Weighed down by equipment and cloying mud, troops struggled from their flooded shell holes and waded vainly towards the German lines. Concrete pill boxes, many so low-lying that they were almost impossible to spot, housed machine guns which poured devastating fire into the burdened attackers. Advances were reckoned in scores of yards and the dead computed in hundreds. It was into this evil slough that the 10/Manchester was thrown.

The 10th was allowed a little longer to train than its comrades in the brigade's other battalions. The time was again spent in practising methods to attack the concrete pill boxes sprinkled along the German lines of defence. On the night of 5 September the men donned full fighting order and prepared to begin the slog towards the front. In a night punctured by squally showers and lit intermittently by the soaring lights of flares, the Oldhamers trudged along the duckboard tracks towards Railway Wood. This much pummelled sector had been just behind the British front line when the offensive began and was, five weeks later, just two miles behind the forward positions. The area was regularly shelled, making conditions among the mere stumps of trees unimaginable. With the water table only some 18 inches below the surface of the fields, trenches in the conventional sense were impossible to dig. Where local conditions allowed, breastworks were construc- ted but most of the work done in and around the wood consisted of shovelling liquid mud from one forlorn position to another. The 10th carried rations and shells to the forward posts and the gun lines, worked on roads and duckboard tracks and suffered. It was not involved in any fighting but suffered losses from the constant attention of the German gunners. Attacks continued on other parts of the front but the task of the 42nd Division was to prepare its sector for an attack at a later date. The flooded shelters and trenches were poisoned by gas and shrapnel bursts above their heads showered them with lethal balls of lead and slivers of red-hot iron.

It was during one such bombardment that Lieutenant-Colonel Lewis was killed. Battalion HQ was housed in the cellar of a ruined farm known as Kit and Kat. The position lay on what in more peaceful times had been the minor road running between Frezenberg and Westhoek. Lewis was hit by a shell splinter when giving orders to a runner and died shortly afterwards. His body was taken back to Ypres and buried in the burgeoning cemetery near to the tumbled central square. Significant though it might have been to the officers, the death of the colonel probably had little effect upon the general morale of the battalion. Having only recently joined the unit, most of the men would have recognised him but would have had little to do with him. Wynne thought initially that Lewis' methods had seemed harsh but later considered that he was a 'thoroughly efficient soldier' who had been 'very much misunderstood'. Bradbury believed that Lewis' one object in life was to kill Germans and that he expected everyone else to hold a similar creed.

One day after Lewis had been buried, another three of the battalion's men were laid to rest close by. Two of them were not Oldham men: Sergeant Thomas Poole came from Manchester and Lance Corporal Robert Roscoe hailed from Wigan. Granville Rourke, who had enlisted in the 3rd Battalion came from Werneth. To the west of Ypres, along the straight road which led to Poperinghe, a number of casualty clearing stations were constantly busy. Several were concentrated at the village of Brandhoek and it was within their tents and huts that another three of the 10th, two of them from Oldham, died of wounds. The other fatality was Lance Corporal John Bliss from Middlesbrough who had come to the battalion with a small draft of men from the Durham Light Infantry. A further five men were also killed or died of wounds during the battalion's short stay in the sector. In addition to this total, at least one former member of the 10th was also killed and buried not far from where Lieutenant-Colonel Lewis fell. William Fisher from Albany Street had enlisted in the 3rd Battalion but probably owing to some medical disability was transferred to the Labour Corps. He was killed while working with the Corps' 8th Company near Birr Cross in early October.

By the time Fisher died the division and the battalion were well away from the hated sector. The 10th handed over to the 9/Scottish Rifles of the 9th Division and marched away to Derby Camp near Brandhoek. Although the men were undoubtedly pleased to be heading away from the Westhoek Ridge, their mood remained subdued. As Wynne recalled, 'Men cannot come through hell unscathed'. They needed time to recover their spirits, to clean up, to put behind them the horrors of the Salient and look forward to mail from home and perhaps a posting to a quieter sector. They probably realised that they had been very lucky. Few battalions went into the maelstrom without having to undertake a major attack and lose in the process perhaps hundreds of men. Two brigades of the division had made a costly and largely abortive advance towards the notorious strong points of Iberia and Borry Farm, but the 10th had been required only to labour and suffer from a distance. As if in partial penance for its good fortune, the new colonel was waiting for the battalion as it marched and slithered into Derby Camp. Lieutenant-Colonel Peel inspected the ranks and promptly ordered two hours saluting parade and platoon drill.

Derby Camp was in range of German guns but the time spent there amidst the sea of mud did begin to heal men's minds. Many might have assumed that this period was merely a respite before the division was again thrown into the cauldron. It was unusual for a division to do only one tour and apart from a critical comment on the 42nd's performance by General Gough's chief of staff, Neill Malcolm, no convincing reason has surfaced to explain why the authorities decided that the division had done enough. Even the divisional historian thought: 'The men were glad to quit the Ypres salient, but they did not leave it in a happy frame of mind. Every one felt that the division was not at its best; that it was capable of better things had opportunity been given'.

Perhaps senior officers did regret the division's departure but most of the men no doubt rejoiced at the news that it was to begin a move north to the quieter coastal sector of the Nieuport front. Bradbury later recorded that 'the battalion had been in many hotter places, but it was the general atmosphere of Wipers which was so depressing and the fact that the fighting was on exactly the same ground as it was in the early days of the war'. When it arrived on the coast the division discovered that it was relieving its own second line unit, the 66th Division. There was little time for friends, brothers and cousins in the various battalions to exchange news of home and recent experiences for the 10th moved in just about as the 2/10th marched out. The senior battalion began acclimatising to an area which fathered swarms of ferocious mosquitoes and sand fleas.

The Second and Third
Line Battalions

The 2/10th battalion manchester regiment had recorded
something of a chequered history since reaching establishment in
late September 1914. As we have seen, it left Oldham in November
1914 dressed in civilian clothes and spent the following winter
and spring in Southport. It gradually acquired the necessities of
war and in May 1915 travelled down to Cuckfield in Sussex. Still
at full strength it moved to the tented camp at Pease Pottage in
June and, in July, despatched Lieutenant Spielman, Wilf Cook,
Jack Street and 300 comrades to the 1st Battalion to make good
some of the losses sustained at Krithia. Afterwards, although the
2nd Battalion did receive a small draft from the 3/10th about the
same time as the two large Gallipoli drafts were leaving, the
strength of the battalion underwent a serious decline.

By August 1915 the unit was only about two-thirds establishment. It had moved to Shoreham-on-Sea and was engaged in
coastal defence. The time was easy and the weather largely kind.
The troops spent their working hours digging trenches in the
sand, laying barbed wire, stretching out on route marches along
the Downs and generally enjoying themselves. The men appear
to have been properly equipped but the transport was somewhat
lacking. The transport section could boast of possessing two
civilian lorries, one milk float, six General Service limbers, 19
horses and 19 mules. The officers shared six riding horses and
two cobs, five of which were deemed unsuitable for riding;
officers leading their companies on route marches therefore had
to walk rather than ride at the head of the column. The battalion
had been allocated to 198 Brigade of the 66th (2/East Lancashire)
Division which at the time was forming at Southport. For the
time being therefore, the 2/10th had little to do with the other
units of the division.

The principal problem facing the battalion was how to achieve
an acceptable degree of fitness for overseas service when so many
of its ranks were being posted. In addition to the drafts to the
1st Battalion, a substantial number of men were returning to
Oldham and civilian employment. Many men with a background
in engineering were recalled or, if army life was not to their

liking, could apply to be released. The Government's drive to improve the manufacture of munitions was in full swing and skilled men were deemed to be more useful in the factories than as cannon-fodder. At least 140 men followed this path during the autumn of 1915, thereby creating something of a crisis for the battalion. Aware of and alarmed at the drain in the ranks, the Council and Territorial Force Association organised a Recruitment Fortnight for the battalion in late September and early October 1915. Colonel Rye and the Mayor together addressed some of the 47 meetings held across the Borough. The object of the campaign, which included posters on Co-op vans, trams and taxi cabs, adverts in newspapers, handbills, concerts, boxing matches and parades in Alexandra Park, was to secure a further 600 recruits. By the close of the rally, only 180 had attested. The campaign was in competition with drives for several other units, not least for the town's own 3rd Battalion. The results were disappointing but came at a time when the Volunteer movement as a whole was showing alarming signs of fatigue. An attempt to delay or put off conscription was about to be launched and many men had decided that they would rather wait and be called than offer themselves voluntarily. While they waited, they could earn better money in the factories than that offered by the King.

Until early November the battalion itself remained working in Shoreham where, periodically, news filtered through of the fate of many who had gone to Gallipoli in July. Spielman's death was certainly widely known of, and those of other comrades were reported in the local papers sent from home. One unknown soldier remembered Spielman as a 'smart, able, thoroughgoing young officer who promised well ... he was withal, a true gentleman – a soldier and a man'. Shortly after his death was announced, another draft of officers followed the path of Spielman and his men. This was the group of nine officers which included Selwyn Rowbotham.

In November the battalion moved to Burham in Kent and then began a five-day march to Crowborough in Sussex. This march of over 70 miles was done in full kit and took its toll of men. On arrival the battalion was housed in huts which had been well used by many units en route for France. The accommodation was adequate but hardly luxurious and there was little opportunity for the troops to enjoy any non-working hours. Holding few attractions other than the countryside itself, Crowborough was a lonely place sited among the heaths and sparse woodlands of the Weald. The men knuckled down to some hard training and received two drafts from Oldham. These 109 newcomers were largely men of the Army Reserve, not of A1 fitness but capable of serving overseas. They were joined in February by a further 172 men of a similar class. So many men of the original battalion had gone to the 1st Battalion or back home to work in munitions that the September 1914 enlistments were now in the minority.

In March 1916 the battalion and its brigade left Sussex for Colchester. A large draft from Oldham arrived on 1 April to make good the losses from postings and transfers and brought the battalion back to full strength. These men were from the 3/10th Battalion which had been raised in March 1915. Recruitment to this unit was, like that to the 2nd Battalion, slow, but it had reached 60% of establishment by June and for a time was ordered to stop enlistments. A few days later recruiting was reopened when the third line battalions (which were intended to be training units to replace losses sustained by the first and second line battalions) were permitted to recruit up to 90% of establishment. The summer months were hard as fewer than ten men per week presented themselves for attestation. It was for this reason that the East Lancashire Territorial Force Association refused a request from the Gordon Highlanders and the Argyll & Sutherland Highlanders Associations to recruit in the Oldham area. A similar request from the 4/Royal Scots, the Edinburgh Territorials, was also denied but the Scots seemed to have ignored the refusal and enlisted a few Oldhamers who preferred trews to coarse serge.

Recruits to the third line remained in Oldham until October 1915. When the battalion marched in full voice down to Clegg Street station the town turned out to wish it well. A watching reporter thought the 'womenfolk who assembled did not appear to feel the strain of their departure, but seemed to be fully incensed by the fact that their men were going away in order to prepare to do their little bit when called upon'. The knowledge that Oldham's 1st Battalion had suffered severely on Gallipoli and that a major battle had taken place with heavy losses and with little apparent success at Loos, was beginning to harden those left at home and confirm that the war was going to last a long time.

With both battalions now posted away from the town, uniformed troops were not seen so regularly on Oldham's streets. A small number remained at Rifle Street but most soldiers seen about were those on leave. The majority of these men were there legitimately but others had left camp without the necessary pass. Several of these absconders ended up before the local Bench. Richard Oates, for example, described by the press as a 'dishevelled-looking soldier of the 2/10th' had gone AWOL on six occasions. The magistrates sent him to Strangeways until a military escort could be provided to take him back to camp. Fred Rourke of the same battalion was treated with greater leniency. He claimed that his name had originally been on the list for Christmas leave and had then been removed. Disappointed, he went for a few pints in a Crowborough pub and then decided to catch a train home to Oldham. He expressed regret for his actions and was ordered to return to camp without an escort. A final example concerned a rather elderly soldier of the 3/10th. James Mason, aged 43, of Shaw Road was brought before the court for disorderly conduct. While on leave he had taken a couple of pints and then set about his wife. His frightened daughter rushed into the street and begged a passing policeman to come and rescue her mother who was 'being killed' by the soldier. On giving a promise that he would never do such a thing again, Mason was discharged and ordered to return to camp.

The 3rd Battalion spent some months at Codford on Salisbury Plain. The village itself consisted of about four houses, a train station and a public house. The troops were bored and the accommodation poor. In early April 1916 it moved to Witley in Surrey, a much improved camp with good facilities and surrounded by beautiful country. The three third-line battalions of the Ardwick, Ashton and Oldham Territorials remained here until September 1916 when, in a major reorganisation, the three units were amalgamated to form the 8th (Reserve) Battalion. Men trained with this unit from enlistment but were liable to be posted to any unit serving abroad which needed a draft.

By that time of course, the Battle of the Somme was reaping its terrible harvest and the demand for drafts was incessant. Fred

Hardman was at Witley and, like several others of the 1st Battalion who were recovering from wounds, was concerned that he might be sent to any battalion of any regiment then serving on the Western Front. Life at Witley was fairly gentle and Hardman had been searching for rooms which would allow Kitty and Rex to come down from Oldham. He had been made up to Captain but despite his now more senior rank and status, his repeated applications to be sent back to the 1st Battalion in Egypt had so far drawn a blank. The rumour about camp was that because all available men were needed in France, there would be no further drafts for Egypt. Confirmation of this policy seemed to come in late June when a large draft left for the Western Front and a further three officers and 150 men departed two weeks later. Hardman was one of several officers who seemed to have been deliberately kept back by the adjutant in the hope that he might at some time in the future be permitted to send a draft to Egypt.

In September the newly created Reserve Battalion moved to Oswestry and then Kimnel in North Wales. Hardman wrote to Kitty that Oswestry was 'a miserable little place ... Royton without the mills'; Kimnel, a huge sprawling camp of hutments, was considered to be a significant improvement. In October 1916 the battalion moved to Southport. Establishing a camp close to a holiday resort started alarm bells ringing in high places. Senior officers of Western Command had already expressed horror at the dress and behaviour of young, junior officers with the training battalions. Their 'general conduct and bearing was ... unsoldierlike and ungentlemanly' and, being 'subversive of all discipline', was deemed likely to forfeit the respect of their NCOs and men. When pulled up and reprimanded by their seniors, the subalterns apparently expressed surprise and ignorance of standing orders. To ensure that the young men should not imagine staying at a seaside resort was a licence to behave in a yet more slovenly or licentious manner, Western Command issued some uncompromising orders. Officers were not to go into cafés before 5.00pm, were never allowed to use any hotel bar, to carry parcels or to wear slacks (as opposed to breeches) before 6.00pm. Finally they were warned that it was an offence against the Defence of the Realm Act to check into an hotel under a false name or to attempt to register any women other than their wives.

In late September, just before the battalion moved from Drenewydd Camp to Southport, Hardman and Gilbert Taylor, another officer of the Oldham Battalion, were ordered to take a draft over to France. He warned Kitty not to be worried as the officers only had to deliver the men to the enormous base camp at Étaples and then return home. The experience had a profound impact on Hardman. While hanging around Étaples station:

> ... watching hospital train after hospital train come through ... one realises that there really is a war on. I saw men coming down from the front line with those glassy eyes which tell of exhausted nerves and sleepless nights, plodding along with their heavy loads, too tired even to speak. I knew what they felt like, each man showed it in his face and my sympathy was spontaneous with them.

As we have seen, Hardman was fortunate and eventually rejoined the 1st Battalion in Egypt. Other officers and men who had originally enlisted in the Oldham Territorials considered themselves lucky to be sent to the 2/10th which, in March 1916, moved to Colchester.

The battalion was by that time such a hybrid unit that A and D Companies were reorganised to contain men who originated from Oldham, and B and C Companies took the men from Manchester and other parts of Lancashire. On 1 July 1916 a draft of 350 men made up of original 2/10th and men of the 3/10th posted to the 2nd Battalion, was sent to the 1/King's Liverpool, a unit then in the thick of the Somme fighting. This drain, along with the number of men of the 2/10th who had left for a variety of reasons, probably reduced the number of original members of the battalion to fewer than 300.

In conjunction with its brigade, the battalion trained and prepared itself for France. The Battle of the Somme ground on amidst the mud and floods of the Ancre Valley and the demands for yet more men remained foremost in the minds of authority.

In late 1916 the second line Territorial divisions were warned that they would be going to France early in the New Year. Remaining at Colchester until March 1917 when it too entrained for Southampton and the Western Front, the 66th Division was one of the later ones to go.

An advance party from the battalion had left for France in February but the bulk of the unit did not depart from Folkestone until 5 March 1917. It landed at Boulogne and marched to St Martin's Camp, the traditional first night's stop for newly arrived battalions. The men spent two days cleaning up, resting and turning out for the odd parade before the battalion then moved to Calonne-sur-Lys. Three days were spent in this small town before the brigade marched a little further south to La Bassée. The other three battalions were first into the line to gain experience, the 2/10th remaining in reserve in the village of Le Quesnoy. The division had taken up position in the area around the infamous Cuinchy brickstacks, a region which in 1914 and 1915 had seen heavy fighting. By 1917 it was considered to be a quiet sector, ideal for new divisions to gain trench experience. The Oldham battalion trained and waited for its turn to take over a sector of the line; its opportunity came in mid-March when it relieved the 2/4 East Lancashire in trenches almost waist deep in mud. As in so many places on the Western Front, the enemy had the advantage of the high ground. The battalion's trenches were largely overlooked and German machine gunners and artillery spotters had the front and rear areas precisely registered. Little could be done in daylight to improve the appalling condition of the trenches so most of the work was of necessity done at night. Casualties were light but still significant for a unit new to active service. Two men were killed on the first night up and Lieutenant Fripp was hit in the hand shortly after. In all, ten men were killed and one died of wounds during the several trench tours of March and April. These fatalities included Corporal Robert Carr from Blackburn, Walter Johnson, the son of a former Colour Sergeant in the Manchester Regiment, and James Hurst of Oldham who had been attached to the 198th Light Trench Mortar Battery. John Cundiff of Gorton and John Holmes of Dewsbury, formerly a member of the KOYLI, were two of the several men in the division who succumbed to pneumonia.

The enemy regularly sent over liberal amounts of phosgene gas. This particular form of gas is odourless and caused casualties among men who, believing the shells to be duds, failed to put on their masks. Soaking into the ground and seeping into shell holes and trenches, the gas could linger for many hours; it caught the unwary, causing paroxysms of coughing and choking. A substantial number of men disappeared for treatment at field ambulances and casualty clearing stations during these early weeks. In early May, Second Lieutenant Shepherd died from the effects of either phosgene or chlorine and Second Lieutenant Mitzakis, who like Shepherd had been attached to the battalion from the 13/London, was awarded the *Croix de Guerre* for helping to evacuate victims of this pernicious weapon. Many other men, and unfortunately the war diary rarely specifies precise numbers, were sent down the line suffering from trench foot and sickness. In addition to those who died from enemy action or disease, Private Thomas Bell fell into the nearby canal and drowned. He was buried in the beautiful little cemetery at Gorre where, following a tumultuous action seven months later, many men of the 1st Battalion were to be laid to rest.

Although the 2/10th was itself not required to attempt one, other battalions of the brigade conducted raids on the enemy lines. On one occasion the East Lancashires went over while the Oldham battalion held the trenches to their rear. The Blackburn Territorials protected parties of Royal Engineers whose object was to destroy mine shafts and dugouts in the German front system. The Oldhamers had earlier spent a very uncomfortable tour listening to the sound of German miners tunnelling beneath them. Every day an officer of the RE would come into the trench, listen and announce that the German mine was not yet ready to explode. It was with great relief that the front companies were eventually replaced by those of another battalion. The engineers frequently discharged gas towards the enemy lines from the front trenches and, with their task completed, hastily withdrew to leave the unfortunate infantry to suffer the inevitable German retaliation. Three men of the battalion, none of whom came from Oldham, were killed during one such exchange on 6 June. Unpleasant and bestial as it was, the use of such weapons was expected. Concern had swept through the companies in May when it was feared the Germans were preparing a new and yet more deadly device. Anxious sentries reported strange noises emanating from behind the enemy lines. With the majority of the men coming from industrial cities, none had recognised the evening calls of bullfrogs croaking contentedly from the marshes and ponds of the sector.

During this period the battalion received a new commanding officer and second in command. Lieutenant-Colonel Burke, who had been with the unit from its earliest days, went home and was replaced by Major Norton who was posted from the West Riding Territorials. Major Shiers, who had similarly been with the battalion for over two years, was replaced by Major Locke of the Royal Warwickshire Regiment. To underline how far the unit was from being a battalion of Oldhamers, in June two large drafts totalling 238 men, described as coming from 'anywhere and everywhere' arrived for duty. With a total strength of about 750 and having lost 19 dead since its arrival, in June the battalion moved with the rest of its division to the coast. It left behind the dreary landscape and crumbling brickstacks of La Bassée and Cuinchy and looked forward to a rest at the seaside.

Much of July 1917 was spent training on the sand dunes near Bray. It was a fairly idyllic existence, with plenty of opportunity for sea bathing and sports. There were few casualties as a result of enemy action, although Second Lieutenant Forth and three men died on 30 July during a German bombardment. A more substantial number of men, however, suffered from the effects of being stung by jellyfish. Battalion bathing parades usually ended rather abruptly; men would wash rapidly and then return to the beach before the swarms of jellyfish made their presence felt. Occasionally a German patrol boat would emerge from the morning mist to spray the bathing companies with machine-gun fire. An absence of casualties from such action suggested that the Germans were merely indulging in horseplay.

The battalion did its turn in the front lines, the left flank of which touched the sea near Coxyde. In early August, 198 Brigade was told that the division on its right was to attack towards Lombartzyde and that the brigade would make an attempt to cross the Yser in support. This was part of a plan intended to regain some ground taken by the Germans in July and as part of the wider scheme to support the British offensive which had opened at Ypres. The 2/10th was designated the reserve battalion in the proposed attack, but spent some time training in the art of crossing an imaginary canal by improvised pontoons. Having successfully completed one such exercise, the battalion marched back to camp. Shortly after, a German aircraft flew over the camp at a height of about 50 feet. The startled battalion regained its senses and opened up with everything it had; rifles, Lewis guns and even an 18-pounder field gun loosed off at point-blank range. Thirteen British planes next swooped upon the lone German and chased him as he droned back towards friendly lines. The planes fired hundreds of rounds at the enemy plane, all apparently to no avail. The end of the chase came when a solitary machine gun in the British front trenches sprayed the aircraft and finally brought it down in flames.

Much of the time behind the line was spent in what the army called 'fostering offensive spirit'. This usually entailed a great deal of bayonet and grenade practice. Fortunately working parties were cancelled and, to maintain morale, concerts and leave passes into La Panne were organised on a regular basis. An otherwise successful brigade exercise using pontoons was spoilt for the 2/10th when the signallers managed to sink one of the rafts ferrying them and their cables across the canal. In early September the battalion moved into the Nieuport Bains sub-sector. With the left flank lying on the sea and No Man's Land being the Yser Canal, this was a unique portion of the Western Front. Dating from an earlier age when the sector was occupied by the French, most of the trenches ran in and out of the ruined sea front houses. The French tended not to take as much care with the construction of trenches as did their British allies, the result being that British units often had to expend a considerable amount of time and energy making the defences rather more substantial. Many of the houses and their cellars were left by the departing French in a rather parlous state. Walls hung precariously above unsupported cellars while loose or absent brickwork threatened the integrity of their connecting tunnels. Although it was a fairly quiet sector German artillery played a regular game of targeting the demolished lighthouse, the tumbled railway station and, even though it was in the words of the adjutant a 'remarkably difficult mark to hit', Battalion HQ.

A patrol went out during the night of 4-5 September to investigate the wreck of a German seaplane which had crashed a little to the front of the battalion's trenches. Seeking a trophy, the patrol was disappointed to discover that the pilot had set fire to the aircraft and all that the looters could recover was a machine gun. Further excitement came two days later when Sergeant Archbold and Private Dawson swam across the Yser Canal with the intention of raising a French flag on the end of a ruined jetty which lay within the German lines. Although frustrated by the strong current, their exploit was subsequently reported in several national papers. The following night the two men tried again, this time with a Union flag. After some time an exhausted Dawson struggled back to the British bank with news that he had lost contact with Archbold. Both men had been linked by a lifeline to their comrades on the bank but somehow both lines had either broken or slipped. Little could be done to organise a search for the missing swimmer but eventually a wounded and unconscious Archbold was pulled from the canal. He was taken to a field ambulance but Archbold, who came from Hertfordshire and had originally enlisted in the Essex Regiment, died of his exertions some days later.

The next few days were ones of normal trench routine. Casualties remained light, there being only 14 fatalities during the entire period the battalion spent on the coast. On 23 September the unit met up with the 1st Battalion and spent a short few hours swapping stories and tales of home. The 1st Battalion had come up to the coast following its short stay at Ypres and was somewhat surprised to discover that the men of its sister unit still had shiny boots and polished buttons. The more experienced members of the senior battalion regaled their junior counterparts with tales of the Salient and how before long the 66th Division must surely take its turn in the slaughter mill. The pessimists were soon proven correct. When out of the line the battalion began training in methods of attacking pill boxes. It soon became clear that the division was preparing for a move and that the only likely destination for a division which had spent so little time in an active sector since its arrival nine months before, was Ypres.

In the time between the 1st Battalion's departure from Ypres in mid-September and the arrival of the 2nd Battalion in early October, conditions in the Salient had deteriorated further. The British offensive had sloshed on through the mud and a few more metres of waterlogged marsh had been captured. The main thrust of the advance was directed towards the Passchendaele Ridge and it was to this sector that the 66th Division marched.

Detaching seven officers and 100 men at Morbecque as battle surplus (these men were to stay in the rear while the battalion attacked and in the event of large casualties would be the foundation upon which the battalion could be rebuilt), the 2/10th marched through the devastation of Ypres and camped in a field beside the Menin road. 'Camped' is something of a euphemism. There were no tents or shelters and the field was nothing but a wasteland of overflowing shell holes. Needles of blinding rain drenched the troops as they sought what little succour they could from the quagmire. Occasional stumps of former spinneys and hedges protruded from the mire and if a man attempted to dig a shallow scrape, he invariably uncovered parts of at least one decomposing body. Without hot food or the means of even brewing up the battalion sat, shivered and half drowned for nearly 24 hours. In theory they were supposed to be resting but as night threw its gloomy cloak over the tortured land, companies were warned for working parties. All night they laboured on the duck-board tracks and roads, carried engineers' stores and dug into the liquid mud. The following day was just as depressing but, according to the war diary, 'the men seemed in good spirits'. As evening fell the battalion drew battle stores and prepared to march off.

The entire brigade assembled and at 5.30pm on 8 October moved off in single file. The rain continued to lash down upon the fully burdened troops, making their passage along the slimy duckboards treacherous. Shells landed around them as Very lights and flares arched and soared around the distant front positions. Progress was slow and fatiguing, with frequent hold ups and confusion. Sometimes the wooden tracks were broken by shell fire and in the dark, vague, shadowy figures of pioneers and engineers laboured to breach the gaps by laying new stretches. The troops waited, fully exposed to the howling shells and rain, until the column again shuffled forward. In front of the 2/10th, two battalions of the East Lancashires (who were to lead the attack) reached the jumping off tapes and advanced towards the slight rise which led towards the now vanished village of Passchendaele. The attack was something of a Northern affair as, on the left of the Blackburn and Burnley battalions, Territorials from Mossley, Saddleworth, Halifax and Huddersfield were similarly slogging their way towards the ridge. The 2/10th was supposed to be in support to the East Lancashires, but as it had taken eleven hours to reach the start line, the 500-odd men of the battalion were ordered not to stop, but to keep going. The barrage had already been lost and, such was the difficulty the field and heavy guns had when firing from less than stable positions, British shells began to land in the mud around the battalion. The troops waded across a flooded valley and came to a halt. A combination of shell fire, machine-gun barrage and the physical elements proved too much. The battalion sank into shell holes and sought what little protection the few shattered stumps of Augustus Wood offered. The only saving grace of the situation was that the mud absorbed the impact and thus the effect of bursting shells. Even so, casualties mounted. One company officer thought he had lost half of his company within two hours of the operation's beginning; and that was only the start. The battalion remained in or around the marsh for another two days. Shrapnel rained down upon them and vicious bursts of machine-gun fire probed for a billet. No rations or water could be brought forward so the men existed on what they could forage from the packs and bottles of the dead. Officers and NCOs crawled from one occupied shell hole to another trying to bolster spirits and comforting the maimed. During darkness a few of the wounded were evacuated but their perilous passage down the line was threatened by the dark and enemy shells. Eventually during the night of 11-12 October, Australian troops moved up to relieve the exhausted survivors of the 66th Division. They struggled back, many with badly swollen feet, along the often broken duckboard tracks towards the dark shape of Ypres. Henry Lawson, a young subaltern later recalled the experience:

I was spent and horror stricken; shaken by the unending experience of apprehension and bloodshed. The survivors, including myself, dragged our feet back to the Menin Gate … I recollect seeing sickening hallucinations on the walls near the Gate as I passed through, images of the carnage, friend and foe dead or dying, stretched in the mud under a leaden, weeping sky.

The weary column of 198 Brigade passed through the martyred city and collapsed in the tumbled ruins of Vlamertinghe three miles to its west. Prayers for rest went unanswered when parties were found for carrying tools and stores to dumps close to the front line. This torture lasted until 17 October when, with sighs of relief, the battalion marched further to the rear and was allowed a period of rest and reorganisation.

The battle surplus rejoined the approximately 250 survivors of the attack. These were soon reinforced by the arrival of eleven new officers and 300 Other Ranks. In the same manner as earlier drafts, these men came from an assortment of units and localities. A breakdown of the places of birth and residences of those men who were killed during the period 8-11 October emphasises how the 2/10th had become a hybrid battalion. A total of 61 Other Ranks were killed or died of wounds during that period. Only 16 of those came from Oldham and another 23 from Manchester; 13 more had addresses in Lancashire towns and nine came from other parts of the country. This final group included Corporal Carolin of Thornton Heath, George Parker from nearby Croydon and Sydney Wheatley from rural Sussex. Many of the dead had been posted to the battalion from other regiments. They included former members of the King's Liverpool, the Royal Sussex, the East Surrey and the Green Howards. It was, like most battalions by the fourth year of the war, one of married and single men, those whose application for exemption had been refused by the tribunals and those whose physical health had prevented earlier enlistment. Only 23 of those who died have a known grave; the bones of the other 38 disappeared into the mud of the Salient or were recovered after the war and laid in unnamed graves. Two officers were also killed and they too have no known grave. Like those of their men, their names were later carved on the panels of the Tyne Cot Memorial to the Missing. Second Lieutenant Gerald Baxter had served in Fred Hardman's company of the 1st Battalion at Gillemont Farm. He had been wounded in March 1917 and on recovery was posted to the 2/10th. The other officer fatality, Second Lieutenant Henry Chapman, seems not to have come from Oldham. In the days after the attack, information was collected about the bravery and tenacity of the troops involved. Eventually, 15 men were awarded the Military Medal and four officers, including Captain Fripp, the son of an Oldham solicitor, were awarded the Military Cross.

From Vlamertinghe the battalion entrained at Ouderdom for Heuringham near St Omer where it spent one month refitting, training and absorbing the recent drafts. War had been a long time in coming for the few remaining originals who had enlisted in those heady days of September 1914 and they no doubt spent some of the time recalling lost friendships and broken dreams. The first ten months of overseas active service had cost the battalion 94 dead, not, in the context of the Western Front, a particularly large number. To that should be added a total of probably around 450 who had left the battalion wounded or sick. However, as so few originals actually travelled to France with the unit, any claim for it to be a battalion of Oldham Territorials had long since been lost. Those who had survived could reflect upon the horrors through which they and their comrades had passed. Many men of the BEF who fought at both the Somme and Ypres believed the Salient to be the worse of the two. The conditions and the frequency with which some divisions were thrown in, mauled, rebuilt and then thrown in again were generally considered to be more difficult and trying than those experienced on the chalk downs of the Somme and in the swamps of the Ancre Valley. The Official Historian recorded as much some years after the war:

> The chief cause of the great discontent during this period of the Flanders fighting was, in fact, the continuous demands on the regimental officers and men to carry out tasks which appeared physically impossible to perform, and which no other army could have faced. It must be emphasised again, too, that in all that vast wilderness of slime hardly tree, hedge, wall or building could be seen. As at the Somme no landmarks existed, nor any scrap of natural cover other than the mud-filled shell holes. That the attacks ordered were so gallantly made in such conditions stands to the immortal credit of the battalions concerned.

The time spent at St Omer was one of rebuilding. Discipline was reasonably relaxed and the men were allowed a fair degree of free time. Platoon and company officers used the opportunity to get to know their men and their backgrounds. With perhaps an element of fallibility in his remembrance of the origins of his men, Henry Lawson recalled:

> There was plenty of time for talk. Reading matter was scarce. The men of my company were all from the Oldham district ...

They delighted in telling me, in effect a foreigner from the south,
the stories of their lives, particularly the gay times spent on
holidays ... We sometimes used to lie out under the stars, and
an almost invariable subject for conversation was the fabulous
delights of Blackpool in wakes week. They gave me a vision of
magic casements, stately pleasure domes and enchanted towers.
I listened in amazement as they talked of driving up and down
the esplanade, spending with gay abandon every penny of which
they were possessed, other than the half crown left under the
clock on the mantelpiece at home for payment of the cab on their
return ... In those dark days they warmed their hearts at the
remembered flame of their Lancashire homes.

All too soon however, the division moved back to the Salient. Although the battle had been officially closed down and the Passchendaele Ridge was in British hands, conditions remained appalling. The onset of winter exacerbated the problems of bringing forward supplies and of merely staying alive in the flooded shell holes which constituted the front and support positions. The battalion alternated between regular turns in the forward zone with providing working parties a little further to the rear. Much effort was expended on trying to ensure that the men had a change of socks every other day and that they daily soaked their feet in whale oil. The rum ration also served to stave off some of the worst effects the elements could throw at them, but there remained a substantial although unspecified number of men who went down the line suffering from exposure. Three men were killed by a short but intense enemy bombardment on 21 November and another four during the remainder of the month. Only one of them, Robert Turner, came from Oldham. At least 25 others, including at least one man who was hit by falling masonry in the ruins of Ypres' infantry barracks, were wounded during the month. The battalion concert party, The Bombs, was in the midst of its routine when a German shell took another few feet of brickwork and tiles off the walls and roof of the building. Even when the battalion was withdrawn to Hondighem for rest and training, German 12-inch shells allowed them little respite. Dispersed over several acres of muddy ground and offering few facilities, Hondighem Camp was a miserable affair. Most of the men were accommodated in draughty barns and the officers in nearby cottages. The sick list did apparently diminish but the war diary suggests that because numbers were so low, battalion rather than company exercises and classes could be held for some skills.

Christmas was spent at this little village not far from Hazebrouck. A layer of snow added to the festive season and the troops enjoyed the contents of parcels sent from home. Comforts committees in Oldham had been collecting cigarettes and seasonal food for dispatch to the front. The men sat around crackling fires, supped beer, smoked, sang and turned their thoughts homeward. They were united by their comradeship in adversity; for now there was little room for pessimistic reflection about what the morning would bring. Troops had learned that, on the Western Front, you seized what few moments the authorities might offer you for relaxation, enjoyed them for what they were, and coped with tomorrow when it came.

The return to the line came on 3 January 1918. The cold was severe and in the posts and trenches of the Frezenberg Ridge the troops suffered terribly. Alternating between the line and Hussar Camp at Potijze (a mile to the east of Ypres), men occupied shallow posts in the snow-covered landscape or provided working parties to dig a new defensive line then under construction. Many of the forward positions were isolated and rations did not always appear. When a thaw set in during the middle of the month, men sank up to their knees in mud. Equipment and kit often disappeared beneath slides of pernicious slime and at least 25 men were sent down the line with trench foot. On the night of 13 January one company was hit by a German salvo as it moved off from Hussar Camp. Five men were killed and at least ten wounded but the remainder of the company struggled along the mule track of slippery duckboards to spend the night working near Tyne Cot.

At the end of January the battalion had reached a strength of 780. In comparison with many battalions of the BEF this was an impressive number. The Battles of Arras, Third Ypres and Cambrai had been so costly that there was an increasingly serious man-power shortage. Rather than maintain the official establishment of overseas units, the Prime Minister was deliberately keeping large numbers of men at home in the training battalions. One former sergeant of the 10th, who was now an instructor with the Reserve Battalion, noted that one of the training companies had no fewer than 40 officers. Lloyd George's motive behind retaining so many trained men in the UK was principally to lessen the possibility of Haig squandering them in what the Prime Minister regarded as further futile attacks. Unable for political reasons to sack Haig, the Prime Minister was depriving him of the numbers of men required to launch another major offensive. There were, so Lloyd George believed, sufficient numbers in the divisions to hold the line for the winter, there being little likelihood of the Germans making a serious attempt at the Allied line until the early spring. Whether aware or not of the political squabbles going on at home, in most battalions of the BEF the reduced numbers meant additional work for those who were there. In an attempt to make more use of the available manpower the Army decided to reduce the number of infantry battalions in each brigade from four to three. In the 66th Division this meant that three battalions would either be disbanded or transferred to another division.

The 2/10th was the unlucky unit in 198 Brigade. At some stage in early February 1918 the battalion was informed that it was to be disbanded and the troops posted elsewhere. In divisions up and down the line the same demoralising news was being heard. Many regiments deeply resented the loss of one or more of their battalions and questions were even asked in Parliament about the likely effects such a move would have on *esprit*. There is no officially recorded reaction to the news in the 2/10th; perhaps the battalion simply accepted it as a necessity or put it down as another example of the vagaries of the Army Council. Perhaps the troops did not care a great deal to which battalion they belonged for many had after all, been posted to the Manchester Regiment from other regiments. What was more important was the way in which the men would be distributed and here there was some consolation in the fact that the men were told they were to be transferred to the 42nd Division. This meant that several platoons of the 2/10th could expect to end up in Oldham's senior Territorial battalion. The more that companies and platoons could be transferred *en masse*, especially if they were moving to battalions of their own regiment, the more likely it was that the men would accept the move with equanimity.

A final concert was given near Poperinghe in early February, after which, various of the divisional staff came to bid the battalion farewell. Something like 250 men were transferred from the 2/10th to the 1/10th, the remainder being posted to the 1/7th and 1/8th Manchester. Nine officers of the 2/10th, including Henry Lawson from Surrey and Jimmy Whitehead from Park Road, made the relatively short journey from the mud-laden Salient to trenches held by the 1/10th east of Béthune. Having lost just over one hundred men killed or died of wounds since its arrival in France in February 1917, and having fought in one of the most soul destroying battles of the war, Oldham's second line Territorial battalion ceased to exist.

WATER, WINTER AND A VICTORIA CROSS

WHEN THE DRAFT from the 2/10th reached its new home, its parent battalion was suffering from the effects of the weather in a collection of partly destroyed former mining and farming villages near Béthune. It had come to the sector from the coast in late November and, although in a quiet area, had won a Victoria Cross and a clutch of Military Medals during a desperate defence of its trenches on 10-11 December. Things had calmed down a good deal since but in the hope that the burden of work might be proportionately lessened, the battalion was pleased to welcome the reinforcements.

The 10th's five-day march from Proven to the Channel coast in September had done wonders for morale. The division had passed through areas untouched by war, where the colours of autumn and the absence of gunfire lightened spirits as well as steps. Villagers welcomed them to their overnight billets and waved them a cheery farewell in the morning. The only discordant note according to Wynne came not from the villagers but from a British Town Major who objected to men of the 10th spending a short march break propped against the walls of his requisitioned cottage. The men enjoyed the spectacle of this puce, rotund and moustachioed individual blasting away at the unfortunate Wynne who had done nothing but obey orders.

With a friend in high places, the battalion was allotted some rather superior billets when it arrived at La Panne. Captain Wilkinson, one of the 10th's original officers who had served with the battalion on Gallipoli, was now a brigade staff captain. It was generally suspected that he had spied some comfortable billets and decided that they would be suitable for his former comrades. The agreeable accommodation and the fact that La Panne remained occupied by civilians allowed the battalion a very pleasant ten days. The Belgian shopkeepers and *estaminet* owners were not particularly hospitable but, with Battalion HQ housed in a sumptuous sea-front hotel, the troops in former boarding houses, an Indian summer and with access to the municipal baths, the troops realised that defending the coast was something of a sinecure. Unfortunately, on 7 October the division was relieved by the 41st and ordered to move up the coast to the Nieuport sector. Here, things took a turn for the worse.

The town of Nieuport was little more than a pile of rubble. Enemy artillery and night-time bombing pounded it remorselessly and gas discharges frequently drenched its tumbled ruins. The 10th went into the St Georges sub-sector which lay to the south-east of the town. As the area was largely below sea level it was impossible to dig conventional trenches. The front line therefore consisted of breastworks and small posts dotted around the flooded, marshy ground. To exacerbate the problems, many of the posts in the St Georges sector lay beyond the conjunction of several canals. To reach the positions, heavily encumbered troops had to make their perilous way along duckboard tracks and bridges which rose and fell with the tide. As the enemy artillery had the tracks and crossing points accurately registered, much effort was expended on keeping them in reasonable repair. The 42nd was one of the few divisions which had not yet been allocated a Pioneer battalion. This meant that all the maintenance work had to be executed by the divisional RE, assisted by working parties from the infantry. The German positions were generally on higher ground than the British so not only were they less affected by the inundated ground but also had observation over many of the British posts. While gas seeped insidiously into posts and hung in clouds above the often fetid marsh, trench-mortar barrages fell upon the exposed crossing points. Reliefs and patrols splashed and sometimes swam their way towards their objectives, arriving wet, exhausted and often without the equipment with which they had started.

The debilitating conditions prompted the resourceful Padre Raymond to resurrect a derelict former Church Army motor canteen. The padre, assisted by Dick Coyne and an assistant who claimed he knew how to drive, supplied grateful nocturnal working parties with coffee and soup. On one such very dark night the driver reversed the canteen into a canal. Accounts vary as to how the vehicle was eventually recovered but it was certainly the navy, or at least several of its exceptionally fluent personnel, which came to the good padre's rescue. Raymond appeared to pick up some of the navy's expressions for when a shell finally put the canteen permanently out of commission, the padre was rumoured to have uttered things 'which', according to Wynne, 'he didn't oughter'.

Casualties during the six-week period in this water-logged sector were remarkably light. Only eight men were killed or died of wounds but a large number of men suffered from gas and the elements. The colonel instructed the quartermaster to 'make every endeavour' to obtain clean socks and regular supplies of whale oil. To provide troops in the line with hot food, additional supplies of solidified fuel were sent up for use in small cookers. It was the responsibility of company cooks to prepare hot food in the cookers but by the time the food was transported to the front positions (enemy and elements permitting) the food was often cold. It was more usual for the troops to obtain hot food when out on rest. It was on such occasions that the long suffering men of the companies vented their sarcasm at the cooks. Their parentage was questioned, the quality of their produce ridiculed and the very term 'cook' described as a misnomer. The thickness of cooks' skin was legendary and was ascribed to frequent applic- ations of their stew pots' contents.

In the second week of November, the 10th left the sector and moved to a village outside Dunkirk. The town was bombed nightly and long-range German guns dropped huge shells into the disintegrating ruins of once fine buildings. The townsfolk were in a state of 'almost utter destitution and appeared to have lost all hope and interest in life'. Understandably perhaps, they were described by one diarist as 'amongst the most inhospitable' the battalion had yet met. A few days were spent in billets before the whole division set off for a seven-day trek south.

Accommodation on the way was often indifferent but at Aire, the division came across an old and much admired French custom. During the festival of St Catherine any youth who presents a girl with a flower can claim a kiss. Once the troops became aware of this right, the local gardens were denuded of anything which might vaguely have been described as a bloom.

On 28 November the battalion settled into billets at Beuvry. It had been a long march, made longer by one of those inexplicable detours which so characterised movement behind the lines. The battalion cobblers had been kept busy repairing boots which had deteriorated from weeks of immersion in mud and salt water.

However, the weather had been generally kind and the two days at Aire had done much to liven the men and rebuild spirits after the sodden period of trial on the coast. Their new home in the Béthune sector was also a largely flat wilderness of marsh and blasted copses. The landscape was dreary and the front positions a combination of blown mine craters, trenches and breastworks. The divisional history later described the area as:

> *'Bairnsfather-land' pure and simple. The trenches deep in melting snow; No Man's Land, with its almost continuous line of craters, full of stagnant, green, stinking water, the sides of crumbling earth and slimy mud converting them into death-traps for night patrols; the front line with its saps — eerie and lonely posts for the sentries who kept watch ... 'Trenches' were little more than parapets of turf and sandbag breastworks ... and, under the influence of rain, frost and thaw, shell fire and trench-mortar fire, duckboards had disappeared under pits of mud, and walls had collapsed and blocked the trenches in a tangle of wood, rabbit-netting and mud. It seemed enough to ask a man merely to keep alive in the awful discomfort of the trenches ...*

In this uninspiring area the battalion was to spend the next three months of monotonous trench routine.

When out of the line troops provided endless working parties. Besides the continual need to keep the forward positions in some sort of repair, a defensive line of concrete shelters and pill boxes was under construction a little to the rear. As the division was still without its own Pioneer battalion, it was loaned the 55th Division's Pioneers, the 4/South Lancashire. These men helped the divisional RE by providing skilled or semi-skilled labour while the infantry did the donkey work. In many ways life in the front line was preferable to being out on 'rest'. Following a spell as labourers, the 10th relieved the 6/Lancashire Fusiliers in the forward positions during the morning of 10 December. Once darkness had fallen and probably aware that a relief had taken place, the enemy launched a sustained gas attack on C Company's position in Red Dragon Crater. Choking and blinded by the gas the company manned the parapet and 'behaving splendidly beat off the attempted raid with ease'. These official words from the war diary give a somewhat simplistic account of the incident.

The Germans were intent on raiding the British line, probably to obtain a prisoner for identification purposes, and had prepared well for the task. The fight lasted for possibly thirty minutes, with heavy casualties on both sides. Lewis-gun and rifle fire poured into the raiders' ranks while those who reached the parapet were blown apart by showers of Mills bombs. Gradually the enemy resistance slackened but by that time a number of the Oldhamers were dead or dying from the insidious gas. When the line quietened down, fifteen men of C Company were dead, most of them victims of gas.

Later accounts of the fight gave the scribes an opportunity to indulge in some understandably purple prose. Wynne described the men as 'forgetful of anything but the security of the line' and of 'disdaining death', while Bradbury wrote of men dying 'on the parapet almost in the act of firing'. The stand by C Company under the command of the Gallipoli veteran Captain Procktor Stott was indeed heroic and demanded recognition. As every man was regarded as having behaved with exceptional bravery, a selection was made as to which of them should receive medals. Private Walter ('Spud') Mills of Smith Street was chosen for the posthumous award of the Victoria Cross and four other men of the company received the Military Medal. In addition several other men, including two officers, received divisional cards in recognition of their action.

The following day a number of volunteers from the 6/ Manchester dug separate graves for the 10th's dead in the local military cemetery. Among those laid to rest with Mills were Corporal John Boyle of Bloom Street, Dick Coyne, the assistant to Padre Raymond's mobile canteen, and Harry Henthorn of Bridgewater Street. Despite the cemetery's proximity to the front lines, the ceremony was conducted with full honours. Mills' wife had 'Death does not part the love that formed the link between us' inscribed upon her husband's headstone and in due course the cemetery at Gorre developed into one of the loveliest on the Western Front.

Supplying hot food to the forward positions remained an intractable problem. The cumbersome containers proved too awkward to carry along slippery duckboards and were substituted by petrol cans wrapped in hay or blankets.

As Christmas approached, speculation grew as to which units of 126 Brigade would be holding the line on the day itself. During the night of 23-24 December the division discharged 400 gas cylinders and fired over 1,500 mortar shells onto the enemy positions. Fearing a raid, a retaliatory barrage crashed down upon the 10th's trenches, killing four men and wounding several others. Among the wounded was Jack Street. Having arrived back from a 'ripping' ten days' leave at home, Street had fallen victim to a recurrence of the malaria he had picked up in the East. The eight weeks spent at convalescence camps meant that he missed the battalion's stint at Ypres and had rejoined it in early November. Street was taken to the 1st Casualty Clearing Station at Cuinchy and then evacuated by barge to St Omer and home. Those who were not as lucky as Street were buried in the same cemetery as their comrades killed on 11 December.

Violent as the German retaliation had been, its conclusion signalled the end of the 10th's trench tour. The battalion was relieved and made its way back to camp in Le Quesnoy. Despite the occasional long-range shell landing nearby, a relatively sumptuous official Christmas dinner, supplemented by parcels from home, was consumed in comparative safety. The divisional concert party performed *Cinderella* and the battalion sang the esoteric, and what the divisional historian described as the 'weird lament', known as *On Owdham Edge beaut 'at*. Further tours in snow-filled or thawing trenches followed, with both sides conducting raids and exchanging regular shell fire. In late January the Germans raided the 10th's trenches but met with little success. An enemy officer and an NCO were killed and instead of dragging an Oldhamer back to the German trenches, two wounded raiders remained in the British lines. A report of the successful repulse of the raid appeared a few days later in the national press. To add to the discomforts afforded by the enemy and the elements, hundreds of rats infested the trenches. One particularly brazen creature consumed Procktor Stott's field cap.

The seemingly endless routine of trench warfare confused the cold, wet and often miserable warriors. Fred Hardman wrote home:

I am altogether lost as regards the date. I am not sure whether this is the 7th or 8th. I have written a letter to my uncle and dated it the 8th and am now writing this one and dating it the 7th.

As regards the day of the week, I am still more at sea for I have not the faintest idea what day it really is.

As a means of trying to keep experienced officers from cracking up, it was fairly common practice by this stage of the war to recommend their return home for a period of six months. Chic Taylor had been told that he was on the list to go but he and Hardman had talked of requesting a transfer to the Machine Gun Corps. The two old friends had decided that if the anticipated German offensive did not come within two weeks, they would place their application on the Colonel's desk. Rumours of the impending request spread among the companies and the two officers were petitioned to stay by some of the battalion's older hands. So impressed were the two men by their men's concern and loyalty that the applications were never submitted.

One officer who was expecting daily to leave the battalion was its MO, Captain Hannagan. Royal Army Medical Corps officers were attached to battalions for a specific period and Hannagan's appointment was rapidly approaching its end. He was hoping for a transfer to the Royal Navy but failing that, rather than do another stint with a front line battalion, he had decided to apply for a position at a base hospital.

In mid-February the division was relieved by the West Lancashires of the 55th Division and the 10th marched back to Busnes, north-west of Béthune. It was here that the draft of men from the 2/10th joined the battalion and infantry brigades were reorganised; the 10th was to be brigaded with the 1/8th Manchester and the 1/5th East Lancashire. The 10th was billeted in and around a dirty farm reeking with the filth of bygone years and whose dishevelled owners were far from hospitable. Shortly after its arrival the brigade was put on the alert and moved up to support the Portuguese divisions holding the trenches near Neuve Chapelle. The British authorities had little faith in the fighting qualities of the Portuguese, whom they considered were poorly led by their officers, so when a furious bombardment hit their trenches on 25-26 February, 126 Brigade was sent to La Couture in case of an enemy attack. In the event nothing happened and the battalion returned to its billets. Hardman wrote of the incident to Kitty:

We had an awfully busy day yesterday. Our gallant allies got the wind up about something and we were rushed up … It was blowing a blizzard ... and as we were not needed we had the pleasure of marching all the way back again about six miles in a blinding snow storm. The French villagers were extremely glad to see us for they have not much faith in the people we went to support and feel more comfortable when they see the cheery face of the British Tommy.

The action demonstrated the nervousness felt by the High Command about the possibility of a major enemy offensive. Rumours abounded that the Germans were transferring huge numbers of men from the now silent Eastern Front in preparation for a decisive breakthrough against the BEF and the French. When not required to labour on defensive lines, 126 Brigade trained in rapid deployment and counter-attack methods. Special classes were held for Lewis-gun teams, signallers and bombers and the divisional commander, Major-General Solly-Flood, toured the units lecturing them on what was to be expected when the weather improved. It was during this time that he coined what later became the division's legendary motto, 'Go one better'.

It was also during this period that the battalion felt the pinch of food shortages at home. Many regiments had Comforts Committees which regularly arranged fund-raising activities to provide the men in the trenches with cigarettes and other luxuries. The increasing success of the German U-boat campaign resulted in shortages in Britain of all kinds. Sweethearts and wives were finding it difficult to buy the ingredients needed to bake the cakes they had been used to sending to their menfolk. The severe winter exacerbated the travails of the men and the absence of the fancies and comforts which made life bearable was sorely felt. The battalion's commanding officer requested that the depot bring to the attention of the townsfolk the problems being experienced by the Other Ranks. Lieutenant-Colonel Rye was elected chairman of a committee which immediately placed appeals for money in the local press. Two years earlier a letter from a wounded Oldhamer in Heaton Park Hospital had complained that he and about 60 other crippled former members of the battalion were being ignored by the town. He had asked, 'Does anyone remember us, or is this a forecast of how soldiers will be treated after the war?' Within a few days the minders of

Collinge's Mill had despatched parcels to the men. Other mills and societies followed suit and soon a regular flow of comforts was being enjoyed by the soldiers. The response to Rye's appeal was equally swift and generous. Nearly £500 was donated in a matter of days and before long the committee sent the first of several batches of parcels overseas to the grateful men of the 10th.

The 42nd Division spent most of March in the area west of Béthune. The 10/Manchester in billets at Lapugnoy absorbed its influx of reinforcements from the 2/10th, trained and relaxed when it could. With a strength of 980 Other Ranks and with a temporary excess over establishment of 24 officers, it waited for the anticipated call. Leave was still open but, as their departure dates drew near, men and officers feared that the German offensive would begin before they had left for home. The local inhabitants certainly thought a German drive was imminent. Those closer to the front line who had been used to the daily rattle of machine-gun fire and the shriek of medium calibre shells, were packing up and falling back. Civilians in Lapugnoy and nearby villages were caught up in the general concern; for the first time in the war, long-range shells and bombs were exploding in the vicinity. To the locals that presaged an offensive and, like their cousins to the east, they began to depart for less noisy pastures.

On 21 March the long awaited German offensive opened. Massive attacks broke through Fifth Army's front north and south of St Quentin while, south of Arras, Third Army executed a more disciplined withdrawal. The BEF fell back in the face of these hammer blows and with the French at first unable to help, depended upon divisions in quieter areas or out at rest to help stem the flood. On 23 March the 42nd Division was warned for a move.

The 6th Volunteer Battalion detraining for the Salisbury summer camp of 1906. A hoarding in the background proclaims the virtues of the New Midland Hotel, Manchester.

Corporal Edward Arnold *(standing right)* who served with the 6th Volunteers is pictured here at Salisbury. He saw action with 10th Manchesters in Egypt and France and was wounded.

Plate 1

In its first year as a Territorial unit the 10th's football team won a league cup. This picture was taken outside the ammunition store at the Rifle Street Drill Hall. After the Second World War the magazine doubled as a wine cellar.

The Battalion and its band marching at ease during the 1911 camp at Dolphinholme, near Lancaster.

Plate 2

The Battalion's officers in August, 1912. Back: Capt. Sutton, Lt. Scott, Lt. Owen, Lt. Sheppard, Lt. Sutcliffe, Lt. Pochin, Lt. Wilkinson, Lt. Griffiths, Lt. Kennedy. Middle: Capt. Fort, Capt. Farquhar, Capt. Leatham, Col. Paterson, Major Rye, Major Taylor, Capt. Newton. Front: Lt. Hardman, Lt. Griffiths, Capt. Smethurst, Lt. Leach.

Colonel Paterson and officers of the 2/10th Battalion at Crowborough, East Sussex in 1915. Several of these officers were attached from other battalions of the Manchester Regiment to the 2/10th and did not go overseas with the unit in 1917. Paterson was too old to go to France and joined the Royal Army Medical Corps. Others, for example, 2nd Lt. Jupp (extreme left, back row), and 2nd Lt. Fripp (fourth from right, middle row) would later join the 1/10th.

Plate 3

A group of the 10th's senior NCOs in Egypt in either 1914 or 1915. RSM Chittenden sits second from the right and Jacob Wolstencroft second from left. Wolstencroft is wearing the ribbon of the Territorial Force Efficiency Medal, awarded to him in 1909. Born in 1863 he had joined the Volunteer Battalion in 1897. His sons, Stuart and Harry, both joined the 10th. Harry was later transferred to the Royal Garrison Artillery but Stuart, after having served with the battalion in Egypt and Gallipoli, was killed in France in April 1918.

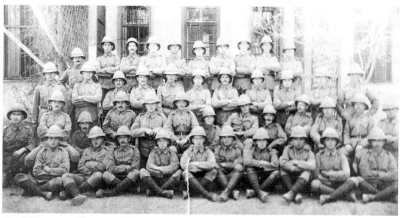

No. 9 Platoon at Abassia in 1914. Lt. James Stott is fifth from the right, second row.

Plate 4

The 10th's officers in Egypt in 1915. The photograph was probably taken at Abassia Barracks a few weeks before the battalion left for Gallipoli. Lt. Col. Rye is seated fifth from the right, with Major Bamford on his right and Capt. de Pentheny O'Kelly on his left. By October 1915 Fred Hardman (fourth from right, second row) would be the only officer still with the unit who had served continuously since its arrival at Alexandria.

Plate 5

Part of the group which manned Garrison Post at Rez-el-Est, near the Suez Canal in April 1915. Lts. James Stott and Fred Hardman are hatless.

Lt. James Stott at Caernarvon in 1914. He was killed in action 18 June 1915.

Lt. Pochin the Transport Officer, shown at Heliopolis in 1914.

Plate 6

Sergeant Frank Miller at Heliopolis. Miller joined the 6th Volunteer Battalion in 1894. He was wounded at Krithia in June 1915 and on recovery became Bandmaster to the 8th (Reserve) Battalion. He rejoined the 10th in 1920 and served until 1936. He was awarded the Meritorious Service Medal and the Territorial Efficiency Medal with bar.

Arthur Kirkbride (seated) and his younger brother George, who joined the 10th under age. Both survived the war.

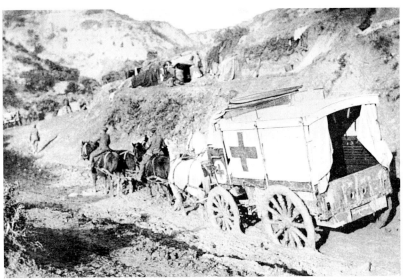

Rain turned the Gallipoli ravines into rivers of mud. An ambulance wagon with wheels and team caked in mud, makes its way down Gully Ravine.

Plate 7

HQ dugouts of the 42nd Division buried into the hills and slopes of Gully Ravine. The gully was a main route up to the front trenches and was an area known intimately to the 10th.

Red Cross flags fluttering above dressing stations near Lancashire Landing. The dominating heights of Achi Baba can be seen in the distance.

Plate 8

Lt. Griffiths and Lt. Stott on Gallipoli in May 1915.

Lt. Harold Spielmann, killed in action on 13 August, 1915 at Gallipoli.

Plate 9

Serjt. E. Drinkwater of the 1st/10th Battalion, The
Manchester Regiment. Killed in action 19 June 1915.

2041 SERJT. E. Drinkwater 1st / 10th BN. MAN. REGT.

Serjt. Drinkwater's Queen's South Africa Medal (bars South Africa 1901, South Africa 1902),
1914-15 Star, British War and Victory Medals and the George V Territorial Efficiency Medal.

Plate 10

Stores piled on 'W' beach (Lancashire Landing) shortly before the evacuation. Much of the material was deliberately destroyed by the departing Allies.

Pieta Military Cemetery, Malta. In contrast to most Commonwealth War Grave Commission cemeteries, the headstones are laid flat and the bodies are usually buried three to a grave. Many of the 10th who died of wounds or of disease contracted on Gallipoli, are buried here.

Plate 11

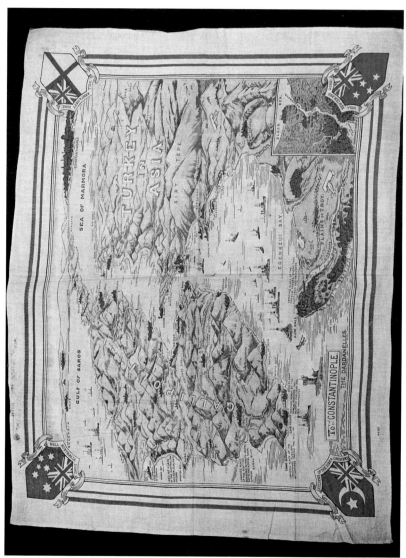

A rare surviving example of the coloured, linen handkerchief which was given to survivors of the Gallipoli landings 'WITH BEST WISHES FROM MANCHESTER GUARDIAN READERS'. It had belonged to Arthur Kirkbride and was kindly loaned by his son Jack.

Plate 12

'A' Company near El Arish. This is typical of the terrain crossed by the 10th during its seemingly interminable marches across Sinai in 1916–17. The broiling heat and unforgiving sand took its toll of men used to working and living in the cold and damp of North-West England.

Lt. Baxter and Lt. Hassall performing their ablutions near El Arish in 1917.

Plate 13

Ensuring an adequate and regular water supply was of crucial importance to the Allied advance towards Palestine. Like all battalions, the 10th had a camel section.

Chic Taylor using some of the precious water supply to brush his teeth.

Plate 14

Once a broad gauge railway line had been laid across the Sinai, water was brought forward by train. This photograph was taken at Romani.

The headstone of Private Thomas Brigham in Warlincourte Halte British Cemetery. Private Thomas Foulkes, the other member of the 10th shot by firing squad, has no known grave and is commemorated on the Loos Memorial to the Missing.

Plate 15

Private Walter Mills, VC. It is generally believed that this photograph was taken after Mills had died of his wounds.

The beautiful cemetery at La Gorre near Béthune. It contains the graves of those of the 10th killed during the German attack of 10 December 1917, including that of Private 'Spud' Mills, VC. There are also many graves of other Oldhamers who were serving with different regiments and battalions.

Plate 16

*Photographed during a home leave, probably in 1917,
Fred Hardman with his eldest son Rex. Hardman died in
1972 and was followed three years later by his wife Kitty.*

The railway cutting north of Achiet-le-Grand as it is today. The 10th rested
here before running up to Ervillers in March 1918. Two small cemeteries lie
either side of the track.

Plate 17

Brigadier John Alexander Chisholm 'Chic' Taylor, DSO, MC and bar. His splendid
medal group is shown below.

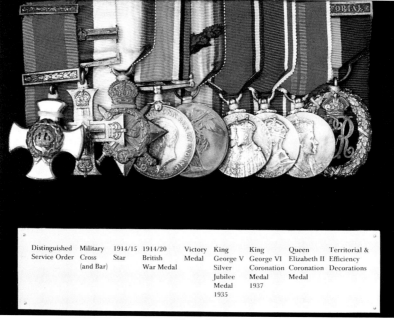

| Distinguished Service Order | Military Cross (and Bar) | 1914/15 Star | 1914/20 British War Medal | Victory Medal | King George V Silver Jubilee Medal 1935 | King George VI Coronation Medal 1937 | Queen Elizabeth II Coronation Medal | Territorial & Efficiency Decorations |

Plate 18

Rossignol Wood, between Gommecourt and Puisieux. In 1918, this area remained criss-crossed by British and German trenches of 1916 vintage. The 10th spent some weeks in this sector during April 1918.

A band of one of the Manchester battalions of the 42nd Division marching past Major-General Solly-Flood, the divisional commander. The photograph was taken near Famechon on 7 June, 1918.

Plate 19

The village of Riencourt near Bapaume as it was in 1919.

Riencourt today. The photograph was taken looking east across the ground attacked by Chic Taylor's and Walter Shaw's companies on 31 August 1918.

Plate 20

The impressive portals of Bancourt British Cemetery, just to the north of Riencourt. The dead buried here were largely those who fell in September and October 1918.

The 42nd Division's memorial on the Trescault-Ribécourt road. It commemorates the division's work in Gallipoli and Egypt as well as the storming of the Hindenburg Line in September 1918.

Plate 21

The ground attacked by the Manchester Brigade and the 10/Manchester on 26–27 September. The trees of Boar Copse are left of centre, with Couillet Wood on the crest of Highland Ridge in the right distance.

Unseen Trench was part of the Hindenburg Line near Highland Ridge. The 42nd Division stormed this and its adjacent trenches on 27 September 1918.

Plate 22

Ribécourt Road Cemetery near Trescault as it was at the end of the war. Most of the graves are those of the 42nd Division killed in September 1918.

The grave of 2Lieutenant Tom Wilson in Ribécourt Road Cemetery. He is the only member of the 10th buried here.

Plate 23

Herpigny Farm, west of Solesmes. Here, on 18 October 1918, Lt. Col. Peel addressed the battalion before it moved off to take part in the 'railway cutting stunt'. The survivors also rested here briefly on their way back to the rear area.

The railway cutting south of Solesmes. The ravine, which saw some of the most ferocious fighting, lay beyond the track to the right.

Plate 24

The small, compact Belle Vue Cemetery south of Solesmes. Many of the 10th killed on 20 October, including Lt. Frank Cook and Lt. Charles Cooper, are buried here.

Lt. Frank Cook MC, killed in action on 20 October 1918.

Plate 25

Hautmont, scene of the 10th's last engagement of the war. Local inhabitants helped Chic Taylor's company to build a makeshift bridge across the river. The more substantial effort seen in this photograph was erected later by the Divisional RE.

Chic Taylor on *Leicester*. The photograph was taken at Gilly in 1919.

Plate 26

Oldham's war memorial shortly after its unveiling.

Major-General Buchanan at the unveiling of Oldham's war memorial in April 1923.

Plate 27

The band with Bandmaster Frank Miller seated to the left of the base drummer. Ramsay Camp, 1923.

Plate 28

The battalion's Lewis gunners stripping their weapons at a camp in the 1920s.

With tents open for airing and bedblocks neatly piled, a company of the 10th await morning inspection at a summer camp in the 1930s.

Plate 29

Some of the 10th's regimental silver. Shooting cups, commemorative tankards, candlesticks and shields were often donated by retiring officers or the relatives of those recently deceased. Much of the silver is on display beside the memorial drums inside the Civic Centre.

The 10th's memorial drums. Now in the Civic Centre, the drums have the names of the battalions' 628 dead inscribed on them.

Plate 30

Huge crowds always turned out to watch the 10th leave for summer camp. Chic Taylor leads his company from Rifle Street *en route* for Bolton-le-Sands in 1928.

Plate 31

The old colours which were severely damaged by fire during the 1933 camp.

The replacement colours on display outside the Rifle Street Drill Hall.

Plate 32

The Duke of Gloucester presenting the new colours at Alexandra Park in 1934.

Chic Taylor receiving the *Daily Telegraph* Cup from Lord Strathcona at the regimental prize giving of 1936. This was the third successive occasion the battalion had won the cup.

Plate 33

The vast interior of the drill hall. The battalion is on parade to rehearse for the visit of the King and Queen in 1938.

The 10th turned out for all civic occasions during the 1920s and 1930s. Chic Taylor watches as the King and Queen descend the Town Hall steps in 1938.

Plate 34

The 10th's officers at Caernarvon in 1935. Major J.C.S. Rowbotham (seated second from left) and Captain J.B. Whitehead (third from left middle row) would both later command the battalion, albeit in its new guise as 41st Royal Tank Regiment.

Tracked vehicles of 41st Royal Tank Regiment ploughing up the ground of Oldham Edge in 1938.

Plate 35

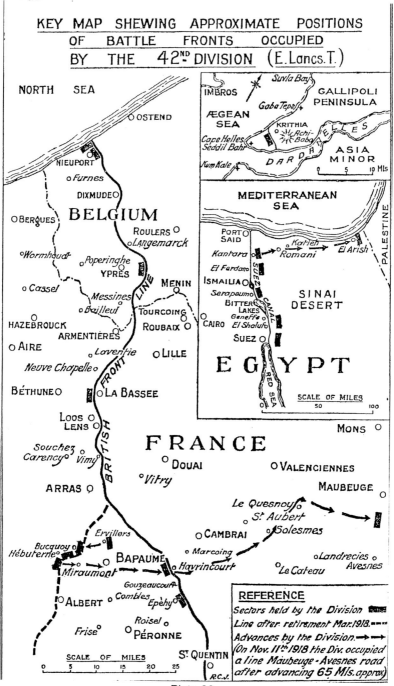

KEY MAP SHEWING APPROXIMATE POSITIONS
OF BATTLE FRONTS OCCUPIED
BY THE 42ND DIVISION (E.Lancs.T.)

NORTH SEA

O OSTEND

IMBROS
Suvla Bay
Gaba Tepe
GALLIPOLI PENINSULA
ÆGEAN SEA
KRITHIA
Achi Baba
Cape Helles
Seddil Bahr
Kum Kale
DARDANELLES
ASIA MINOR
0 5 10 Mls

NIEUPORT
o Furnes
DIXMUDE O
O BERQUES
BELGIUM
ROULERS O
o Langemarck
o Wormhoudt
o Poperinghe
YPRES
o Cassel
MENIN
Messines
o Bailleul
TOURCOING
ROUBAIX O
HAZEBROUCK
ARMENTIÈRES
O AIRE
o Laventie
o LILLE
Neuve Chapelle o
BÉTHUNE O
o LA BASSEE
LOOS O
LENS O
Souchez o
Carency o Vimy
ARRAS O

MEDITERRANEAN SEA
PORT SAID O
Katieh
El Arish
Kantara
Romani
El Ferdan
ISMAILIA O
Serapeum o
BITTER LAKES
Geneffe
CAIRO O
El Shalufa
SUEZ O
SINAI DESERT
EGYPT
RED SEA
PALESTINE
SUEZ CANAL

SCALE OF MILES
0 50 100

MONS O

FRANCE
O DOUAI
o Vitry
O VALENCIENNES
MAUBEUGE O

Le Quesnoy O
St Aubert
o Solesmes

Ervillers
o CAMBRAI
o Marcoing
o Landrecies o
o Le Cateau
Avesnes

Bucquoy o
Hébuterne o
BAPAUME
Havrincourt
Miraumont
Gouzeaucourt
o ALBERT
o Combles
Epéhy
Roisel o
Frise o
o PÉRONNE
St QUENTIN O

SCALE OF MILES
0 5 10 15 20 25

BRITISH FRONT LINE

REFERENCE
Sectors held by the Division
Line after retirement Mar.1918.
Advances by the Division.
(On Nov. 11th 1918 the Div. occupied
a line Maubeuge-Avesnes road
after advancing 65 Mls.approx)

R.C.J.

Plate 36

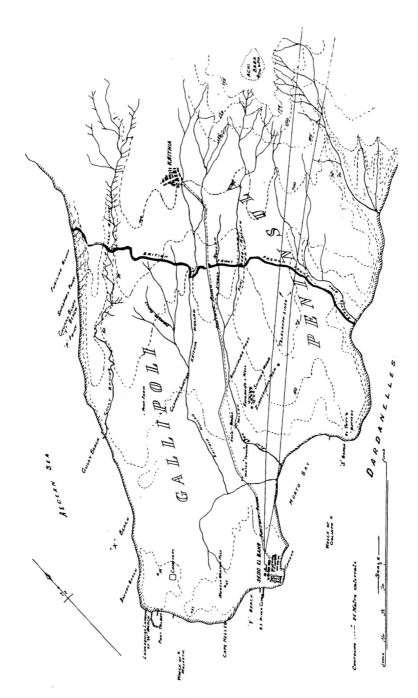

Plate 37

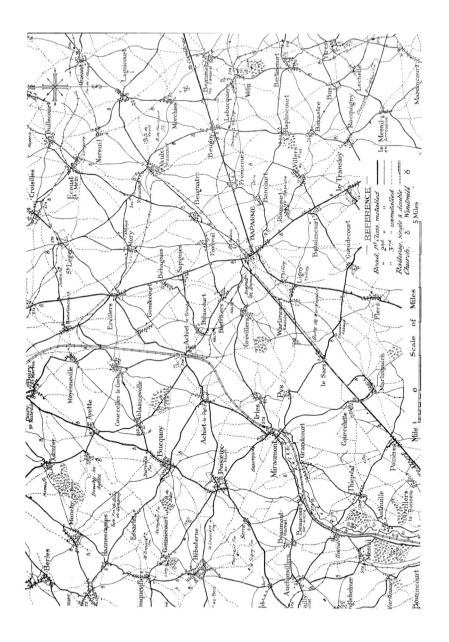

Plate 38

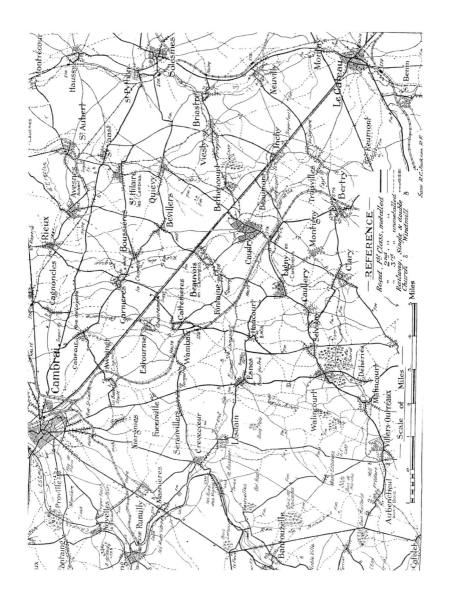

Plate 39

'GOT THE BLIGHTERS'

As THE TROOPS of the 42nd Division busied themselves and prepared to move at 30 minutes' notice, swelling gunfire could be heard to the east. A few letters were hurriedly scribbled home to loved ones and in the early dawn of 23 March the division embussed at Burbure a few miles from Lillers. A huge convoy of London motor buses awaited the troops' arrival and, amid much cursing and shouting, the three brigades crammed themselves and their bulky equipment into the open-topped vehicles. None of the troops yet knew the destination, although the peacetime posters on the buses advertised '1d all the way'. Sardonic comments from battalion pessimists probably suggested what lay at the end of the journey.

The weather was crisp and dry, the morning mist soon dissipating to give way to a watery spring sun. The buses roared off in a southerly direction, careering along the busy roads with almost reckless abandon. Men of the Motor Transport were commonly believed to live an easy and indolent life, enlivened by occasional periods of manic driving. On this occasion they excelled themselves. Frozen men on the top deck were buffeted by branches from overhanging trees while those on the inside were thrown against the windows and each other as one bus swerved to overtake another. Many broke down and when repaired raced back through the column, often with two wheels in the roadside ditch, to regain their places in the line. Rumour abounded as to the eventual destination but, oblivious to the cries and oaths from those behind, the drivers sped on. St Pol and Doullens, where evidence of long-range German shelling was all too obvious, were left behind. The column then turned on to the old Roman road between Arras and Beaumetz before next turning south-east towards Ayette. A quietness fell on the passengers when long straggling columns of refugees passed in the opposite direction. Pathetic sights of families with their worldly goods piled high on farm carts persuaded the troops that something serious was happening further on. Ignoring regulations, a few men threw tins of corned beef to the forlorn and pitiful refugees.

The column sped on, passing through pretty, unspoilt villages where the men hoped the buses would halt for the night. South of Arras the men saw more evidence of how serious the German threat was and, when the buses passed a divisional staff using a barn door as its map table and signals centre, the men imagined the sort of billets they would be using that night. As night fell the men disembussed at Adinfer Wood. Having tossed and tormented their passengers for the previous few hours, the drivers climbed down from their cabs, nonchalantly lit cigarettes and then regaled the waiting troops with harrowing tales of how the day before they had taken up the Guards. On arrival the Guards had piled out, fallen in and then immediately advanced into the wood to throw out the Germans.

Interspersed with showers of rain, the night was bitterly cold. Fires were forbidden, blankets had not arrived and enemy planes droned overhead searching for targets. As it was too cold to sleep men kept on the move, huddled in groups or found what shelter they could. Before dawn the battalion fell in and marched towards the Arras-Bapaume road. Fred Hardman left a hastily penned letter to his wife with the post corporal before the battalion moved off. Hardman, like many of the older hands, realised that they were occupying the same ground where they had rested and played football the previous July. He told Kit not to worry if she did not hear from him for a few days:

We don't know very much of what is happening out here and you probably know far more at home than we do here. You see our activities are confined to the few miles in our vicinity and for the rest, we have to rely on rumours.

It was perhaps predictable that Hardman really knew little of the situation; the front was in turmoil and the lines fluid. The German penetrations had won several miles of ground and thrown the British rear areas into chaos. While divisional, corps and army staffs tried to make sense of the situation and issue orders accordingly, wounded and exhausted troops trudged back along roads congested with field ambulances and casualty clearing stations withdrawing to quieter areas. Communications were so bad that on many occasions orders were out of date before they had been issued. In an attempt to restore a line and halt the German thrusts against Third Army, the 42nd and its fellow Territorials of the 62nd Division had been ordered up from First Army to reinforce and eventually replace those units which had borne the brunt of the German offensive. However, so important had been the need to get the infantry brigades to the danger area that the divisional artillery and transport had been left behind to battle their way along the over-burdened roads. Until several beasts had been borrowed from neighbouring units, there were insufficient horses for the staff officers directing the battalions to the areas where they could be of most use. Third Army instructed the 42nd Division to relieve the 40th Division during the night of 24/25 March but the position was so obscure that Major-General Solly-Flood decided to take up a line roughly north-south through Sapignies and wait for the 40th Division to pass through.

Lieutenant-Colonel Peel and the company commanders reconnoitred the high ground east of Courcelles as far as a now deserted former British aerodrome. Chic Taylor noted 'considerable panic' among the gunners who were desperately dismantling their heavy guns and hooking them up to the waiting tractors. At 2.15pm the battalion was ordered to move forward to Logeast Wood and become advance guard of 126 Brigade; the division's other two brigades went into the forward positions. The sun came out as the men marched off but as the road was full of wheeled traffic the route up was spent largely in the adjoining gutters and ditches. Logeast Wood was discovered to be far from the pleasant spot it had been when the 10th had enjoyed its leafy canopy in the summer of 1917. The trees were down and salvos of German shells screamed overhead. Unsure of what was to happen next, the battalion boiled canteens over small fires, filled water bottles and tried to make themselves comfortable.

The QM stores and the battle surplus under Fred Hardman were to remain in Adinfer Wood until the situation became clearer. It was known that heavy fighting was continuing around the village of Mory but as 125 and 126 Brigades were getting into position a staff officer, probably of the 40th Division, informed the columns that the enemy was through at Sapignies and ordered the 10th and the other battalions to head south-east. The information of an enemy breakthrough was not subsequently confirmed, but it does illustrate the difficulties faced by the 42nd Division in trying to ascertain just what the position was. With the 10th's transport still adrift somewhere to the west, Wynne and the four

CQMS waited for two days at Ablainzeville hoping that rations and ammunition would appear. Knowing how short the battalion was of the essentials, Wynne purloined a GS wagon and loaded it with rations and small arms ammunition from a nearby dump. When the driverless cart was full and ready to leave, the harnessed horses charged off and were not seen again. Acquiring next a shabby but serviceable two-wheeled country cart, Wynne loaded it with what few salvaged boxes he could find and was about to haul it himself to the front when a messenger arrived with orders for the CQMS to proceed to Essarts.

At about 9.30 on the night of 24 March the battalion collected its equipment, fell in and marched out of Logeast Wood. Word was received that Mory and Ervillers had fallen and that the 10th was to move into the line to prevent any German move out of Ervillers. The first halt came at a railway cutting north of Achiet-le-Grand but, just as the Lewis guns had been dug in and the men had begun to brew up, an order to continue the march came through. Abandoning what meagre rations there were, and under cover of a spluttering barrage from 18-pounder field guns, the battalion advanced through Gomiécourt and took up a position to the south-west of Ervillers. Lieutenant-Colonel Peel borrowed a bike and cycled ahead to see who was actually in possession of Ervillers. He was told that it was held by the enemy but that remnants of the 31st, 40th and 59th Divisions were holding a line of sorts just to its west. Those divisions were in a state of exhaustion. Three days of continual fighting, want of rations and a prolonged lack of sleep had reduced their numbers to handfuls. Instead of somewhere around 10,000 infantry, the nearby 19th Division for example claimed a fighting strength of only 2,200. One battalion of 58 Brigade was down to a junior subaltern and 29 men. In comparison the battalions of 126 Brigade were fresh and up to strength.

Chic Taylor was ordered to take his company into trenches occupied by men of the 40th Division and a Labour Company. Warned by a staff officer not to allow any of these troops to retire, Taylor moved along the trench to ascertain strength and morale. The Labour Company was in a state of near panic. When it had arrived, the firing line was four miles to the east; now it was virtually the front line. The Labour Company had a Lewis gun trained along the road leading into Ervillers so, leaving a reliable sergeant to 'stamp on their heads' should they open fire on him, Taylor and Private Weston crept along the road and into the village. Instead of finding it teeming with Germans, Taylor stumbled across Peel, still with his borrowed bike, and Captain Bletcher. Peel had discovered that the village was still in British hands and that elements of the 31st Division were holding a line on a reverse slope to its east. Returning to the battalion, Peel ordered two companies to move forward into the village and take up position about 150 yards behind the line held by troops of the 31st and 40th Divisions.

Enemy artillery soon turned its ferocious attention to Ervillers. Pounding the village with salvos of 5·9-inch shells and under cover of the barrage, German infantry were seen to be massing on the Mory road. As the transport had still not appeared and there seemed to be no reserves in the trenches, the Oldhamers had only the ammunition carried in their pouches. In the nick of time, Lieutenant Truman and three loaded limbers galloped up Ervillers' main street. Now replete with small arms ammunition and the knowledge that a machine-gun company, having man-handled its guns and ammunition for some eight miles across country, was holding a trench to the left, the two companies awaited the expected onslaught. Instead of the anticipated attack however, Taylor saw British troops retiring across the Arras-Bapaume road. Bewildered as to why they were withdrawing, Taylor sent an officer to round them up and bring them into his trench. When questioned the troops told Taylor that they had been ordered to retire to the Corps Line. Thinking quickly, Taylor replied that they had reached it and should now turn and face the enemy. About 300 men, largely of the 31st Division, were collected in this way. Just as the recent arrivals were taking position a British aeroplane flew low over the trench. With his observer slumped in the rear seat, under fire from both German and British guns and over the noise of his stuttering engine, the pilot shouted that German infantry was again massing east of Ervillers.

At about 8.45am, 125 Brigade reported that troops from other divisions were falling back and questioned whether the 42nd was to conform. Solly-Flood informed all brigades that until other orders might be received and irrespective of what might be happening on its flanks, his division would fight where it stood. Plenty was happening. The Lancashire Fusiliers were being hard pressed about Sapignies and the Manchester Brigade about Bihucourt. Several counter-attacks, supported by tanks and troops of the 62nd Division restored the positions, but it became clear that the enemy was making a very determined attempt to break through towards Achiet-le-Grand. The fall of Behagnies around midday threatened the rear of the 10th in Ervillers but another counter-attack by details of the 5/East Lancashire halted the German drive at least for the time being.

In Ervillers the Oldhamers were under huge pressure. While the 10th was deluged and pounded by shell fire, groups of enemy infantry filtered into dead ground, formed up and swept over the ridge in front of the village. Still without artillery support, the Oldhamers poured Lewis-gun and rifle fire into the Germans who approached in small sections giving each other fire and support. Time and time again the German assaults were frustrated but during the afternoon the young subaltern in command of the machine-gun company to A Company's flank ran down Taylor's trench firing his revolver as he came. Hit in the head, he blurted out that the Germans were in the trench to the right and then passed out in Taylor's arms. The gun crews were close behind their officer and merely wanted someone to tell them what to do. Taylor ordered them into positions with good fields of fire and they immediately opened up. Erupting into a 'terrible row' and 'having killed everything that lived within 600 yards', Taylor had some difficulty in persuading the gunners to stop firing. So intent were they to prevent a German advance that machine-gun crews stole Lewis-gun pans to fill their belts while the Lewis-gunners stole belts to fill their pans. Hunched over their Vickers, the gunners fired madly at anything that moved in the general direction of the enemy. So hectic and exciting was it that Taylor resorted to hitting the gunners on their backs with his stick to calm them down. However, if the battalion's left flank was not to be turned, the positions vacated by the gunners had to be filled.

Taylor ordered Henry Lawson and his platoon to plug the gap developing on the battalion's left. Although Lawson did not realise it at the time, Taylor never expected to see him or his men alive again. Having positioned his platoon, Lawson waited for the next attack to develop. Some hours passed and the only movement he witnessed was troops either side of him withdrawing. By early evening he realised, with something more than alarm that his platoon, with half the German army massing in front of it, was now entirely isolated. No orders arrived for him to withdraw his men, so they stayed put. A little to their rear, Peel was also in a quandary. During the heat of the earlier engagements the colonel had dispatched a defiant message to Brigade: 'Got the blighters. Can hold as long as you want'. Despite Peel's optimism, troops to the left and right were in the process of withdrawing. Communication with Brigade had been lost but because the 10th held good positions, Peel decided to remain where he was. There was also some disquiet from several of the troops whom the battalion had 'captured' earlier in the day. When they saw other units withdrawing they felt it was time they rejoined their own battalions. Officers told them that for now, whether they liked it or not, they were honorary members of the Oldham Territorials and that they were to remain with their adopted unit. The men quietened down and awaited the Germans.

At about 8.00pm a runner arrived with news that the corps on the left was under orders to withdraw further and that the 10th would have to conform. Company and platoon officers carried the orders to their men who began to collect what little equipment they retained. While the attached Machine Gun Corps officers were provided with compasses and sent on their way, Taylor took it upon himself to go forward and see if Lawson and his platoon still existed. Much to his surprise they did. Lawson, who was at that moment contemplating whether to order his men to stand to the last or surrender when the enemy next attacked, was delighted to see Taylor appear at his side and order him to extricate his men. They needed no second telling and headed back to rejoin the rest of the battalion.

Conducting a fighting withdrawal the battalion fell back on Courcelles. There was some disappointment at having to withdraw because the 10th had held its ground against no less than eight determined attacks. Pressure on the 31st Division, however, had grown to such an extent that its battered units could not hold. The 42nd and 62nd Divisions were to provide a defensive screen behind which the tired 19th, 25th, 40th, 41st and 51st

Divisions would collect and reorganise. Ervillers was to be abandoned to the enemy and by what James Bleakley described as a 'series of perfectly organised withdrawals', the battalion and the division took up a new line. Protected by the divisional artillery which had struggled through the congested roads to position itself in the rear of the new line, the 42nd Division occupied the ground between Bucquoy and Ablainzeville.

Although shielded by morning mist, the enemy was cautious and did not launch a major attack against the new position until the early hours of 26 March. Taylor's company was most heavily involved, its Lewis guns doing thorough execution of the advancing hordes. Amidst the activity Private Pearson, an Old Contemptible who had somehow ended up in the battalion as one of A Company's cooks, discovered some water and coolly brewed up a dixie to sustain the men. Lawson's platoon was ordered to take up position on a reverse slope but as it was only some 40 yards from the crest its field of fire was severely limited. It nevertheless poured bursts of fire into any Germans appearing over the hill and brought their advance to a halt. During a lull in the fighting Lawson decided to visit the troops on his flank. Crossing the open ground and a gap of some distance between the two units, Lawson discovered his neighbours to be a battalion of the Coldstream Guards. Unshaven, dishevelled and having fought for 36 hours with little food or water, Lawson looked every bit the tired but resolute warrior. He was greeted with a look of horror from an immaculate Guards officer. This young man (who had been fighting for a similar if not longer period of time), listened politely to Lawson's thoughts on the perilousness of their mutual position. After a few minutes he brought Lawson's monologue to a conclusion by wishing him 'Good afternoon. Nice of you to come over. We don't need anything, thank you. Goodbye'.

Fortunately the enemy showed no further desire to test the mettle of the defenders. Snipers ensconced in a nearby wood caused some difficulties but their enthusiasm waned after the trees had been sprayed with several prolonged bursts of Lewis-gun fire. Further to the rear Lieutenant Faulkner was severely wounded and several other wounded men were killed when their ambulance was hit by shell fire just outside Courcelles. Enjoying a brief respite of 24 hours in some reserve trenches near Essarts, Hardman seized the opportunity to write a letter home. Having been in command of the divisional battle surplus for what he called the 'six most atrocious days of the war', Hardman rejoined the battalion as it bedded down in Essarts:

> *The battalion did some very good work ... and managed to hold the blighters up. We have lost a few officers but they were not Oldhamers. The fight lasted a lot longer than it did in Gallipoli but our casualties were only about half as many so we have not done badly ... This battle is more a case of numbers ... I should think we were outnumbered 6:1 and he keeps rolling up wave after wave of fresh troops. We have only weary and tired troops to stand against him so you can understand how bitter we are just now against men of military age at home. Our men are doing wonders but they can't work miracles.*

The battalion's return to the forward positions coincided with a deterioration in the weather. Rain fell in torrents, flooding the posts and shell holes and drenching the already exhausted men. Unknown to the man in the line, the troops of the 42nd Division and the other three tired divisions of IV Corps, were opposed by nine enemy divisions with another five in support. The odds were heavily in favour of the enemy but with the roads to the rear clearing and the staffs getting more of a grip on their dispersed units, the British position was not without hope. An attack by the enemy from Logeast Wood against 126 and 127 Brigades was halted when the Mancunians lay on top of their trenches to obtain improved fields of fire.

Unprotected by wire or local artillery the Oldhamers occupied a line of shell holes and trenches of 1916 vintage. Every night Major-General Solly-Flood visited the line to encourage his men to 'go one better'. The General knew how perilous was the state of play, for all three of his brigades had an effective strength of fewer than 1100. The Oldhamers' brigade, 126, was officially described as: 'Much shelled, ready to fight, but cannot march' and the division as a whole was listed in a GHQ report dated 1 April as one of the 15 'exhausted divisions still in or near the line'. Knowing that there was little prospect of immediate relief or rest the men hung on, sheltering where possible from the German shells, snipers, gas deluges and the seemingly endless rain.

When the rain eventually stopped the nights turned cold. With no greatcoats or blankets and with sharp hoar frosts filling their earthen scrapes, the men struggled to keep their limbs from freezing. During one bright, bitter night, as the guns were crashing around them, the post came up. Touched by the brutality of his surroundings and the emotion evident in a letter from Kitty, Hardman rushed off a note in reply:

> *My thoughts are deep and true dear. My mind is full of retrospect and I want to rush home to you, just to see you once again and kiss the tears from your hot cheeks. But that is a joy to be when victory is won and any fighting is over. I will come back dear! Back to my heart's home, to be comforted and give comfort by passion and love.*

At times of extreme stress and self-doubt, Hardman tended to unburden himself not to his wife but to his father. Two days after writing the passionate and assured note to Kitty, he penned an introspective letter to Hardman senior:

> *I wonder sometimes how it all comes about and why it is my lot to continuously see my friends go down while I come through. Sooner or later it seems that my luck must change and in those moments of uncertainty which seem like years, I am afraid that I am sometimes a coward and wish that it would.*

Hardman and his men had to endure another 48 hours of torment before they were relieved by troops of the West Yorkshire Regiment. Even when the battalion was finally out of the immediate firing line the enemy did not leave it unmolested. As they struggled to squeeze into some completely inadequate dugouts in Essarts, over 70 men were badly gassed. Another three were killed and nine wounded when a barrage of 5·9-inch and 8-inch shells smashed down to supplement the gas. During a six hour bombardment, an estimated 5,000 enemy shells and canisters were put down on an approximate square of 500 yards. Already a foot deep in mud the trenches were described as 'slime and blood, carpeted with bodies'. Those six hours, during which the battalion lost more men than in the previous twelve days of battle, was according to Wynne 'probably one of the worst experiences of the war'. It was not until some hours after the shelling had ceased that Fred Hardman realised he had not masked promptly enough. Next morning his eyes were closed and weeping, his throat and chest wracked with pain and his heart feeling it was about to leap through his rib cage. The battalion's Medical Officer had already been evacuated with similar symptoms so Hardman took himself off to a nearby aid post. Blindfolded against the light, he was put into a lorry for evacuation to the railhead. The following day he settled into a bed with clean, crisp sheets at a Boulogne hospital.

Meanwhile, after fourteen days and nights, the battalion was ordered back to Souastre. This village was behind the line now manned by the divisions for which the 42nd had been buying time. For the moment the Lancastrians had done all that had been asked of them. In a stupor, unshaven, unwashed and with eyes sunk deep into their sockets, the Oldhamers stumbled into the village to be greeted by the sights of steaming cookers and wooden huts. The survivors filled their stomachs, wrapped themselves in blankets and curled up on the boarded floors. The following day they fell in and continued the march another few miles to Pas. Here, far behind the lines, comfortable billets, real baths and a beautiful, fully leafed wood, 'gave Pas the appearance of Paradise'. With stubble and mud still adorning their faces and tunics, the column was dismissed. Sections filed into the waiting *estaminets*, ordered egg and chips, talked quietly or simply engrossed themselves in their own thoughts. After a good night's sleep they smartened up, sorted equipment, cleaned their weapons and took greater stock of their environment. Besides the joy of the pleasant surroundings, of hearing birds twittering in the trees and only the faintest sound of gunfire, the post had arrived. So too had a draft of what Wynne described as 'mere boys'. They appeared to have been well trained and were 'most enthusiastic' but, 'Poor lads! Within a few short hours of their arrival, many of them were laid low'.

There was time for reflection before the battalion would return to the line. Letters and parcels from home, baths, football and rest cheered the men and restored morale. There was also time to take stock of casualties among the other platoons and companies. Despite the severity and the length of time the battalion had been engaged, fatalities had been remarkably light. For the period between 25 March to 7 April, 19 men had been killed and another

15 died of wounds. The number of wounded and captured is unrecorded but it was probably considerable as the division as a whole lost just under 3,000 men in almost exactly the same period. Two of the battalion's dead were from the KOYLI draft which arrived while the 10th was still in Egypt and another, Alfred Viner, had arrived from the Ox & Bucks Light Infantry. Several of the dead, including James Wood who succumbed to gas, died in the large base hospitals on the coast, while others, including a Gallipoli veteran John Cadman, died of wounds at a Casualty Clearing Station some miles behind the lines. At least three other men who had been wounded on Gallipoli were also killed: Herbert Ogden of Mount Pleasant Street and James Stansfield were buried in a British cemetery at Couin while James Platt of Chadderton was buried with four other members in the small village of St Amand. Among those whom the fortunes of war did not honour with a known grave were John Coates from Failsworth and George Drayton from Sheffield.

Casualties among officers are easier to determine. No officers were killed, but three, none of whom came from Oldham, joined Fred Hardman in the hospital at Boulogne. Captain Redmond the Medical Officer was hit at the same time as acting RSM Smith; Lieutenant Jackson was wounded soon after. Captain Bletcher was wounded but remained at duty. Procktor Stott was away on a course and safe; Chic Taylor, although knocked around a little, Alfred Butterworth and Jimmy Whitehead were also unwounded. Although the war diary makes no note of their arrival, it seems likely that several new subalterns arrived with the draft of Other Ranks to replace the commissioned wounded.

The respite was short lived. At 4.00am on 14 April the battalion again fell in and marched off towards the front. It was a foul day, with drenching rain and a howling wind. What good the inadequate time spent at Pas did was soon undone by a tiring day and an uncomfortable night spent huddled beneath the dripping branches of Henu Wood. The sound of battle to the east rose and fell during the interminable, miserable hours. With the coming of another black and mournful night, the battalion again set off. As it passed between the tumbled buildings and martyred church of Fonquevillers, salvos of 5·9-inch shells ripped open the pouring heavens. Lieutenants Selwyn Rowbotham and Finch were hit by shrapnel and, what the war diary recorded as 'many' Other Ranks were also wounded. A proportion of the wounded, although again one which is impossible to ascertain accurately, was certainly from the draft which had only just arrived. These young boys had not even reached the front line before being cut down. The evacuation of Rowbotham and Finch necessitated a change in the companies. Lieutenant Chapman became OC D Company to replace Rowbotham and Second Lieutenant William Norris from Bristol replaced Finch as OC B Company.

Having relieved units of the 37th Division, the battalion spent the next three weeks in and out of the front line posts and trenches to the north-east of Rossignol Wood. The battle surplus under the command of Chic Taylor had a fairly easy time but the men in the trenches suffered badly. The weather was atrocious and many of the trenches little more than mud-filled ditches. The British reserve trenches were the former German front line system of 1916; these were deep, well revetted and furnished with good dugouts. By contrast, the British front positions were now in what had been the German reserve lines; these were shallow and possessed nothing which could be described as a strongpoint. The shelling was incessant so what little work could be done to improve drainage or revetting was frequently undone by the next salvo. As they dodged the shells the troops laboured on improving the drainage, laying wire, digging communication trenches and gas-proofing dugouts. Once the former German narrow gauge track had been relaid through and beyond the ruins of Gommecourt, engineers' stores, rations, water and ammunition could be brought up by railway.

On 18 April, Intelligence reported that the Germans were about to launch a major assault. The troops waited with anxious anticipation but nothing came of the alarm. Ten days later the battalion was ordered to extend its frontage by taking over some of the sector previously manned by the 62nd Division. Envious Lancastrian eyes were cast at the West Yorkshire Territorials as they filed out of the trenches to take a long-delayed rest. Fortunately, envy soon turned to joy. Troops of the 57th Division appeared in the forward trenches and on 6 May, weighed down by cloying mud and equipment, the battalion dragged itself back the few miles to Pas Wood.

During its absence the wood had blossomed. Branches were full of youthful leaves and the ground carpeted with colourful and fragrant blooms. Amid the trees were tents, cookhouses, huts and the many various buildings which typified a rest area. As they threw themselves into their canvas accommodation, even the sun came out to welcome the weary men. Within a few days the ground had dried out, the men were playing cricket and football and once again bore the appearance of soldiers. Colonel Peel had had the foresight to request a piano from the Mayor of Oldham and this arrived soon after the 10th took up residence in the wood. Sitting in a tree-shaded natural amphitheatre, the battalion listened to performances given by the concert party and generally enlivened each others' spirits. Laughter, ribaldry and ridicule could again be heard from throats and lungs which until recently had been more used to grousing and cursing. The time was, according to Wynne, 'one of the few pleasant interludes' of the war.

Fred Hardman rejoined the battalion as it revived its *esprit* among the glades of the wood. Having spent a few days at a convalescence camp on the coast, a Medical Board at Boulogne had finally decided Hardman was fit to return to duty. He returned to command D Company but could find only six of its original 1914 members still serving. His officers too were a mixed bunch. His second in command was a Cornishman, with the subalterns hailing from Scotland, Wales and Liverpool. Despite the very non-Oldham character of his company, and indeed the entire battalion, Hardman retained his confidence in its fighting abilities. What had annoyed him during his recovery period were the reports he had read about the enemy in the British press:

> I see that half the papers are still spouting about the poor quality of the Boche ... it makes me sick to read it. I can't tell what they mean to convey by talking as they do, for you can take my word that their material is just as good physically as ours and that they are brave men into the bargain. But thank God! They have got their match when they come up against our boys.

Despite his admiration for the bravery and tenacity of the enemy, his antipathy for them had not abated:

> There can be no truce between God and the devil and we have got to fight this lot out to a finish. There can be no half measures and the more I see of the handicraft of the damnable Boche, the more firm my resolve ... Whatever the cost, those who come after us shall at least be free of a foreign yoke and a conqueror's heel.

The relaxation generated during their arboreal sojourn allowed officers to get to know their men. Closer links were forged between worldly, slum-raised Lancastrians who ranged in age from 18 to 41, and relatively innocent 19-year-old officers from public schools and leafy Surrey lanes. It was an officer's responsibility to care for the welfare of his men. This did not mean that he had only to consider the state of the men's feet or their rations, but also their spirits and domestic concerns. Coming from the higher echelons of society had its advantages when it came to pulling strings or using people in positions of authority. For example, Hardman wrote to his father asking him to speak to one of his fellow magistrates on behalf of one of his men. The man was losing 2/6d per week from his pay to his estranged wife. While the soldier had been in Gallipoli his wife had been regularly picked up by the police for drunkenness. The Bench had given custody of the man's three children to his mother but the wife still received a separation allowance. Now that she had given birth to another man's child, the soldier wanted the payments to cease. Two weeks later Hardman had a personal reply from Oldham's Chief Constable explaining that the matter had been resolved.

Life in the wood was not all pleasure as the serious business of war had still to be practised. Enemy planes flew over at night and occasionally dropped the odd bomb; long-range shells searching for Divisional HQ and other worthwhile targets regularly whistled overhead and crashed a little to the rear. Training, mostly in the form of company and battalion counter-attacks and other field firing schemes, was continued. On one occasion Lawson's platoon was picked to demonstrate the art of fire and support. His men had to manoeuvre for about 1000 yards up a grass-covered hill, firing live ammunition at targets as they went. On successfully reaching the objective Lawson presented himself to the watching General to receive his plaudits. As he began to compliment the young platoon commander, the General suddenly stopped and demanded, 'What is the matter with that cow?' First one and then another beast collapsed and fell to the ground, picked off by Lawson's men. The staff jumped up and down; a puce-faced, stick-brandishing farmer advanced and there was general commotion. An enquiry was conducted into the affair but no culprit was ever discovered. The farmer received heavy compensation and an apology. Lawson felt humiliated but his company commander regarded the matter as a huge joke, ceasing to laugh only long enough to offer caustic comments about the priorities the staff seemed to have about casualties.

On a beautiful late May morning, with mist hanging evocatively between the stately boughs, 126 Brigade held a medal parade. Accompanied by his gilded staff, Solly-Flood emerged from the trees seated on his prancing steed. A bugle sounded and three thousand bayonets flashed in the sun as the hollow square came to attention. Each recipient's deed was read aloud by an immaculate staff officer and one by one those men who were still alive were presented with their medal ribbon. Colonel Peel accepted the VC ribbon on behalf of 'Spud' Mills' widow and, as the first note of the *Last Post* rang out, the parade came automatically to attention. Peel received a bar to his DSO and Chic Taylor the DSO which had been awarded him for his part in the March fighting. Captains Frank Howarth from Newton Heath and Fred Hardman each received a Military Cross, the latter having earned his for his work during the Gallipoli campaign. On presenting Hardman with the ribbon, Solly-Flood commented 'Somewhat delayed is it not?' Lance Sergeant Robinson and Privates Davies, Hulme, Hutchins and Spink were awarded a Military Medal while Sergeant Haslam and Private Coulson were presented with the Belgian *Croix de Guerre*. The parade was brought to a conclusion with the recipients standing beneath the flag and the troops, led by the General, marching past.

Captain Redmond's replacement for the post of Battalion Medical Officer was Captain Harvey, an American from South Georgia. Like many American doctors attached to British units he was eager to gain experience in treating combat injuries but was less willing to endure the camp's Spartan facilities. One day in Pas Wood he decided to construct what he described as a 'Turkish bath'. Inside a cubicle made of suspended blankets were placed several Primus stoves; once burning, these appliances generated a prodigious heat. A perforated biscuit tin was hung from an overhanging branch and periodically filled with cold water to function as a shower. Delighted with his creation, Harvey invited his fellow officers to benefit from the ingenuity of the New World. Apparently everyone except the battalion's drummers enjoyed the novel experience; the jobs of filling the biscuit tin and pulling the string fell to members of the band.

In mid-May Harvey was joined in the 10th by several hundred of his compatriots. Battalions of the 307th Infantry Regiment were attached to units of the 42nd Division for training and trench experience. Other US regiments, artillery and engineer units were being similarly paired with British divisions out at rest. The 307th was a New York regiment and when the MO discovered the imminent arrival of a Northern regiment he let fly some uncharitable remarks about these 'Yanks'. Somewhat bemused by these unexpected criticisms, the 10th's officers asked for clarification. The 'Doc', whose language was at times apparently sufficiently colourful to make a Billingsgate porter 'hang his head with shame', explained that anyone who came from north of the Mason-Dixon Line was little better than an uncivilised thief. It was with great pleasure therefore that Harvey listened to the Oldhamers' band, which essentially meant the drummers augmented by a few buglers, play the Americans into camp. The band met the column of Americans some distance from the wood, took position at its head and commenced playing. It was a long, weary march, capped by a stiff uphill climb into Pas. Having virtually played itself to a standstill, the band girded itself for a rousing finalé and began to crash out *Marching through Georgia*, one of the 10th's favourite tunes. Not realising its significance to Americans from the Northern states and ascribing Harvey's delirious cavorting to his usual eccentricty, the band blew and beat as it had never done before.

Despite the unfortunate introduction, the Americans appreciated the hot meal prepared for them by the 10th's cooks. It did however take some time for the US troops to fraternize freely with the Oldhamers. There were many doughboys of Austrian and German descent which, according to one somewhat tongue-in-cheek source, required US platoon sergeants to give instructions in 16 different languages. Hardman was certainly initially surprised at the polyglot nature of the 3rd Battalion, describing the American as 'the most complete mongrel that nature ever blended'. Other Oldhamers were rather taken aback at the number of Irish in the ranks. At a concert given by the American battalion for its British hosts, almost every other song was an Irish ballad and every soldier seemed to have been called Murphy or O'Brien.

The Americans were very green but eager to learn. There were a few of what Hardman called 'typical Yanks', but most realised that they could teach the veterans of four years of war little about training and trench warfare. They seemed mystified by the lack of offensive action and champed at the bit to be given an opportunity to test themselves. When the chance came, the inexperience and reckless courage was to cost them dear in the Argonne and the trenches of the Hindenburg Line. Their impatience impressed Lawson and other experienced British officers who felt that the newcomers brought a refreshing and optimistic outlook to the ingrained acceptance of static trench warfare. So inexperienced were the Americans that they assumed the occasional appearance of bomb and long-distance shell constituted their being in a battle zone. Wynne relates a story of how one of their officers awakened from his slumbers by the drone of an aeroplane mistook the noise for a strombos horn used to give warning of a gas attack. Seizing his revolver, donning his box respirator and struggling into an exceptionally gaudy dressing-gown, the officer rushed from his tent and tried to gain access to the HQ mess by way of the stove pipe. He was rescued from his undignified predicament by Colonel Peel who then guided him into the mess through the more conventional entrance. He was soon restored to a more appropriate demeanour 'in the usual way'.

Towards the end of May, the 10th engaged in a baseball match with its pupils. The Divisional General was invited to attend, a pitch was marked out and a team of Oldhamers instructed in the rudiments of the sport. When the day came troops from both battalions lined the diamond and Solly-Flood appeared mounted on his shining charger. Play commenced but during the Oldhamers' innings a heavy shell was heard shrieking in the general direction of the camp. The shell exploded harmlessly some 60 yards away but it was sufficiently close for the General's horse to leap into the air and gallop off. It was later alleged that it took three miles of rough riding before Solly-Flood regained control of his truculent steed. On the pitch, the American team and most of its supporters had disappeared and the Oldhamers were left to roll around laughing at the now empty positions of their allies.

In return for instructing the Americans in the arts and science of modern warfare and in how to run a mess, the New Yorkers taught the Oldhamers how to jazz. Shortly before it departed, the 3rd Battalion treated the 10th to a concert. On a summer's evening beneath a canopy of leaves and a star-studded sky, an alleged $20,000 a year ragtime pianist, a cornet, trombone and two drummers entertained the battalion for an hour. The 'music' and the antics of the 'musicians' at first bewildered the Oldhamers, but once they comprehended that there was nothing to understand, they roared with approval and laughter at the pianist's increasingly more eccentric behaviour. Eventually, after absorbing sounds which no Lancastrian would probably have believed could have come from five human performers, the battalion cheered the drained artists from the stage. Upon recovery the pianist was invited into the mess where revenge was sought. He was forced to endure endless renditions of *Three Blind Mice* and *Who Killed Cock Robin?* To the surprise of the mess, the American showed no signs of alarm or discomfort, commenting instead that the dirges were 'real music', whereas his was 'only a collection of syncopations'. Wynne believed that 'no one professed to know what he meant but *Robin* was killed and the *Mice* blinded for some hours'.

The coming together of representatives of the Old and New Worlds in the glades of Pas Wood was of benefit to all so it was with genuine regret that the companies paraded at noon on 6 June to wish the Americans 'good luck' and 'farewell'. The 307th had been ordered to move at short notice, an enormous pile of discarded equipment testifying to their hasty departure. The Oldhamers descended upon the abandoned piles of boots, socks and shirts like vultures on a corpse. By the time the Salvage Officer appeared to lay official claim to the pile the 10th's packs had been filled to unlikely limits with plundered goods.

The Americans' departure coincided with increasing signs that the battalion's rest period was approaching an end. Warning orders arrived instructing the division to be prepared to relieve the New Zealand Division and on 5 June the advance party went into the trenches of the Hébuterne sector to reconnoitre. Two days later the battalion marched out of its idyllic home of Pas Wood and once more moved towards the front.

By this stage of the war, four members of the 42nd Division had been shot by firing squad for desertion and a fifth for leaving his post. Two of these five men, Privates Thomas Foulkes and Thomas Brigham, were from the Oldham Battalion. As the two men are not listed in *Soldiers Died* and the Commonwealth War Graves registers are of little help, information about the pair is sparse. Foulkes was a conscript and had originally served with the 21/Manchester. At some stage of the war he was posted to the 10th, from where he deserted. He was shot at Zermezeele in November 1917. Thomas Brigham's army number suggests that he was probably originally a member of the 8/Manchester, the Ardwick Battalion. He certainly joined the Territorials before the war and had served in Egypt and Gallipoli. He deserted twice in 1917 and was given a suspended death sentence. It is unclear whether he was serving with the 10th on these occasions, but it was from the Oldham Battalion that he had deserted for a third time. When he was again captured, there was little chance that he would be saved from the firing squad.

As Brigham had served in Chic Taylor's A Company, it fell to an officer and firing party of the company to perform the execution. In a slightly confused reminiscence, Henry Lawson believed that the death sentence for desertion was justified; however, as an officer of A Company he dreaded that he might be required to command the firing party. It was to his great relief that another officer was chosen but Lawson later considered that the procedure requiring men of the condemned man's company to carry out the deed was 'wholly repugnant'. The officer selected told Lawson that Brigham had been strapped to a chair near Pas Wood with a piece of paper over his heart. The execution took place at dawn on 4 June. After firing the volley the officer and firing squad reputedly dropped their rifles and fled from the scene 'running away because they dare not look upon the consequences of their deed'. If the execution was supposed to act as a deterrent to others, Lawson concluded it failed. He claimed that only a small proportion of the officers and men of the company had ever 'heard of him or his desertion', and that probably no more than ten per cent of the battalion knew of his execution. This statement is a little difficult to accept. Word of a man's execution would inevitably get about the companies and battalion Daily Orders within the BEF often announced the execution of condemned soldiers. Nevertheless, and aware or not of Brigham's fate, the 10th returned to the trenches near Signy Farm south of Hébuterne.

THE ADVANCE TO VICTORY

Brigham's execution coincided with the third anniversary of the battalion's attack at Krithia. There is no record to suggest that the battalion itself officially acknowledged the event, although in the shade of Pas Wood many of the survivors no doubt turned their thoughts to absent friends and several officers were invited to a fine commemorative dinner hosted by the 6/Manchester. Three hundred miles away in Oldham the tradition of remembering the 10th's bloody encounter with the Turk had already been established. In May 1916 the local press had carried letters from discharged or wounded soldiers of the 10th suggesting that there should be some recognition of the battalion's arrival at Gallipoli to 'honour and respect the few that are left'. An unnamed mother who had lost her son at Krithia pointed out that the ANZAC landing had already been officially commemorated by the Dominions but that 'our lads' landing seems to be passing unnoticed'. The swell of opinion within the town was such that on 5 June 1916 a service of commemoration was held in the Empire Theatre. About 160 of the 10th's Gallipoli veterans were present. So too was their former CO on the peninsula, Lieutenant-Colonel Rye. He was accompanied by Lieutenant-Colonel Bamford, now of the 2/10th, Captains Leach and Newton and several other officers who had landed with the battalion. In an address Reverend Sunmars declared that the service was not concerned whether the campaign was a 'stroke of genius or a huge blunder', but that they had simply gathered to remember the gallantry and patriotism of their townsfolk. Other dignitaries delivered similar speeches before a procession through the town centre brought the proceedings to a conclusion. The precedent had been set and for many years after the tradition of commemorating the battle was maintained.

By the time the 1918 service was held, the town knew of the battalion's exploits in March and April 1918. The 10th was one of the very few units singled out for individual praise in Douglas Haig's official despatches and Oldham's press naturally trumpeted the battalion's collective and, when details became known, several individual successes. Local churches and schools often presented former members who had won awards with certificates and gifts as a token of their former link and Chic Taylor received several congratulatory messages when news of his DSO was known. Lieutenant-Colonel Rye wrote from his home at Albert Mount to say that as Taylor's former commanding officer, the award gave him 'great satisfaction'. Taylor's current CO, Lieutenant-Colonel Peel, wrote: 'To my mind it is one of the best DSOs there has been and no one deserved it more than you did'. A less formal note arrived from one of Taylor's former colleagues then serving with a Training Brigade at Blackpool:

> ... *you casual old blighter. I can just see you Chic, being bored to tears shooting the swine, the whole thing nothing but a beastly bore, and you wondering all the time when the beastly affair would be over and you could get back under your eiderdown quilt.*

Equally delighted was Taylor's sister Dorothy. Writing to her parents from the military hospital where she worked, Dorothy exclaimed, 'I can think of nothing else ... can you wonder ... a DSO in the family!'

A few hours after the 10th had moved back to the front positions near La Signy Farm, a violent bombardment crashed down on C Company's sector. Second Lieutenant Stanley Gregory from Northwich and seven other men were killed, nine wounded and John Bardsley of Chadderton Road died of wounds four days later in a CCS at Bagneux. Gregory and the other fatalities were carried back to Bertrancourt and buried in the military cemetery just outside the village. Until the plots were laid out and organised in the years after the war as a typical Commonwealth War Graves Commission cemetery, Gregory's grave was marked by a tall wooden cross and plinth surrounded by chained posts. Four of the Other Ranks dead were from Oldham, one of whom was Lance Corporal Albert Wright. He was buried next to Private Herbert Wright who came from Crewe. The steady, although undramatic toll of casualties and the continued strain of commanding a company, caused Fred Hardman to ponder on his own fortunes:

> *I take up my company of 'Britain's Best' and come back fewer in number ... I sometimes wonder if the generations of the future will appreciate the sacrifices of the present. Of my three subalterns, two have been wounded and one is back in Blighty ... I wonder whether I am the lucky one to be still 'carrying on' or whether*

I should have been the lucky one to be back in England ... The soldiers' spirits are good ... we will have nothing else but victory. But if you want to betray us, keep at home the men who have so far sacrificed nothing and only shelter their miserable bodies behind the better men out here.

Life for Hardman and his men in the Hébuterne sector was hectic. Shelling was almost continuous and there were constant demands by the RE for the infantry to provide working parties. Trench-mortar crews on both sides were very active and trenches were frequently blown in by sustained and accurate fire from enemy *minnewerfers*. During the night of 17-18 June a working party of the 10th was caught by German shells as it laboured a little behind the front line. Five men were killed and at least two wounded. Like Gregory's party ten days earlier, the dead were taken back and buried in Bertrancourt's expanding cemetery. Four nights later another bombardment killed a further five men. Four of them came from outside the Oldham area but Corporal Harry Kirkman lived at Hollinwood. Three men were killed on 18 July (one of whom was certainly the victim of an enemy air raid on Bertrancourt village) while the battalion was out at rest. The casualties of these two months indicate the variety of areas of origin and former regiments of recent drafts; fatalities came from as far apart as London and the Midlands and the men had previously served with battalions of the East Surrey and Border Regiments.

Apart from the shelling, another feature of life in the Hébuterne sector was the frequency of raids. The 42nd Division maintained heavy pressure on the enemy lines by regularly sending men over the bags under cover of a trench-mortar barrage to grab a prisoner. Some of the raids involved nearly one hundred men while others, such as one undertaken by the 10th in June, involved only five.

Besides the enemy's attempt to kill and maim, the division experienced a substantial drain of men in June when scores were admitted to hospital with flu. The 10th's war diary records that in a nine day period ending on 3 July, 120 Other Ranks had gone to hospital. After the war Wynne believed that the total was sometimes 60 admissions per day. Whatever the precise figure, the reduction in strength meant more work for those who remained. It was with some relief therefore that the division heard that the New Zealanders were returning to the line; this enabled the 42nd to reduce its long frontage to a more acceptable one of 3,800 yards.

On the other side of No Man's Land the Germans too were suffering. Their hammer blows against the Allied line in March, April and May had dented but not broken the defences and, following a lull which allowed reorganisation and regrouping, the Allies were in a position to launch their counter-offensives. The 42nd Division was edging its way forwards, little by little, taking a hundred yards here and a hundred yards there of the German front. There was still a possibility of another strong German offensive so as the line progressed communication trenches and strong points were established across the newly captured ground. By August the piecemeal advances became a little easier. Although it was clear that the Germans were withdrawing to better positions, they continued to harass and delay the patrols probing their evacuated positions. A small road named Watling Street by the British ran up and across the crest of a ridge west of Serre village. This village had been the objective of the Barnsley and Sheffield Pals on 1 July 1916 who, as they plodded towards the village, had been torn to shreds in the tempest of oncoming fire. The tumbled buildings had remained in German hands until the enemy evacuated them during his staged withdrawal to the Hindenburg Line in February 1917. Lieutenant-Colonel Peel decided that Watling Street should be captured by a well rehearsed attack of two companies. The companies were taken out of the line to practise their roles and were promised extra rations and cigarettes on completion of the stunt. Unfortunately for A and C Companies, Captain Selwyn Rowbotham commanding B Company, decided not to wait for the official attack and despatched a daylight patrol of his own men to investigate the German position. The patrol returned with the news that Watling Street was empty save for enemy corpses. To the disappointment of the other companies the men of B promptly claimed and were awarded the extra rations. Besides the natural glee at getting one over on another company, the men of B appreciated the cigarettes. Joe Humphreys of C Company wrote to his wife in mid-August complaining that he could not get cigarettes for love nor money.

He implored Flossie to send any she might be able to procure as he and his mates were contemplating smoking dried tea leaves.

The British artillery gave the retreating Germans no respite. As the 42nd Division's infantry advanced into the evacuated areas the damage wreaked by the artillery on the enemy's wagons, gun teams and infantry became evident. Roads were littered with dead men and animals, abandoned equipment and demolished dugouts. By 20 August Serre was in British hands and the division had pushed on almost to the Puisieux-Beaucourt road. The ground gained was not of particular military value in that it was simply the land devastated and destroyed during the Battle of the Somme, but it did have tremendous symbolic importance. This was the land for which thousands of British troops had died between July 1916 and February 1917. Now, and for very little cost, it was once again in British hands. The Allied offensives had opened to the south and although the Germans were still fighting hard, it was becoming clear that they were being beaten in the field. The divisional history summed up this stage of the campaign:

For seventy-five days the Division had been in the line, an unusually long period. The heavy work upon the defensive system, the numerous raids and minor operations, the constant harassing of the enemy, the consolidating of the new positions gained, the advancement of the line with its added difficulties of transport and supply, all these — in the hottest months of the year — had imposed a great strain upon all units. But the troops were fired by enthusiasm, and had no desire to be relieved at such a time as this. Their one desire was to get the Boche on the run; and when the rumours of impending advances finally gave place to definite detailed orders and preparations, the weariness and strain were lightly cast aside. The Germans had done their worst, and had made deep impressions on the allied front. The 42nd Division now meant to go for the Hindenburg Line — and to 'go one better'.

Although the formidable and intimidating obstacles of the Hindenburg Line still lay some distance to the east, everyone from the mightiest general to the lowest private knew that at some stage of the battle they would have to be breached. Before the line's acres of wire and concrete blockhouses could be traversed and stormed, there were many miles of wasted land and areas of determined resistance to be negotiated.

The return to what had almost become a war of movement necessitated different tactics. Officers and men who had grown used to trench warfare had to learn new offensive and flexible means of movement. Experience and the improved quality of guns and shells had allowed the artillery to perfect the creeping barrage. This expertise allowed the infantry to advance about 25 metres behind a line of bursting shells designed to keep the Germans cowering in their trenches until the British were upon them. The shrapnel burst forwards and although there were occasions when the artillery fired short, the troops had confidence in the accuracy of the gunners. The golden rules were to keep as close behind the barrage as the terrain permitted, and to keep going. The first waves pressed on, allowing the following waves to mop up, until either the natural momentum of the advance petered out or they lost the barrage. Then the priorities were to consolidate the captured ground, make sure Brigade and the artillery were aware of the new line and await the anticipated counter-attacks.

On 20 August the 10th was temporarily attached to 127 Brigade to provide working parties. Two brigades, 125 on the right and 127 on the left, were ordered to attack the high ground above the ruined village of Miraumont. If the village (which straddled the River Ancre) fell, the enemy would be compelled to evacuate the whole of the defended Ancre line. In the early hours of 21 August the brigades attacked but failed to take their final objectives. In the afternoon the Lancashire Fusiliers finally secured the Dovecot, a collection of shattered trees which had once surrounded a now obliterated dovecot. It was during this action that Sergeant Edward Smith of the 5/LF performed deeds of outstanding bravery which were later recognised by the award of the Victoria Cross. Appreciating the critical importance of the position the Germans launched ferocious counter-attacks. Two platoons of the 10th were sent up to assist the 7/LF but the enemy numbers were so overwhelming that the Territorials were forced to withdraw from the Dovecot. The enemy success was, however, to be short-lived. Despite the heat, the gas and the debilitating cost of battle, the division knew that it had achieved a significant advance. Spirits were high and the consciousness of what had already been achieved helped men to overcome their physical and mental weariness. At 2.30am on 23 August, A and B Companies of the 10th attacked in conjunction with two companies of the 8/LF and threw the enemy out of the Dovecot.

Searching to establish bridgeheads across the Ancre, patrols advanced down the slope towards Miraumont. Fierce machine-gun fire from the village confirmed that the enemy was alert and prepared to fight. The artillery was brought up and preparations put in train to execute a set-piece manoeuvre to pinch out the village. On the morning of 24 August, as heavy shells pounded the centre of the village and shrapnel rained down on the heads of the defenders in its outskirts, the 5/East Lancashire and the 10/Manchester worked around the village from the north. They met up to the east of the buildings with 127 Brigade which had approached from the south. Caught in the trap, many of the German garrison simply threw up their arms and surrendered. Some did however continue to resist. Henry Lawson, who claimed to be the first man into the village, believed that his men took no chances and tossed grenades down cellar steps. Once the village had been cleared the battalion pressed on and finally halted close by the ruins of the nearby hamlet of Pys.

In view of the strategic importance of Miraumont and the number of prisoners taken, casualties in the 42nd Division were described as 'light'. The 10th had captured 40 Germans, 18 machine guns and a wireless set. In return, its casualty list for the two days amounted to eight dead and 28 wounded. Among those killed were Second Lieutenant Frank Elliot, who had only arrived at the battalion two days earlier, and Lance Corporal Harvey Lewis of Godson Street. None of the other fatalities was from Oldham. Graves of two of the fallen were not identified after the war and their names were later engraved on the Vis-en-Artois Memorial to the Missing. Four of the men, including Elliot, were buried at the pretty Sucrerie Cemetery near Colincamps, and the other two a little outside the village of Bucquoy.

The 10th was withdrawn to rest while other battalions continued the advance. Units of the division crossed the Bapaume-Péronne road north-west of the small village of Riencourt but attacks on the village by the 5/East Lancashire and the 8/Manchester were beaten back by the German defenders. The divisional artillery turned its attention to the buildings but when patrols ventured towards them they were again driven off. It was decided that the 10th should be brought forward to attempt to take the village as darkness fell on 31 August. The omens were not encouraging. The battalion was shelled as it crossed the main road to its assembly positions, machine-gun bullets whistled past the troops as they shook out into artillery formation and an enemy spotter-plane buzzed and swooped above their heads.

The village was about 1,000 yards in front across a fairly flat approach. The objectives were first to capture the village and then press on to establish a line on rising ground 500 yards to the east. As Fred Hardman was ordered to remain with the 'beastly battle surplus', command of D Company devolved upon Lieutenant Walter Shaw attached from the 2/Royal Fusiliers. His company was to attack on the right, while A Company under Chic Taylor would approach from the left.

At 7.00pm on Oldham Wakes Friday the two companies began the advance. The village was pummelled by the divisional artillery, but as soon as the troops showed themselves, they were met by a hail of machine-gun bullets and a counter-barrage. They passed by numbers of wounded men of the East Lancashires and 8/Manchester who had lain out in the open for 24 hours. Many begged for help but steeling themselves against their entreaties and tilting their helmets towards the storm, the companies kept going. D Company came up against belts of uncut wire and suffered as the men desperately struggled to find lanes through them. Within five minutes one platoon which had started with 23 men was reduced to nine. Despite the intensity of the defence, the 10th fought its way into the village and began to clear the buildings. Dumps of trench-mortar and smoke bombs ignited by the barrage exploded as they passed through adding to the general mayhem and confusion. Lieutenant Shaw was everywhere, encouraging and organising his men. His coolness, bravery and sheer hard work saw his company through the worst. The second wave came up through the centre and fanned out to support the companies on the flanks. Minutes later C Company under Captain Butterworth came through to link up with A and D; B then passed through to continue the advance on the left. Threatening to halt the charge, German machine guns and a field gun opened up at almost point-blank range. Chic Taylor led a Lewis-gun section against the enemy nests, driving the enemy from a trench and then from a sunken lane. The worst was over but as isolated parties of Germans attempted to regain their own lines, sporadic fighting continued throughout the night:

The dawn broke on hungry, tired, battle stained men with a look of something indefinable in their eyes ... (there were) too many huddled khaki figures dotted about the field who had read letters from wives and mothers round the previous night's camp fires ... and the saddest of all was to take the rifle and bayonet from the clenched stiff hands of the man whose face was towards the enemy. (Bradbury)

Impatient for news of how the operation had gone, Hardman went up to the front to seek information. If he had been allowed to take part, he rather than Taylor would have been in command of the attack. He regretted the chance had passed him by but took succour from the knowledge that Shaw and the men of his own company had 'done splendidly'. Shaw and Taylor were later awarded the Military Cross. Lieutenant-Colonel Peel recommended Taylor for a bar to his DSO and, although the recommendation was rejected by Division, scribbled a note to Taylor congratulating and thanking him for his performance:

The staff are very bucked and the success of the operation was entirely due to you ... I think you know that I have implicit confidence in you and always feel that everything is all right if you are there.

In view of the ferocity of the engagement the battalion had escaped lightly. Two days after the battle the companies went back to collect and bury their dead. The nine fatalities included James Aspin, one of the draft which had arrived from the disbanded 2/10th and Sergeant Thomas Clutton MM, an original member and Gallipoli veteran. Another long serving member, Sergeant Charles Langley DCM of Anchor Street died of wounds at a CCS in Bagneux. All of the dead, six of whom came from Oldham, have a known grave; so too do the four men who later died of wounds. In addition, about 80 Other Ranks were wounded.

Lieutenant Gregston and Second Lieutenant Wignal were also wounded and evacuated. Fred Hardman's friend and subaltern, Jimmy Whitehead, received a 'pleasant little wound' in the arm and also disappeared off to the rear areas.

Besides the Military Crosses to Taylor and Shaw, almost a dozen men were awarded the DCM or MM. CSM Toogood, an original member who had been acting RSM for some weeks, received the DCM and Private Macnamara, one of Sugden's party in Havrincourt Wood which had captured the division's first prisoner, received a bar to his Military Medal. Another MM was awarded to the erstwhile reporter of the *Oldham Standard* and Gallipoli veteran, Maurice Bradbury. In a later article Bradbury reflected upon the Riencourt engagement:

> *Men who pass through such ordeals should be very strong afterwards for they have seen souls and hearts laid nakedly bare, have glimpsed hell, and have had one foot over the border of beyond.*

For its success on 31 August and subsequent night attacks, the battalion acquired the nickname of the 'Night-jars'. Pleased with the sobriquet and praise from Solly-Flood, the battalion was relieved and marched back the two miles to rest near Thilloy. The division attacked again during the following days, pressing on towards the next heavily defended villages of Villers-au-Flos and Metz-en-Couture. Sixteen days of fighting had taken the division across the worst of the Somme wilderness and a few miles closer to the Hindenburg Line.

Divisional HQ moved to occupy a large former German ammunition store in Riencourt and, once the infantry had been relieved, the brigades were scattered in other nearby villages. Although the villages themselves were in ruins there was plenty of material with which the troops could improvise shelters. The 10th for its part spent most of the next two weeks in and around Haplincourt Wood a little to the east of Riencourt. The battalion practised assaulting machine-gun posts and attacks in conjunction with trench-mortar and machine-gun units. Lessons had been learnt from the recent operation and emphasis was placed on rehearsing the almost forgotten tactic of sectional attacks using fire and movement. So successful were they in these manoeuvres that other brigades were sent to observe how the Oldhamers had perfected the art. There was also plenty of time devoted to sport and other competitions. Three new second lieutenants arrived, one of whom was an Oldhamer called Travis.

Hardman had recently written to his father about the quality of officers then being posted to battalions. He told his father that 'the stamp of an officer today is very poor, at least as far as being a gentleman is concerned'. By 1918 this was a regular complaint of serving officers across the BEF. Junior officers were being turned out from training units by the hundred and many of them would not, for social reasons, have been commissioned in earlier years. Many of these largely young officers had previously served in the ranks so when commissioned and posted abroad they brought with them valuable trench experience. They may not have come from the more usual social classes and probably had attended their local elementary school, but they knew more about warfare and what motivated the men under their command than many of the young officers who came from the greater or lesser public schools.

Second Lieutenant Travis was described by Hardman as a 'rather peculiar person'. Travis said he came from 'behind Park Road' but claimed he did not know any of Hardman's family. This caused Hardman to conclude that the subaltern probably came from Waterloo Street. It is fairly close to Park Road but did not have the rather grand detached and semi-detached villas of Oldham's upper middle class. Of greater cheer to Hardman was the reappearance from hospital and convalescence of Selwyn Rowbotham and Jimmy Whitehead and yet another letter from Kitty. He replied in vibrant tone:

A day of trial has been crowned by the arrival of the mail and that mail contained a letter from the dearest in the world to me. How nice it is to get a letter amidst the carnage and cares of war, to feel that the world is not all cruel and that there is love and kindness in the world afterall.

Comparison and contrast between the bestiality of war and the incongruous beauty of its setting is a constant theme in Hardman's letters home. In an undated missive to Kitty he enclosed several roses gathered from among the detritus of a ruined cottage:

*There is something beautiful even in the battlefields of France
... these roses I have plucked for you were struggling to live
among the nettles and thorns of this devastated village. As they
have lived, so you must live and lift up your heart when the
world is lonely and sad, for after all, there is something beautiful
in this troubled universe of ours.*

Besides the arrival of the post another cause of celebration was
a dinner given by Lieutenant-Colonel Peel to commemorate the
completion of his first year in command of the battalion. In a
damp, cramped dugout in the midst of Haplincourt Wood, Peel's
servant prepared a meal for the senior officers. Details of the
menu have not survived but it was eaten, enjoyed and, as a
reminder of trials past and those yet to come, a toast to absent
friends was made within the sound of distant gunfire.

On the night of 21/22 September the battalion relieved the
8/Lincoln at Butler's Cross in Havrincourt Wood. It was 15
months since the 10th had occupied the same sector of line and
it appeared to have changed little. The trees were rather less dense
and the trenches not so robust but the old hands recognised the
landmarks and remembered with affection the quiet times of June
1917. In front of them then, as now, was the Hindenburg Line.
Its Havrincourt defences had been breached by Territorial troops
in November 1917 during the Battle of Cambrai and it was clear
to the 42nd Division that Territorials would be expected to do
it again.

Once the battalion had settled into its new positions Hardman
continued with a letter to Kitty he had begun earlier in the day.
He had expressed the opinion that: 'The Boche by now is just
a bit 'dizzy'. He certainly is not fighting with the same spirit but
he can still effect considerable carnage with his artillery and
machine guns'. Within a matter of minutes those words were to
be proved very true. As Hardman wrote, enemy gunners began
to deluge the wood with mustard gas. Somewhere between 2,000
and 3,000 canisters drenched the area with choking and burning
fumes. Although most men seemed to have masked in time, a
number of headquarters' personnel were overcome. Fred
Hardman was evacuated that night and Lieutenant-Colonel Peel
the following day. Hardman's letter to Kitty was later completed

for him by a fellow patient at the Number 8 British Red Cross Hospital. Peel returned to the battalion in October but one man who was not so lucky was Walter Scott of Ardwick. Scott was evacuated from the wood and sent down the line to the coast. He hung on for nearly a week in a British hospital near Calais before eventually succumbing to gas poisoning.

The 10th moved into the front line near Trescault during the night of 23-24 September. Its task was to patrol No Man's Land and, where possible, to improve the impending jumping-off line by extending saps and posts. On the night of the attack the battalion, less four platoons under the command of Rowbotham, was to withdraw as battalions of 125 and 127 Brigades lined up on the tapes. Three men became fatalities during these minor operations. One of these was Second Lieutenant Tom Wilson of B Company. Although his chronology is a little at fault, Henry Lawson remembered the circumstances leading up to Wilson's death. Several officers were talking quietly in a large dugout when Wilson began to reminisce about his past life:

From his first few sentences I knew he was telling me that he would not live the night ... something about him, his manner, his voice, his words, his spirit, utterly different from his ordinary character, all conveyed an intangible finality with life here on earth. He was of course killed.

As part of a major assault against what the Germans considered to be the impregnable defences of the Hindenburg Line, the 42nd Division was to attempt to break through to a depth of two miles. In front of a double row of trenches and concrete bunkers protected by acres of barbed wire, was the German outpost line. During the morning of 27 September the attacking brigades would be assisted by eight tanks and a heavy barrage of field guns and howitzers. Followed by other battalions of 125 and 127 Brigades, the 5/Manchester and 8/Lancashire Fusiliers were to open the attack; their companies would leap-frog each other towards the final objective of Welsh Ridge. The division did not like the scheduled timetable as it meant that if the 5th Division on its right failed to take the high ground around the village of Beaucamp, the Lancashire Fusiliers could be caught in enfilade as they advanced towards Highland Ridge. Unfortunately, the division's fears were fully justified. The 5th Division failed to eject the enemy from Beaucamp and only two of the brigades' tanks remained operational long enough to offer substantial assistance to the infantry; the Fusiliers and Manchesters were consequently badly cut up in Beaucamp Valley. Although progress was made the objectives were not gained and it was decided that 126 Brigade should attempt to continue the advance in the early hours of 28 September.

The 10/Manchester moved up to the jumping-off tapes after darkness fell upon the battlefield. A waning moon shed a ghostly light upon the trenches and occasionally a nervous machine-gunner fired a traversing burst from an unseen pit. German guns fired a few desultory shells towards the British rear areas but for some hours there was an almost unbroken silence. It seemed as if both sides were girding and conserving themselves for the tumult which must certainly come. While NCOs and officers passed among them, men dozed, smoked, chatted in hushed tones and checked their equipment. They rose from their scrapes to wait for the barrage in No Man's Land, passing words of encouragement, offering prayers and muttering jests from anxious lips. At 2.30am the guns opened with a roar which dulled senses and shook the ground. The troops rose to their feet, lit cigarettes, tilted their helmets and moved forward. Shrapnel bursts showered the ground thirty yards in front of the first wave; seventy yards further on explosions rocked the German trenches and blasted the wire; the heavens and horizon were riven by flame and explosions. The scream and whine of shells, the chattering of machine guns and soaring flares fired by desperate defenders added to the maelstrom and cacophony of violence. The waves advanced, crested Highland Ridge, chased the Germans through Couillet Wood, crossed a single track railway and reached the lower slopes and abandoned trenches of Welsh Ridge. The 10th halted as the 8/Manchester passed through to ascend the slope and take the crest. Parties of bewildered, anxious Germans were rounded up and pointed to the rear as the Manchesters and Fusiliers dug in and consolidated. German counter-attacks were expected but the enemy contented himself with shelling his lost positions. At 3.00am on 29 September the New Zealanders passed through the Manchesters and swept on towards La Vacquerie. For a loss of under 200 dead and 900 wounded the 42nd Division had broken the vaunted Hindenburg Line and was now approaching villages and fields largely untouched by war.

The weary yet immensely proud troops of the 10th moved back to their old haunt of Havrincourt Wood to regroup and rest. Congratulations poured in from Corps and Army, but what the men needed most was hot food and sleep. In view of the difficulty of the operation the casualty list was surprisingly light. The battalion had captured 248 Germans for the loss of five dead and about 30 wounded. Lieutenant William Norris from Bristol would die of his wounds two weeks later and it is possible that at least one other man also succumbed. Of those killed during the operation, three have no known grave and their names were later inscribed on the Vis-en-Artois Memorial. The only Oldham fatality was Harold Platts of B Company. His body was later recovered and buried in a secluded cemetery bound within the gentle folds of Villers-Plouich.

The battalion spent nine fairly relaxed days among the turning leaves of Havrincourt Wood. Dirt was scraped from uniforms, baths taken and a fresh issue of underclothing made. As there is no record of any draft arriving, it is difficult to estimate the size of the battalion as it licked its wounds and rested. Most infantry units were by that stage of the war well under establishment and divisional returns suggest that the 42nd was no different from other divisions. It is probable that the 10th had an effective strength of around 600 men.

The other divisions of IV Corps had continued the advance in the general direction of Maubeuge. On 9 October, the 42nd was ordered to begin its march to relieve the New Zealanders near Briastre, about ten miles south-east of Cambrai. The Germans had massed troops and artillery on the River Selle and the New Zealanders' attempts to cross the river had been met with deter-mined resistance. To the Germans, the River Selle line was of crucial importance; if it were crossed, the Allies would directly threaten the enemy grip on the important communications centre of Valenciennes and on the industrial towns of Maubeuge and Mons. As it moved towards the river the 42nd Division marched through areas where villages, although looted, were intact and where fields were largely undamaged by shellfire. During the cold and squally night of 12-13 October, the 42nd Division relieved the New Zealanders along the banks of the swollen Selle. Opposite the Lancashire Territorials was a renowned and fresh division. The claim of the German *25th Division,* which had been moved into the line to bolster the existing defences, was that it had never been defeated. It certainly held its carefully selected positions in strength and was apparently under orders not to yield them under any circumstances. Patrols of the Lancashire Fusiliers did succeed in crossing to the eastern bank and established tenuous footholds under direct observation of the enemy. Shortly after, they and their comrades on the western bank were treated to liberal doses of gas, shells and machine-gun fire. Division had decided that 126 Brigade, with the 5/East Lancashire on the right and the 10/Manchester on the left, should cross the river and attack the defended railway cutting south of Solesmes. The attack would go in with the 5th Division on the right and the West Yorkshire Territorials of the 62nd Division on the left. To intimidate and demoralise the defenders, a massive creeping barrage moving at a rate of 100 yards every five minutes and interspersed with coloured incendiary shells to guide the infantry, was to smother the enemy positions. All troops knew that this was going to be a hard fought battle.

As the gathering gloom of an October night descended, Lieutenant-Colonel Peel addressed the battalion at Herpigny Farm near Quievy. He told them of their objectives and of the difficulties they were bound to encounter. When the parade dismissed, the men shouldered their packs, adjusted their webbing and in drenching rain and enveloping mist, moved off towards the front. German shells crashed down among the files as they reached the forward zone, causing 27 casualties among the leading two companies. Lieutenant Charles Cooper of A Company who had been attached to the battalion from the 2/Manchester was among the several who were killed before the attack began. When they reached the jumping-off tapes many of the weary troops lay down in a sodden beet field and fell asleep for an hour. The only consolation, as Rowbotham later recalled, was that the Germans were 'probably as miserable as us'.

At 2.00am the barrage opened. To some observers it was even more magnificent than that which had preceded the assault on the Hindenburg Line. The thermite explosions illuminated the parameters and the troops followed. The two leading companies were to get into the cutting, B Company would mop it up and establish a relay centre, D would pass through to the final objective.The battle which developed was the most intense yet experienced by the 10th on the Western Front. It degenerated into a series of bitter hand-to-hand struggles where, in the darkness, men lost touch, lost the barrage and where officers and NCOs led by example. When the momentum broke down, someone stood up, rallied his comrades and charged with the bayonet; when uncut wire proved an obstacle, a soldier would cut a path and lead his section or platoon through; if a machine gun held up the advance, someone would grab a satchel of grenades and hurl its contents towards the nest.

Guided by the barrage, A and C Companies hit their objectives to the inch. According to one officer, 'considering the night and the chaos of our friends (4/East Lancashire) on the right who appeared to think anywhere along the British front was good enough', this was a remarkable achievement. The bank of the cutting had earlier been reported as being about six feet high; it was therefore a shock for the troops to discover it was closer to a steep 50 feet of mud, scrub and German machine-gun nests. Firing Lewis guns and rifles from the hip, the companies rolled and slithered down the slopes and put the bayonet to use. Chic Taylor and two men tried to knock out a machine-gun post with their Lewis; when it became clogged with mud, Taylor brought up a captured German weapon. When it too jammed, Taylor searched for some rifle grenades and despatched the machine-gunners at a range of 50 yards. He then led a charge into a sunken road beyond the railway. On his left Sergeant Lees cleared a machine gun from the depths of a crater with a Lewis and then proceeded to mop up an area known as the 'railway triangle'. His platoon cleared over 1,000 yards of the cutting and gained touch with the 2/4th York & Lancs of the 62nd Division in Solesmes. Although wounded, Private Chapman advanced over 1,500 yards at the head of his section, bayonetting several Germans on the way. Corporal Fisher, in charge of a Stokes mortar, used his weapon against a German *minnewerfer* emplacement and then led a charge against the stunned crew. At the head of his section

Sergeant O'Connell captured five machine guns and their crews while Corporal Martin and two men confronted 50 Germans, charged them and put them to flight. Selwyn Rowbotham captured two machine guns and personally accounted for 24 of the enemy. His batman, Ernest Hutchins, 'put quite ten of them out with a beautifully placed bomb' just before he was himself cut down. Rowbotham established the relay centre and attempted to despatch messages to Battalion HQ. His notepad was soaked and the pencil merely added to its destruction. Concerned at the lack of decipherable intelligence, Peel went forward to see what was happening. He arrived to discover that the cutting was secure and the final objective about to be taken.

The 'railway cutting stunt', as Bradbury later called it, was a supreme test of discipline and leadership. When officers and NCOs were hit, privates led sections and kept the men going. In battalions where morale was good and men confident in their ability and training, this could be done. In units where this was not the case, night operations often bogged down in confusion. The fighting in the ravine lasted for five exhausting and bloody hours. With the final objective (the ravine which ran parallel to the railway), having been cleared by Lieutenant Beveridge and CSM Toogood of D Company and with the enemy on the run, 127 Brigade passed through. The 10th consolidated its ground, saw to the wounded and sent its prisoners to the rear. At 5.00pm on 22 October New Zealand troops completed the relief and the Oldham battalion marched back along congested roads to its temporary home of Herpigny Farm.

Even allowing for some jubilant exaggeration, the slaughter had been prodigious. Rowbotham remembered:

The number of Boche that kept turning up was wonderful. Firing his Lewis from the hip Whitehead seemed to think he was mowing corn. We got fed up with killing them (particularly when it came to burying them). If they had made a determined stand we might have had a bit of a job on as we (B Company) numbered 85 all told and I should think we laid out 150 before daylight finally settled the matter.

In contrast, the 10th had lost a total of 19 dead and another two who would die of wounds. In addition five officers and 91

Other Ranks were wounded. The battalion's dead and those of the other units involved were buried the following day in a field alongside a ruined cottage named Belle Vue. They included Lieutenant Cooper, Second Lieutenant Frank Cook MC, Rowbotham's servant, Ernest Hutchins (an original member who was awarded a posthumous MM), two men from Chadderton, Fred Etchells and Sergeant Joe Milner (another of the 1914 enlistments and holder of the MM) and Corporal Robert Whitmore from the Spinners' Arms on Lees Road. The remainder of the dead came mainly from Manchester, Ashton and Salford; several of them had served with other regiments, such as the Loyal North Lancashire and the Duke of Lancaster's Own Yeomanry. One man who had trodden a slightly unusual path on his way to joining the battalion was Lewis Sheppard. Sheppard lived in rural Wiltshire and had travelled to Gillingham in Kent to enlist in the Army Ordnance Corps. As the demand for ever more infantry developed there were periodic clear-outs of non-infantry depots and training units and any surplus men were posted to France. Sheppard was probably picked up in one of these sweeps and had arrived at the 10th in April as it rested in Pas Wood.

Among the wounded was Second Lieutenant Henry Lawson MC. He had gone over with his platoon but had been hit as he attempted to get over the German wire. He collapsed on the wire and was hit again. Falling into unconsciousness he lay exposed with the battle raging around him. He came to as he was being carried by German prisoners to the dressing station where his wounds were bound up. A chaplain took one look at him and began intoning the last rites. After several large doses of morphine, at least one operation and months of convalescence, Lawson recovered. His mackintosh and map case, both ripped to shreds by bullets and grenades, were eventually returned to him.

After one night at Herpigny Farm the battalion moved back another three miles to the village of Beauvois. A cheerless few days in poor weather and indifferent accommodation were spent there in reorganisation and general cleaning up. Company training usually occupied the mornings and specialist classes the afternoons. On 31 October the battalion, looking as spick and span as the conditions allowed, turned out for a medal parade. Among the awards distributed was a bar to Chic Taylor's MC and MCs to Alfred Butterworth and Lieutenant Walter Shaw. Three nights later 126 Brigade marched out of Beauvois and formed up on the Solesmes road.

That same night a superb attack by the New Zealand Division captured the walled town of Le Quesnoy. On 5 November 126 Brigade trudged through the town, marvelling at the strength of the ramparts scaled by the New Zealanders during their assault. The Kiwis had forged on and for the moment 126 Brigade followed in their wake some three miles behind. In front of them the Oldhamers could see the looming mass of the Forest of Mormal. The sound of firing and a steady procession of walking wounded and ambulances heading back towards Le Quesnoy indicated that the New Zealanders were encountering stiff opposition. In August 1914 the forest, which covers about 34 square miles, had caused some difficulties to the BEF; now, just over four years later, it was to do so again.

The roads leading towards the forest were in poor condition and those inside had been all but obliterated. Their ill defined routes were cratered by mine explosions and trees felled across their path. As it was impossible for wheeled traffic to negotiate the obstacles, the 10th struggled through the mire, manhandling their awkward Lewis guns and clumsy accoutrements. The surviving trees were blasted into grotesque parodies and as testimony to the ferocity of the fighting, German crews lay sprawled beside their now silent machine guns. To help clear routes, platoons were issued with billhooks and hatchets but the bulk of the repair work was done by the divisional RE and Pioneers. They scurried about laying plank roads around the larger craters and filling the smaller ones with whatever materials could be found. Prostrate trunks were sawn into manageable sizes and hauled off the main routes. Shells whined and crashed into the forest, splintering yet more boughs and creating yet more obstacles. It took the 10th nearly three hours of floundering through the mud to clear the forest. It was tiring, depressing and drab work.

By 3.30am on 6 November, 126 Brigade had passed through and relieved the New Zealanders. The relief, already hampered by the clogged roads, was made more difficult by an impenetrable darkness and torrential rain. Platoons had lost touch while traversing the forest, and locating and assembling them once clear of it delayed the continuation of the advance. While the brigade's other two battalions kept going, the Oldhamers sought what little protection the hedges, trees and roadside ditches, 1,000 yards east of the forest could offer from the elements and enemy gunners. Second Lieutenant Gordon Thorley and 16 men of B Company were hit when one salvo landed among their meagre shelters and earthen scrapes. To add to the misery, a chill wind developed to lash their faces and huddled bodies with needles of penetrating rain.

The 10th was ordered to leapfrog the 4/East Lancashire and seize the high ground overlooking the River Sambre. Difficulties when forming up caused Zero to be delayed for nearly two hours but once the whistles blew, German resistance proved feeble. The village of Mesnil was taken easily but when the enemy gunners realised their infantry had crossed to the river's eastern bank and that the British could now overlook Hautmont and their battery positions, they began a ferocious bombardment. The 10th was ordered to press on and cross the river. Corporal Lane of C Company led a patrol into the western part of Hautmont and sent back a runner requesting support. It arrived some time later in the shape of Chic Taylor and A Company. Assessing the situation Taylor ordered his men to improvise a bridge across the river which was, in total, about 50 yards wide. To their amazement scores of inhabitants poured out of their houses, bringing with them mattresses and other materials to ford the river. Within 30 minutes the company was across and engaging the enemy on the eastern bank. Grim hand-to-hand fighting developed among the streets and housing but gradually the Germans fell back to an old fort lying to the east of the town. Shells smashed into the town square and nearby houses, killing several of the inhabitants in the hour of their deliverance. German resistance remained strong but with 125 Brigade approaching their stronghold from the south, the fort's garrison withdrew along the undamaged Maubeuge road and left the town in the hands of the British and its jubilant denizens.

Other battalions crossed by way of 'Taylor's Bridge', followed closely by cavalry and cyclists who pursued the Germans into Maubeuge. For the 10th the battle, and indeed the war, was over. This final battle had cost the battalion a total of 15 dead or mortally wounded. Not a huge total in view of the novelty of urban street fighting but perhaps the more tragic because the armistice was only four days away. Gordon Thorley of Newton Heath and Harry Knott of Chadderton died of their wounds in casualty clearing stations a few miles to the rear. Lance Corporal James Harrop of Greenacres and most of the other slain were later buried in Maubeuge or in Hautmont's communal cemetery. Two of those who were laid to rest within the confines of the historic walled town of Maubeuge were Lieutenant Walter Shaw MC and Sergeant Thomas Walker. Shaw, a married man from Surrey, had been attached to the battalion from the Royal Fusiliers for six months. He was exceptionally well liked by his own men and, unlike many officers, was well known throughout the entire battalion. His death was genuinely regretted by all. Shaw's stature and importance to the battalion was summed up in Wynne's short obituary: 'To know him was a privilege, to associate with him an education'. Thomas Walker was not the last man of the 10th to die before the armistice but his death was felt more keenly by its original members than even the well-respected and honoured Lieutenant Shaw. Walker had won no gallantry medals and was only an 'acting' sergeant; he did not have the benefit of Shaw's education or of his middle-class background and upbringing. He was born at Waterhead and lived with his parents in a terrace house in Stoneleigh Street. In 1914, probably before the outbreak of war, he enlisted at Rifle Street and became a Territorial. He went with the battalion to Egypt, spent gruelling weeks in the desert and landed as a private on Gallipoli. He fought at Krithia and was wounded later in the campaign. At some stage he rejoined the battalion and eventually put up three stripes. He was never mentioned in the war diary or in any of the several reminiscences written after the war. He was, in fact, the epitome of hundreds of thousands of men who volunteered to serve and, if necessary, to die for their country. It was men such as Walker who made the Oldham Battalion and the scores of other battalions, artillery batteries, RE Field Companies and the rest, what they were.

THE ARMISTICE AND POST-WAR YEARS

THE ENTRY IN THE BATTALION'S WAR DIARY for 11 November 1918 is succinct: 'Orders received 0900 that hostilities cease at 1100'. That was all the official record had to say about the order which finally silenced the guns. Little is known of how the men of the battalion spent the momentous day. They might have been given a few hours off but it is likely that most of the time was spent in cleaning up and possibly helping the inhabitants of Hautmont put some of their streets in order. The town was in a mess, but not to the same degree as the scores of others through which the 10th had advanced during the previous few weeks. In the following days roads were cleared of rubble and accommodation found for the troops in cottages and public buildings.

Two days after the armistice the battalion and town were sufficiently back in shape to permit a solemn parade to honour the Allied prisoners of war who had died in Hautmont during its German occupation. There was a lighter feel to the day on 16 November when the town put out the flags and organised a fête to honour its liberators. Looking as spruce as circumstances permitted, the battalion, together with representatives from other units of the 42nd Division, paraded in the town square to receive accolades from the local dignitaries. Lieutenant-Colonel Peel presented the town with a German howitzer and field gun captured on 6 November; in return the Mayor presented a huge bouquet of flowers and delivered an emotive speech. For the benefit of the listening troops, a translation of the address was later delivered to Battalion HQ and distributed to the companies. The speech reflected the tribulation and terror through which the townsfolk had passed during the four years of German occupation:

It is with great joy that the population of Hautmont congratulates and thanks you, your valiant officers and splendid men who have delivered us from the hordes of bandits and robbers which for the last four years have imposed upon us a reign of terror, stripping our factories, pillaging our homes, taking our youths, and even the girls from their mothers, and forcing them to perform work against their native land. Those who failed to report were promptly thrown into prison, outraged, and then sent to a

disciplinary detachment. For about two years there have been
Russian, Italian, Rumanian, English and French prisoners here.
The Bosches have treated them like beasts of the field, have
employed them to destroy our establishments and let them die
of hunger.

Notwithstanding the very meagre rations they themselves
received, the population was most anxious to … relieve their
sufferings. But alas, many of these unfortunate men sleep their
last in the town's cemetery.

The crimes cry out for vengeance and we hope that in the
settling of accounts which is approaching, the authors of this
terrible war will be charged with their barbarous actions before
the tribunal of the Allies.

We have kept firm hold on our French nationality, we have
never given up our faith in our soldiers and our sympathetic
allies and we have always known of a surety that the Entente
Armies were fighting for Justice and Right, Humanity and
Liberty, against Despotism and Slavery.

Vive les Allies, Vive la France notre Patrie.

The locals celebrated long into the night but troops of the
10th returned to their billets, under orders that training would
recommence on the morrow.

The six weeks spent at Hautmont were pleasant and reasonably
comfortable. Talk of demobilisation was on everyone's lips but
the unexpectedly swift end to the war had taken the authorities
rather by surprise. Schemes were soon in place however, and by
mid-December the first men were on their way home. The
remainder were occupied by route marches, football and even a
visit from the King. On 14 December, amid scenes of great
emotion on the part of its inhabitants, the 10th marched out of
Hautmont and moved by easy stages to Gilly near Charleroi.
Despite the lying snow, the citizenry of this small Belgian town
accorded the battalion a warm reception. Here, according to
Bradbury, 'the rough edge of war was worn away'. Christmas
was enjoyed by the dwindling number of men, while concerts,
education classes and, of course, yet more football passed the time

for those who were still waiting for their number to come up. Word of men who had died of wounds received during the closing stages of the war no doubt reached the battalion from the hospitals on the coast. The harshness of winter was also to take its toll among those who had survived the fortunes of war. Richard Walmsley from Hindley and Frank Dodgson from Leeds died of disease in casualty clearing stations at, respectively, Solesmes and Charleroi. Several members also eventually succumbed to wounds in the UK. Harry Heywood from Werneth died on the day the armistice came into force and Peter Yates, a married man from Beever Street who, like Heywood, had enlisted in the 3rd Battalion in 1916, died some weeks later. The effects of war would continue to take their toll of men of the 10th well into the next decade.

It was not only wounded, sick and demobilised soldiers who returned to Oldham in the weeks following the armistice. Harold Clarke of Oldham Road, Failsworth, had been one of the early enlistments to the Oldham Comrades' Battalion in November 1914. Admitted to hospital and then sent home in the early months of 1917, Clarke was posted to the 1/10th in 1918. Captured during the battalion's frantic rearguard actions around Ervillers in March, he spent the next eight months undergoing privation and ill-treatment. He arrived home on 26 November 1918 looking like 'a bag of bones' and with an abiding hatred for his German captors. His anger and vehemence is apparent in this diary entry written shortly after his return:

If they (his parents) had only seen me two months before there isn't a soul about that could have recognised me. Talk about human hairpins, I knew I was thin then but called myself fat when I got home. May the Germans be slowly brought to death by hunger and thirst as I have seen our lads too weak and helpless to do anything only wait for death as a relief and be bashed about with whips and sticks and bash the butt of the rifle in your back till you thought it was going through your stomach … if I only met that big fat bellied goggle-eyed square headed son of a lunatic, I'd cut him up in little pieces just for kicking me and bashing my ribs in and that snotty little pig of a (sergeant) that made me nearly six inches shorter with hitting

*me on the head with a big stick well I'd just tie him up and I
wouldn't half lay in to him I'd make him a foot taller before I
done and then I'd knock them off and as many German swine
as they brought to me I would do the same and think I was doing
a good thing in getting this world rid of them. Got strafe the
Alleman, may they die awful deaths as our prisoners have done.*

By the time of Frank Dodgson's death in March 1919 the
battalion in Gilly numbered just over 300. Peel had gone at the
end of January, followed shortly by several other long serving
officers. By the third week in March all of those men eligible for
demobilisation had left. The 24 officers and 260 Other Ranks
who remained, mostly men who had enlisted in 1917 and 1918,
were earmarked for the Army of Occupation and soon departed
for the Rhineland towns. Of more immediate concern to the
cadre of the 10/Manchester in Gilly, was when it would return
to the UK. The colours had already been brought from Oldham
in preparation for the return and on 4 April 1919 the remaining
six officers and 46 men embarked on the SS MAGILOFF at Antwerp
and sailed to Southampton. From the south coast the party
travelled by train to Oswestry where the necessary formalities
were performed. On Thursday 10 April, four years and eight
months after the battalion had marched away from Rifle Street
en route for Bury, Egypt, Gallipoli, France and Belgium, the cadre
of Oldham's Territorials marched back with colours flying and
band playing to its home town.

The cadre's forthcoming arrival had been announced in the
local press some days earlier. There was time to organise an official
welcoming party of local worthies and those men and officers
who had already been demobilised or who were home on leave.
Colonel Rye, Major Bamford, Major Wilde and many other
Egypt and Gallipoli veterans waited to greet their returning
comrades. Despite typically Oldham weather, a huge crowd
thronged to the area around the Town Hall, spilling down
Greaves Street and Clegg Street. The train carrying the cadre was
supposed to pull into Mumps but in the event stopped at Clegg
Street. Having heard nothing about any change in plan, hundreds
of townsfolk waited at Mumps; fortunately the official welcoming
party, which included the regimental band, did know of the

alteration and lined Clegg Street's platform. On spotting the train Bugler Denville blew 'Fall in', fog signals exploded along the track and the band struck up the regimental march. Detraining, the cadre of six officers and 38 men, under the command of Lieutenant-Colonel Kelly, a former Mancunian journalist, and his second in command the one-time architect Chic Taylor, marched up Clegg Street towards the Town Hall. Behind the colours and the escort marched a substantial number of the 10th's demobilised and discharged soldiers. Among the small, smart colour party were eleven men who had left with the battalion in those far off days of September 1914. Hundreds lined the route to Rifle Street and whilst there was little cheering, (one reporter explaining that 'Lancashire people are not over demonstrative' and that the 'warmth in people's faces was a sufficient welcome'), the observers did raise a cheer when the party disappeared into the drill hall.

The return was merely a precursor to the town's official welcoming celebration held on Saturday 12 April. The town centre was dressed in flags, the Town Hall decked with flowers and hordes of Oldhamers filled the area in front of the Town Hall and the streets leading up to Rifle Street. In the drill hall demobilised and discharged soldiers were arranged in five companies: No.1 comprised original 1914 members under the command of Fred Hardman, No.2 original men of the 2/10th under Captain Gillespie, No.3 members of the 3/10th under Captain Sutcliffe, with Nos.4 and 5 being discharged men under Captains Pochin and Leach. Crippled and badly wounded servicemen were conveyed to the Town Hall by lorry. To the accompaniment of the regimental band and the occasional ring of church bells, the colours and companies marched off through the thronging, albeit strangely muted crowds. Only rarely did the multitude cheer, preferring instead to give thanks for deliverance in a dignified and restrained manner. There were too many widows and orphans in the crowd to allow great scenes of jubilation.

On arrival at the Town Hall the townsfolk listened to speeches from the Mayor, his deputy and Colonel Rye. The 10th's deeds were recalled, praised and honoured, but among the crowds, bereaved relatives and those whose wounds precluded the likelihood of work, no doubt wondered what the future held.

Lieutenant-Colonel Bamford echoed their thoughts in his few words to the masses. He was determined to impress upon his listeners how prosperous the town had been while its battalions were fighting in foreign fields. Those who had marched away had enjoyed nothing of that wealth. Now, Bamford insisted, the citizenry should 'look after those men ... as they deserve and never forget what they owed them'. Wynne, who was listening to Bamford's speech, reiterated these sentiments when he concluded his series of articles on the 10th in June. He expressed the hope: 'Those who reaped the fruits of victory will see to it that the dead are honoured for all time, their dependants will never want and no returned fighting man will be dependent upon doles. Is the public memory long or short?'.

With the speeches over, the main concern that night was not to count the cost or worry about the time to come but simply to give thanks and enjoy the moment. Fred Hardman, Frank Howarth, Procktor Stott and Selwyn Rowbotham were among the hundreds who turned up that night to celebrate and renew friendships and associations with former comrades. Colonel Rye and those other senior officers who had been invalided from the battalion during its time in Egypt and Gallipoli and who had then done so much to raise and train the Second and Third Battalions, looked down with fatherly eyes upon their laughing and dancing protégés. Several of those more ancient warriors had themselves lost sons: young men who, but for the fates of war, could too have been bantering and joking with their more fortunate comrades.

The euphoria of victory lasted several months. Plans were drawn up to create lasting memorials and reminders of deliverance and it was decided that the town should have a tank as a permanent exhibit to recall its municipal achievement in raising over £3m during Tank and Gun Weeks. A temporary platform to house the monster was built near the Glodwick entrance of Alexandra Park. It was intended to flank the tank with two German guns and the War Office agreed that the town could have a 77mm field gun captured by the Oldham Comrades in Italy. Under pressure from Alderman Charles Hardman, the War Office eventually allowed the second gun to be one captured by the 10th in the Hindenburg Line.

On 14 May, Oldham's tank was shunted off a flat car at Glodwick Road Goods Yard and draped under a protective tarpaulin. Three days later and with an escort of mounted policemen, the tank commenced its grinding, tortuous way towards the park. True to form the engines needed some encouragement to heave the machine up the slope to the park where, surrounded by huge crowds, Colonel Rye officially presented it to the town. In due course the engines were removed and a more permanent plinth erected. For nearly 20 years the tank was crawled over and examined by young boys and curious adults until, the elements having taken their toll, the War Office allowed the Council to sell the hull and its accompanying guns for scrap. One gun was kept by the 10th and the proceeds from the other two items donated to charity.

Of more lasting remembrance were the various memorials erected in the years after the war to honour the fallen. In compliance with the suggestion made in 1915 the Council established a War Memorial Committee in May 1919, the same month as a stone cross was put up in St Mary's Churchyard and Alderman Berry launched his Mayor's Appeal. The local press was full of suggestions as to what form the memorial might take, how subscriptions should be raised to pay for it and where it might be put. The Oldham Master Spinners' Association for example proposed that its members donate £1 for each 1,000 spindles they worked. Contemporary opinion was divided as to whether the memorial should be erected in front of the Town Hall, near Tommyfield Market or in Alexandra Park.

Although local parish councils were formulating plans to erect memorials to their own men, there seems to have been widespread acceptance of the need to construct one for the town as a whole. The sum of £20,000 was fixed as the minimum subscription from which it was intended the memorial could be built, educational scholarships for the children of fallen servicemen founded and, should there be any residue, a donation made to the Oldham Royal Infirmary. This was to be done with a recommendation that preferential treatment be afforded to former servicemen and their dependants. By the time the peace treaty was signed at Versailles on 28 June 1919, £9,000 had already been collected. Donations had flooded in from individuals, sports clubs, churches, factories, foundries and mills. Chic Taylor's father was hired as the architect and Albert Toft, who was responsible for several memorials across the country, as the sculptor.

Preparations proceeded at a fairly leisurely pace. The principal cause of delay was indecision about where the memorial should be placed. Initially the committee wanted to erect it near the parish church on land owned by Oldham Brewery in front of the Greaves Arms. When approached by the committee the brewery declared, perhaps with commendable prescience, that the site was unsuitable. It suggested instead that the plot currently occupied by the Platt memorial at the top of Clegg Street would be far more appropriate. The Council demurred, preferring instead a site at the Old Market Place but, for reasons which are not altogether clear, the brewery eventually donated the land in front of the Greaves Arms and building work began.

Until the memorial was completed the town's post-war com-memoration services were generally held in the parish church. The initial Krithia commemoration held in the Empire Theatre in 1916 was replaced by one in St James's Church in June 1918; in 1920 the service was moved to St Mary's. Although it was held on Krithia Day, this occasion was expanded to embrace a service of remembrance for all of Oldham's fallen. The Council's principal representative at this service was Mayor Charles Hardman, Fred's widower father. The 1920s were to witness the unveiling of several memorials and commemorations but, as the decade opened, there was great concern about whether the town would still have a battalion of Territorial infantry to maintain the traditions established so expensively during the war.

In the parsimony of the immediate post-war years the War Office and Government struggled with the question of what to do with the Territorial Force. Various options were reviewed but the need to save money and the belief that should a further emergency arise the Territorials would revert to their pre-war role of home defence, meant that whatever form or shape the TF might adopt, it would invariably be smaller than it had been in 1914. Advances in technology also suggested that new arms or units might have to be created from existing units. The organisations responsible for raising and maintaining the Territorials were the County Associations and it was to the East Lancashire

Territorial Force County Association that an unwelcome letter arrived from the War Office in February 1920.

The War Office suggested that in a reformed East Lancashire Territorial Division, the Ashton and Oldham Territorials would convert from infantry and become respectively, the divisional signals and one of the two divisional RE battalions. This suggestion came as a bombshell to the two units. At the time they technically did not exist as recruitment to the TF had not officially reopened. However, the drill halls remained open, with officers, Permanent Staff and former soldiers coming and going. All were waiting for the anticipated announcement that the TF could again begin attestations. Major L.C.Wilde, the 10th's temporary CO, immediately informed the County Association that local sentiment was strongly against conversion to an engineer battalion. Such a move would, he believed, result in a detrimental effect on recruiting. He suggested that if one battalion had to convert, a more suitable candidate would be the battalion of the Border Regiment which was rumoured to be about to join the division.

In an effort to appease the County Association the War Office asked the committee to enquire of the battalion whether it would be prepared to accept a revised title. Instead of becoming the No.2 Battalion East Lancashire Divisional RE, it was asked to consider whether it might prefer to be known as the 2nd (Manchester) Battalion East Lancashire Divisional RE. Having consulted with his officers, Wilde replied that if the die of conversion was cast, the battalion certainly did not want the word 'Manchester' in its designation. However, he pointed out that notwithstanding the attempts to sign up officers with suitable engineering experience, only one man (who had subsequently withdrawn his application), had shown any interest. In contrast, 28 officers, all with active service experience as RE, had offered their services to the 1st Battalion RE then being raised in Old Trafford. The lesson, Wilde considered, was obvious; recruit the division's 2nd Battalion from Manchester rather than Oldham. The Ashton Territorials were similarly insisting that it would be impossible to raise the signals unit in their town.

As far as can be gauged, feeling in Oldham was behind Wilde and his officers. The Corporation's Finance and General Purposes Committee aired its concern and Lord Emmott, one of the local cotton magnates, announced that he had written to Winston Churchill, the Secretary of State for War, urging him to reconsider. Emmott's letter to Churchill was in turn supported by three visits from Oldham's senior MP, Bartley-Denniss. The main argument expressed by the battalion's supporters was that despite the existence of many engineering firms in the town which, it could be assumed, might provide suitable men, the Territorials had served with enough distinction and sacrifice to warrant their rebirth as infantry. One writer to the regimental magazine believed that the attempt to get 'rank and file for the Engineers was a hopeless task, as the glorious 10th had established such a great name, and the spirit was far too strong for it to be crushed'.

In the face of such determined resistance the War Office backed down and gave permission for the battalion to reopen recruiting as an infantry unit. On 24 September 1920 its strength was one officer and 58 Other Ranks but within days of the announcement many of the 10th's officers reported to Rifle Street: Chic Taylor, Fred Hardman, still badly gas burned about the face, Procktor Stott, Jimmy Whitehead, Selwyn Rowbotham and Arthur Wynne were among the 19 officers who had served overseas with the 10th. To encourage the enlistment of Other Ranks, recruiting adverts appeared about the town and a 'smoker' and later a dance were held at the drill hall. A letter from Oldham Corporation published in the local press informed its employees that any member of the Territorial Army (as the new force was known), would get 15 days' paid leave in order to attend annual camp; crucially, those days were to be in addition to an employee's annual holiday entitlement. Several of the town's engineering firms followed suit but the response from the borough's young men was tardy. By January 1921 only 19 officers and 170 men of the peace-time establishment of a TA infantry battalion of 28 and 680 respectively had attested.

The principal reason behind this less than overwhelming support for the reconstituted battalion lay in the composition of the unit at the end of the war. So many of its members had come from outside Oldham that when it reformed few of them would be able to attend evening drills. Some men who had served in other wartime units might have wanted to maintain a military link and join their local TA, but many who survived the war merely wanted to swap their khaki for mufti and reclaim their civilian life. Whatever the multitude of individual reasons, the result was that it took the 10th, like most TA units, a number of years to reach establishment.

The battalion seized whatever opportunities offered themselves to publicise its existence and continue the close links forged between itself and the town. The unit proposed the purchase of a set of commemorative silver drums and bugles inscribed with the names of its 628 fallen. When the decision became known, subscriptions from townsfolk poured in. In a well reported ceremony at the Town Hall in June 1924, General Solly-Flood presented the instruments to the battalion; led by the drums the parade then marched to the parish church for the Krithia commemoration. The battalion accompanied the mayor's procession around the town during the annual 'churching' ceremony and the battalion's own yearly prize-giving was given full coverage in the press. The mayor was often a guest and could usually be relied upon in his address to commend membership of the battalion to the young men of the town. The divisional general paid a well publicised annual courtesy visit to the mayor, an occasion to which representatives of local employers were also invited.

Great stress was laid upon the relationship between the town, its principal employers and the battalion. In 1934 the divisional general spoke of the 'happiest relations' between the TA and the town's civic heads, a sentiment which echoed those of a visiting brigadier a decade earlier. The brigadier had talked of the 'keen interest the leading citizens continue to take in their local battalion' and of the 'close liaison which exists between the town and the battalion'. The *Daily Telegraph* contrasted this co-operation with that experienced by some southern TA units: 'Lancashire employers and Lancashire men must have a more realistic view than Londoners of the Terriers' value'. Mr Duff-Cooper, the Secretary of State for War in 1935 and a former MP for Oldham, also believed that if all employers appreciated the value of the Territorials in the same way as did Oldham's, the Government's problems in financing the TA would be 'much simplified'. While successive COs frequently referred to the generous support offered by local employers, those in other parts of the country were not, according to the *Manchester Gazette,* so 'broad minded'. In the opinion of

Chic Taylor, however, not all local mill and factory owners were quite as 'broad minded' as they might be. In his report of 1935 Taylor thanked the owners of several large firms for granting their men permission to attend camp but complained that some of them seemed to be unaware that managers and foremen did not always carry out their wishes. At shop floor level 'men dare not ask for leave of absence for fear of losing their jobs'.

Although official propaganda repeatedly underlined how useful it was for employers to have certain of their staff in the TA, in some quarters the message took time to sink in. As late as 1935 General Buchanan, GOC 42nd Division, thought that 'some public acknowledgment in concrete form' of the Territorials was required and that the country was 'only just beginning to realise' how the force protected 'our industries, our trade and our freedom'.

On its departure for annual camp huge crowds turned out to watch the battalion march from Rifle Street to one of the town's stations. On its return, again watched by hordes of onlookers, the column always halted to lay a wreath at the war memorial. So popular was the occasion that in 1932, when owing to financial stringency camp was cancelled, the *Manchester Gazette* was prompted to note how the 'town's people missed seeing their battalion'. Krithia Day similarly drew large crowds. In June 1925, 6,000 people crammed into the area between the Town Hall and the war memorial and in 1932 the band led over 370 veterans and over 300 of the current battalion to Alexandra Park. Enormous crowds watched the procession, some of whom attended the All Ranks' Dance at the drill hall later that evening.

In May 1934 Alexandra Park was also used for the solemn yet splendid occasion of the presentation of new battalion colours. In the space of five tragic minutes during the camp of 1933 the Regimental and King's colours, which had been presented in 1909 by Edward VII, were destroyed. A pressure lamp hanging in the ante-room of the mess exploded and burnt the marquee. Despite what were reported as 'heroic efforts', the colours, which held immeasurable sentimental significance, some silver and the mess furniture went up in the blaze. The gramophone and several records, most notably *Keep the Home Fires Burning,* were salvaged. The battalion immediately decided to replace the colours and subsequently invited the Duke of Gloucester to present them.

Planning for the formal ceremony began in January 1934. It was to be a wonderful opportunity for the battalion to show off its ceremonial skills and the silver drums and for the town to demonstrate its loyalty and affection for its Territorials. Invitations went out to the youth organisations and associations representing medal holders, limbless ex-servicemen, the Oldham Comrades and other ex-servicemen. In case the weather or the crowds should prove too much, nearly 100 St John's Ambulance personnel were to be deployed in the park and along the royal route. The whole affair was to fall under the supervision of Oldham's Chief Constable. So great was the turnout expected to be that he was to employ virtually all of Oldham's force and 50 additional men from Manchester.

The weather on the morning of 5 May was not encouraging. The rain had ceased by the afternoon but a chill wind compelled the ladies to enclose themselves in fur coats and warm wraps. Flags flew from many of the town's buildings, a peel of bells rang from the parish church and 5,000 people watched the battalion march and manoeuvre in the park. To the strains of *Auld Lang Syne* the tattered remains of the old colours were marched to the rear and their replacements laid for consecration on the piled silver drums. Among the onlookers were former Colonels Hardman, Newton and Stott and many other ex-members. The Duke had brief conversations with William Knight, a private of the 10th who had lost both legs in France, and ex-CSM Cox. Cox had gone out as a lance corporal in September 1914 and returned, having suffered only one slight wound, as a CSM in 1918. Besides Chic Taylor, Selwyn Rowbotham and other familiar names, Clr.Sgt J.Dunkerley, CSM Lees DCM, MM and Band Master Frank Miller MSM also played a major part in the proceedings. At the conclusion of the parade the battalion marched back to the drill hall for a well-deserved drink. So pleased was he with the parade that Major-General Buchanan wrote to Taylor congratulating him on the battalion's 'remarkable' handling of arms and in the hope that the CO had the 'comfortable feeling of satisfaction at having produced … a really good show'.

Regimental dances at the Town Hall were a regular feature of Oldham's social life. The Annual Officers' Dance was always a sell-out, the colour scheme and lighting, in the words of the press, regularly winning the 'admiration of all the ladies'. On what were occasions for Oldham's middle class to dress in its finery, the hosts were sensitive to the feelings of the town's less fortunate citizens. When the borough wallowed in the depths of the economic slump, the dance's decor was rather more modest and the festivities low key. A less formal occasion was introduced to the town's social calendar in 1927 when the battalion resolved to host a Christmas party for for some of Oldham's younger inhabitants. One observing officer later mused over the unlikely image of 'stern sergeants, the RSM, Adjutant, the CO and QM, all floating softly around the drill hall, cooing like doves amidst a seething mass of the very young'.

The battalion played a major part in the Prince of Wales' goodwill visit to the town in July 1921. The Prince, who during the war years had become something of the nation's favourite, met many disabled and crippled former members of the 10th and was introduced to the young daughter of 'Spud' Mills VC. Fred Hardman commanded the Prince's guard of honour and Lieutenant Fripp the colour party.

In September 1928 the papers carried lengthy, emotive reports of the first reunion of those men who had left for Bury in 1914. In purple vein the *Standard* observed how 'broken by war and age (Colonel Rye) looked down the tables on the remnant of that once proud battalion and his kindling eyes showed that memory was at work and that he could see beyond those about him the ghostly faces of those who did not return'. Rye presided over the telling of tales and a silent tribute to fallen comrades. As he hobbled towards the door the battalion sang *For he's a jolly good fellow* and cheered him to the rafters. Times were hard in the 1920s but the spirit and comradeship of Krithia and Ervillers were again evident in the banter, songs and talk of the evening.

The press also reported the funerals of former battalion members. Four years after the veterans had watched him walk painfully across the floor of the drill hall, large crowds turned out to pay their respects to Colonel Rye as his draped coffin was carried by gun carriage to Greenacres Cemetery. Smaller but still significant numbers attended the funerals of Rye's predecessor, Lieutenant-Colonel Paterson and the long-serving Captain Fripp. Officers were usually buried with full military honours and even former Other Ranks were sent on their way with a firing party.

Publicity of a less welcome kind came in 1929 when the court martial of Lieutenant Alfred Winterbottom MM was reported at some length. Winterbottom, a regular who had been the 10th's Quartermaster for nearly four years, was accused of false accounting and other misdemeanours. In the findings of his initial report Fred Hardman, as CO, made his displeasure abundantly clear. Winterbottom initially pleaded his innocence but Hardman was having nothing of it. The disgraced QM was hauled before the brigadier, found guilty of 15 offences under the Army Act and promptly cashiered.

In the post-war years, when universal disarmament and peace remained seemingly realistic ambitions, the TA could not afford to become involved in contemporary political machinations. Colonel Newton refused invitations to speak on political platforms during the 1924 election campaign, a decision endorsed by Duff-Cooper the town's senior MP. Despite having one of its own officers, Lieutenant John Dodd, elected in 1936 as one of the town's two MPs, the battalion could not be seen to be partisan. It was therefore with some embarrassment that in 1935 the 10th became embroiled in a significant political controversy.

The roots of the matter lay in the provision of Poor Relief. A few days after the presentation of the new colours, Cllr Whittaker described the ceremony as 'nothing but a recruiting campaign for the TA'. He went on to suggest that the Territorials were merely 'playing at soldiers' and that the town should not be expected to subsidise their annual camp. The difficulty lay in the lack of separation allowances for married men under 26 years of age. If these men were unemployed their families became dependent upon the town's Public Assistance Committee. Twenty-nine applications totalling £20 were made for the 1933 camp. Cllr Whittaker and several other committee members who believed that the practice was putting additional strain on the already overburdened Poor Rate, insisted that the money should come from the battalion's own distress fund or from the War Office. Miss Martland spoke up in favour of the Territorials and was supported by a series of letters in the local press. Martland called Whittaker's comments 'very objectionable' and was echoed by ex-servicemen who described them as 'insulting' and asked whether the graves in Gallipoli, France and Belgium were those of men 'who played at soldiers'.

Things came to a head the following year when the battalion sought permission to use Alexandra Park for the King's Silver Jubilee parade. Although the Council was not opposed to the TA *per se*, it voted against allowing the use of the park in the hope that it might force the Government to remove the anomaly in separation allowances. Furthermore it claimed that if 6 May was not declared a public holiday, any unemployed Territorial taking part in the parade could not be 'genuinely seeking work' and was thus liable to have his benefit suspended for six weeks. Anthony Crossley MP was so perturbed by the statements that he wrote privately to Chic Taylor protesting that he had 'no idea that Oldham's Labour Party was so mean-minded'. Once details of the dispute fell into the public domain the response was immediate.

Many letters to the press were from genuine pacifists while others objected to expenditure on the armed forces at a time when the spectres of unemployment and distress haunted working people. Several suggested that there would be no harm in holding a parade for ex-servicemen but believed that the young Territorials of the day had only enlisted for a free holiday. In contrast there were many correspondents who had 'fought for freedom' and condemned the Council for its attitude. However, the Council remained firm and the parade took place in front of nearly 12,000 spectators at Watersheddings rugby ground. The *Chronicle* decided it was 'debatable' whether all of them, and the several thousand others who lined the route, were exclusively Liberals or Conservatives. One huge streamer on the way to the ground, emblazoned with 'Honour our Territorials', convinced the *Manchester Gazette* that 'whatever our city fathers might decree, we are confident in the belief that the town of Oldham is still behind us'. The Mayor and many councillors did attend the parade and watched with the 400 ex-servicemen as the battalion was presented for the first time with the *Daily Telegraph* cup. Under a scorching sun and as the band played *The boys of the old brigade,* Arthur Wynne led the march past of ex-servicemen. They were followed by the battalion which, to the sound of tumultuous cheering, made its way back to the drill hall. The 10th had had its day of celebration but it left Taylor fuming that 'never again will any party attempt to drag this battalion into politics'.

Camping and Conversion

LIFE IN THE INTER-WAR TERRITORIAL ARMY was demanding of men's time and energy. Besides the set-piece parades and the annual camp, men were required to attend a certain number of evening drills each year. The drill hall was open most nights and after the parades men were encouraged to remain and socialise. The messes had pianos, bars, billiard tables and, as the decades passed, also acquired easy chairs and carpets. The Officers' Mess had fine canteens of cutlery and quality collections of dinner service, some of which had been presented by retiring officers. Any officer joining after 1922 was required to provide himself with mess dress and the officers' committee annually decided how much each member should pay in mess subscriptions. The subscription of £5-7s-0d for example in 1937 provided for three mess dinners a year. In addition to the formal mess dinners, menus for which could include lobster and oysters, there were also reunion dinners. The first such gathering took place at the Albion Club in 1919, but in 1925 the event attracted only 27 diners. It was suggested that as Oldham offered such poor overnight facilities former officers might be more inclined to attend if the function were held in Manchester. The following year the meal was held at the Midland Hotel but as the attendance was again poor, Colonel Rye proposed that the reunion dinner should be replaced by an annual regimental dinner open to all officers who had served with any of the three battalions. The battalion's Officers also received regular invitations to the annual 42nd Division Dinner Club, the Oldham Royal Infirmary Dance and prize-giving evenings of other units in the division.

Officers of all battalions of the Manchester Regiment were members of the mess and former officers could be nominated as 'Members of the Battalion'. The bar was under the supervision of ex-RQMS Trevitt, and would remain so until his eventual retirement in 1937. Trevitt had enlisted in 1894 and by 1914 had risen to the rank of Sergeant Cook; he served throughout the war and returned with the cadre. When unable for reasons of age to re-enlist, he was appointed caretaker of the drill hall. While Trevitt served them drinks, officers could relax with *La Vie Parisienne* and other popular journals. Perhaps as an acknowledgment of their part-time métier, in 1929 the *Bystander* was replaced by the *Army and Navy Gazette*. From 1922 officers paid a 2d levy on drinks and on games of cards and billiards; this tax was used to swell the coffers of the battalion's distress fund. Unemployed members and former members in financial straits could apply for a small benevolence to the committee of four officers and four NCOs who administered the fund. The committee answered many such calls during the trade slump of the 1920s.

Officers engaged in an annual shooting and billiards competition against members of the Albion Club. The relationship between the club and the battalion dated from the early days of the war when officers were not permitted to stray far from Rifle Street. The Albion offered meals and drinks to officers who wanted to escape temporarily the clamour of the drill hall yet remain within hailing distance of their charges. The sergeants also held regular matches against members of the Oldham police. In 1929 the *Manchester Gazette* reported that the police 'won the shooting by seven points and the billiards by seven miles'.

As befitted an infantry unit, the battalion spent much of its time on the ranges. Various competitions were held throughout the year, several of which carried monetary prizes. In 1925 for example, the parents of the late Lieutenant James Stott donated £100 and a cup for the purpose of 'encouraging the young privates to take more interest in shooting'. Similarly, in the year following Captain Fripp's sudden death, his mother gave a cup which was competed for by the rifle grenadiers. To foster *esprit* men were also encouraged to join the battalion's boxing and occasional football teams.

Men enlisted in the TA for different reasons but the social attractions of the drill hall and the opportunity to earn a little extra cash were certainly motives for many. Few in the 1930s appear to have conscientiously joined 'to serve King and country'. Jim Street was probably fairly typical. He enlisted with two friends from the same warehouse largely because he liked the idea of military service and the chance to wear a uniform. Matt Cowell, who like Street joined the signals section, similarly held no great patriotic ideal but enjoyed the comradeship and social activities. As an aid to recruiting and as part of its service to the community, the drill hall, one of the largest in the country, was opened to keep-fit classes for the unemployed. In 1935 the CO believed that about 25% of his men were unemployed and that the majority of the battalion came from within a one mile radius of the drill hall.

No matter how dynamic or popular the unit might be, recruitment was necessary to replace time-expired men and those who left Oldham to seek work. Figures varied from year to year but, on average, a total of about 140 men became time-expired each year. A proportion could be expected to re-enlist but the majority would have to be replaced by new recruits. However, even when they migrated to the Midlands for work, men were not inevitably lost to the battalion. They often joined a local TA unit for drills but returned to Oldham and the 10th for the summer camp. Commanding Officers' reports make fairly regular mention of men compelled to leave for business reasons but it was not until 1933 that the number of officers fell below establishment. This was the first occasion since the war when there was not a waiting list for officers.

There was probably more of a concept of duty and responsibility among the officers than the men but it is clear that a principal motive for enlistment among all ranks was the annual camp.

Life in the Territorials during the financial retrenchment of the 1920s and 1930s was far from glamorous. The TA came at the bottom of the list when weapons, pay and equipment were under consideration; on the plus side, however, was the prospect of two weeks at camp. Accommodation and food in the 1920s were basic but if the camp was held close to the coast there was the added attraction of visiting the nearby resorts. The officers certainly made the most of the local opportunities. They were usually made members of any nearby golf club and were granted fishing permits in salmon and trout rivers. Messing increased from a total of fifteen shillings for the fortnight in 1922 to nine shillings per day by 1933. Catering firms sent their propaganda weeks before the actual event. Mess kits, which included blankets, camp bed, matting and folding chair and table, were hired individually, while card tables, floor boards, cooking ranges, colourfully lined marquees and coconut matting were hired for the mess. Following the disastrous fire in 1933 which destroyed the colours, electricity replaced hurricane lamps and hot showers replaced Heath Robinson contraptions which emitted at best a trickle of luke-warm water.

When relaxing in the mess, papers ranging from the *Mail* to the *Mirror* cluttered the hired tables and the bar was filled with bottles of 40% proof and mixers supplied at wholesale prices by Lea & Perrins. As an everlasting reminder of the officers' sojourn, local photographers were invited to submit estimates for mounted and unmounted group photos. In the weeks before camp the Sergeants' Mess was inundated by flyers from breweries and in an attempt to acknowledge the inevitable and avoid financial embarrassment at the bar, a savings club was inaugurated in the 1930s.

Many men enlisted just before the battalion left for camp and on some occasions left Rifle Street wearing civilian clothes. The crisis was particularly severe in 1936 when the battalion, already 5% over establishment, was 'staggered' to learn that it could recruit up to 10% over. This put a tremendous strain on the QM and his staff. One hundred and ten men offered themselves in three days, 40 were selected, 38 of whom spent the first few days at Kinmel in mufti. These men received uniforms a few days later but another two men were not so lucky. As the special uniforms ordered for them some six weeks earlier had been lost at Abergele railway station, the pair were condemned to wear out their civilian suits in the appalling weather of the first week of camp. Taylor paid the men compensation of over £3 but, when he attempted to reclaim the sum from the East Lancashire Territorial County Association, he was told by the committee not to show such benevolence again. Problems with clothing and equipment were not the only difficulties experienced when taking recruits to camp. When one such man was bawled out for not saluting a general, the bewildered and indignant youth retorted 'He's nowt to do with us. He's not in our mob'.

An advance party usually left Rifle Street for camp three days before the battalion. For the 1936 camp the QM, a lieutenant and 30 Other Ranks between them erected five large marquees, several smaller ones, 124 bell tents, deployed almost 600 blankets and groundsheets and nearly 10 tons of assorted stores. The difficulties of the advance party were exacerbated at Ripon in 1925 when the approach to the camp was a sea of liquid mud; as the wagons sank to their axles the stores had to be man-handled for several hundred yards across the marsh. When the site was completed cookers were lit and a hot meal prepared for the men's arrival. The quality of the food was sometimes variable but when the divisional general demanded 'any complaints?' the response was invariably in the negative. The division's senior medical officer also inevitably expressed himself 'satisfied' with the diet and provisions. One visiting reporter to the camp at Kinmel in 1930 decided that the 'days when eight to ten men sat around a dixie in a bell tent and took turns with a spoon are well past'. To his surprise, 'everything' was done to encourage good table manners and mess tables were adorned by oilcloths and cruets.

The extent and nature of the training depended upon the weather, the location, with whom the battalion was brigaded and the composition of the battalion. In 1933, 60% of the men were recruits who had to spend a good proportion of their time doing basic drills. Providing local farmers were willing to allow the use of their land, trained men practised company attacks, while specialists such as signallers and machine gunners performed their routine drills, often under the supervision of regulars. In 1928 the skill and efficiency of the machine-gun section so surprised Captain Grant and Sergeant Riches of the Coldstream Guards that the training schedule was hastily redrawn. At the 1930 camp a Cardon-Lloyd carrier was demonstrated to the curious machine gunners. The company commander and his second in command had such difficulty in squeezing their rotund frames into the driver's seat they concluded the vehicle was fit only for the young and active. By 1933 the reliability of the internal combustion engine and other technology had sufficiently overcome the machine gunners' innate conservatism for an officer to remark that 'the old regrettable occasions when the Lewis-gun section gave one the impression that they would be happier with bayonets at the end of their weapons, seems gradually to be dying away'.

The transport section remained largely immune to innovation. It usually went to camp with only one limber and horses which had been borrowed from milk floats or Corporation carts. Sergeant Edwards had joined the battalion before 1914 and served right through as the CO's groom and later as transport sergeant. His experience was vital, especially in 1929 when, following the departure of several time-expired experienced drivers, the section went to camp with men who had little or no knowledge of working with animals. These innocent troops had to work with a group of animals which were described as 'a good average collection of working cattle'. Drivers were also responsible for looking after the officers' mounts. The officers often amused themselves in contriving competition courses for the Falling Off Club. The winners being those riders who could most completely fail to demonstrate any level of equestrian skill. In 1936 Lieutenant Brewer won a special award for successfully crawling under a jump, over which his mount had sailed without difficulty.

In the sunshine, camp was idyllic. At Ripon in 1925 one officer was moved to comment: 'The trees are in full leaf, the fruit trees are loaded with blossom, the birds are singing from morn till night, and no true lover of Nature could wish for a more delightful environment'. The weather that summer proved to be exceptionally hot, two men succumbing to heat-stroke despite shirt-sleeve order and regular bathing parades in the River Ure. Similar weather prevailed at Kinmel in 1933. The 10th was the envy of other units when it was again allowed to parade in shirt-sleeve order; their jealous comrades in other battalions sweated through their drills in coarse serge. Unfortunately, good weather at camp was more the exception than the rule. Kinmel was often wet, with Salisbury, Troutbeck and Halton little better. The first week at Kinmel in 1936 was completely washed out and, following the departure of one man to hospital with pneumonia and the wartime soldiers claiming conditions were worse than at Ypres, the authorities were forced to issue new blankets and tent boards. To make matters worse, the lack of uncultivated land in the vicinity meant that troops were restricted to a limited area of degenerating bog.

When the elements were kind and the ground usable, the battalion trained. One of the most adventurous schemes was instigated by Chic Taylor at Caernarvon where the camp was only one hundred yards from the battalion's tent lines of 1914. Having split the battalion into defenders and attackers, Taylor planned to launch an amphibious raid across the Menai Straits on a supposed enemy radio mast and observation point. Acquiring the services of a pilot's cutter and a dozen rowing boats, Taylor led his 80 raiders against Selwyn Rowbotham's defences. Under cover of smoke and the flash of rockets the raiders destroyed the mast but were jumped by the defenders as they regained their craft. Taylor was captured but by hurling himself head first into one of the retreating boats made good his escape.

In their leisure time the men could obtain concessionary rail fares to places such as Morecambe and Fountains Abbey, hang around camp and even help local farmers dip their sheep. Afternoons were generally devoted to sport which, in the early 1920s, included a regular rugby match against the Wigan Territorials. In 1925 Private Hollingworth played in his fourteenth successive match of the fixture. Five had been played in Egypt, one in Gallipoli, three in France and five at home. A football match against a team from Caernarvon in 1935 was abandoned 'owing', as one report explained, 'to an untimely accident to the bladder'.

Many evenings were spent in cleaning and preparing equipment for the following day. The hard work, long hours and fresh air usually ensured there were few problems with regard to drink, sickness or crime. However, the Salisbury camp of 1929 seems to have been exceptional. One officer decided that the 'quietness of the lines at night and the alacrity of all ranks in the morning have been most unusual'. When the cleaning was done, platoons would sit around the fires and sing. Frequently the songs were, in the opinion of one sufferer, 'mostly pathetic ballads, sung with facial expressions which brought tears (not always of sympathy) to the eyes of the audience'.

On the middle Sunday Oldham's civic dignitaries visited the messes. In addition to the Chief Constable and the Mayor, officers' wives were joined by those of the senior NCOs and by former members of the battalion who arrived to enjoy a buffet and to renew old friendships. The Gallipoli veterans, who in 1935 amounted to four officers, two CSMs, two RQMS, three sergeants, one lance corporal and two privates, usually assembled for a group photo. In 1937 the seven officers and 50 Other Ranks still serving who had seen wartime service with the battalion were visited by Fred Hardman, Procktor Stott and several other former officers. Stott was the last of the pre-war soldiers to command the battalion. In 1926 the General Strike had caused the cancellation of the official camp and in 1932 financial stringency demanded that year's camp should be similarly abandoned. It was unfortunate for Stott that his sole year in command coincided with the Treasury's insistence that the Territorials would have to forgo their camp fortnight. Although the national coffers gained over £1m, recruiting in Oldham and elsewhere was hit badly.

Although the 10th went to camp 57 men short in 1925 the battalion compared well with other units of the 42nd Division. The 5/Manchester was over 200 short of establishment and the 8th and 9th Battalions were both more than 100 understrength. In 1935 Taylor claimed that in the post-war years the battalion had not only taken more men to camp than any other unit but that it had also consistently been the strongest battalion in the division. In 1925 the *Daily Telegraph* had announced that it would award a trophy to the Territorial unit which took the greatest percentage of its strength to camp. For three successive years the 10th came second in the competition. Some Territorial units used nefarious means of securing a high percentage of attendance, even enlisting groups of itinerant ex-soldiers who hired out their services from one unit to another. As different County Associations sent their men to camps during different weeks, these men could spend most of their summer under canvas with different battalions and batteries. When in 1933 it came second for the third time Taylor decided that because any man who was unable to obtain leave from work would invariably be granted leave of absence from camp, the 10th would find it 'practically impossible' to achieve 100% attendance. However, to confound Taylor's own pessimism the battalion won the cup the following year. Ignoring his previous comments, Taylor announced 'given that the battalion (is) considered to be the strongest unit in the Territorial Army', the win was 'not altogether unexpected'. He went on to reveal that the secret behind the success was the battalion's continuity of tradition and membership. The town's employers were doing their bit in allowing men to attend camp and Oldhamers wanted to join because they were proud to belong to the only Territorial battalion to be mentioned in Haig's Despatches of March 1918. The divisional commander added to the general satisfaction when he told the battalion that it was 'one of the best … in Western Command (and) the signallers were the best in the division'.

The battalion's official establishment was 603 but by taking 605 men to camp for all 15 days and four for four days, the 10th won the cup with an attendance of 100.7%. The following year, with 100.3% attendance, it carried off the cup again. This success was achieved with 11 men being excused camp, (seven of whom were in danger of losing their job) and 'in spite', according to Taylor, 'of the opposition of the Labour members of the Council'. This second success caused something of a problem to the editor of the *Daily Telegraph*. As no unit had previously won the cup on successive occasions the paper wondered whether the battalion would repolish and engrave the trophy itself or send it to London. While decisions were being made, congratulations poured in. They included letters from the County Association, other units of the Manchester Regiment, Oldham's MPs and its Chief Constable. The *Daily Telegraph* lauded it as an example to the nation and to the concept of a citizen army. The paper also took the opportunity to condemn the comparatively poor performance of the London Territorials. It suggested that the Londoners (no unit of which had ever achieved more than 90% attendance) should adopt the 10th's innovation for anti-aircraft drills. This involved an aerial runway slung under the drill hall's ceiling along which dummy aircraft were flown for target practice. The paper also praised the battalion's large sand pit in which toy soldiers were employed in theoretical exercises of troop deployment but decided that the 'major factor' in the battalion's success was Taylor's 'own enthusiasm and strong personality'. In 1936 the 10th won the cup for the third time and once again a shower of congratulatory telegrams and letters deluged Rifle Street. Among them on this occasion was a letter from H.B.Shaw, Headmaster of Hulme Grammar School. Shaw, whose former battalion, the 5/DLI, had won the cup in 1927, called it a 'magnificent achievement ... particularly in these modern days when the TA is so misunderstood'.

Shaw was largely correct when describing the Territorial Army as 'misunderstood'. The prevailing national sentiment remained one of war weariness and the belief that money expended on defence could be better applied elsewhere. Although Hitler had reoccupied the Rhineland in March of that year, few people in Britain regarded him as a threat to European peace. The TA was again seen as largely irrelevant and, although not subjected to the same degree of ridicule it had suffered before the war, was seen by many simply as a means by which young men could obtain a paid holiday. Even though the establishment of infantry battalions had been reduced in 1929 to 25 officers and 588 Other Ranks, nationally the TA remained 30,000 under strength. In 1932 its Director-General, General Sir William Thwaite, bemoaned that years of retrenchment had brought the TA 'down through the bone to the very marrow'. On the positive side however, some units, including the 10th, were allowed to recruit up to 10% over establishment. Finding recruits in Oldham was not difficult in the 1930s and in 1936 the battalion took an impressive total of 21 officers and 638 men to camp. Despite what Taylor was still darkly describing as the 'deliberate obstruction' of the Labour Party, his own enthusiasm remained the principal reason for the battalion's success. Taylor's personal contribution was supported by what the *Daily Telegraph* believed was the whole-hearted and unselfish co-operation of local mill owners. Taylor himself ascribed the success to the battalion's family and team spirit, the town's 'intense loyalty' and because all but two of the officers came from Oldham. This, Taylor emphasised, was an essential aspect in fostering local pride and in understanding the men under their command.

The battalion remained up to strength for camps at Abergavenny and Redcar in 1937 and 1938 but by the time it returned from Redcar, significant changes were afoot. British rearmament was under way and, with the Munich crisis in September suggesting that Hitler was unlikely to remain content with the Sudetenland, the Territorial Army was about to undergo a reorganisation. On 1 October 1938 Chic Taylor relinquished command of the 10th and was succeeded by his old friend Selwyn Rowbotham. Taylor assumed command of the newly raised 71st (Anti-Aircraft) Searchlight Regiment at Failsworth and Rowbotham took command of an infantry battalion which was about to be converted to an Army Tank Battalion. The change had come swiftly and unexpectedly. On 31 October six TA infantry battalions were disbanded and re-raised the following day in a new form; the 9/Manchester became a Machine-Gun Battalion and the 10/Manchester became 41st Army Tank Battalion. The Army Council apologised to the County Association for not having consulted before announcing the changes but excused itself on the grounds that the seriousness of the international situation meant that the Council had to act decisively and with expediency. The establishment of the new unit was smaller than that of an infantry battalion, necessitating the loss of 105 Other Ranks but requiring an additional two officers.

However, the battalion was without tanks, without any real experience of what to do with them and, when they arrived, without anywhere to train.

Lieutenant-Colonel Rowbotham immediately began negotiations with landowners with a view to acquiring training areas. Huddersfield Corporation refused land off the Holmfirth road because the tanks would damage the gathering ground for the town's water supply. Rowbotham next attempted to persuade private landowners above Marsden and at Preston but with little more success. Eventually, Oldham Edge became the area where townsfolk were most likely to observe the Territorials manoeuvring with their light tanks. In April 1939, following Hitler's annexation of the rump of Czechoslovakia, a second line unit known as 47th Royal Tank Regiment began recruiting. With its temporary HQ at Waterhead Liberal Club and its QM stores at St Mary's Club in Oldham, it reached establishment in June 1939.

Nearly eighty years after the battalion of Volunteers had first formed, Oldham's Territorials again marched off to war. On this occasion they moved by lorry; in 1914 they had marched to Bury. The type of war the two tank battalions were about to fight was to differ hugely from the experience of their infantry predecessors of 1914-1918. Yet there was one significant similarity: like their fathers, the Territorials of the Second World War would spend a lengthy time in the Western Desert. In the Great War the 10th had suffered badly on Gallipoli but had missed the attritional slaughter of the Somme and most of Third Ypres. Out at rest when the German blow fell on 21 March 1918, it avoided the heavy losses common to many battalions that day. Furthermore, because it joined in the assault on the Hindenburg Line on the second day of the operation, the battalion suffered fewer casualties than its comrades in the Manchester and Fusilier Brigades. Similarly, the 2nd Battalion spent so long in and around La Bassée and on the coast that it too experienced only one set-piece battle. In comparison to many other Territorial regiments, the 10th came off lightly. In the Second World War its successors would not have to endure a similar casualty rate but their experience was to be equally traumatic. The Territorials of 1939 did not belong to the same regiment or wear the same badge as their counterparts of 1914, but they had their traditions and reputation to preserve.

POSTSCRIPT

IN THE EARLY STAGES of the Second World War, 41st and 47th RTR (TA) trained in the United Kingdom. Meanwhile, former members of the 10th who were too old for military service joined units of the Civil Defence or the Home Guard. Fred Hardman was appointed CO of the 23rd County of Lancaster Battalion, Home Guard, a unit which by 1944 boasted 87 officers and 1780 Other Ranks. Among Hardman's officers were his former Gallipoli friends Procktor Stott and Herbert Sutcliffe. Selwyn Rowbotham had relinquished command of the 41st in April 1940 but Jimmy Whitehead remained with the unit and served under its new commanding officer, Colonel R.Farrington.

The regiment remained in Oldham during the Phoney War and in June 1940, as part of an anti-invasion force armoured column, moved to Otley. In September 1940 Rowbotham visited the regiment's training area in an attempt to retrieve the 10th's memorial drums and bugles which Farrington had removed from Oldham. The colonel claimed that he needed the drums for church parades and as 'an inspiration to the young soldiers'. He considered it better to use the drums rather than, as he wrote to the trustees, have them 'entombed' inside a church or bank. Not wishing to have the drums 'banged about from camp to camp' Hardman was incensed by Farrington's unauthorised action. Hardman believed the drums were 'memorials first and drums afterwards' and should only be used on 'sacred and memorable occasions'. Rowbotham came away from Otley empty handed but, after a further exchange of letters and as the issue was becoming general knowledge about Oldham, Jimmy Whitehead was ordered to placate his former comrades of the 10th. In February 1941 he informed Hardman that as the 41st was about to move, the drums would be deposited in the vaults of the County Bank, Oldham. The following month Whitehead himself assumed command of the 41st and the drums returned. Three decades later, as one of the senior regimental trustees, Whitehead arranged for the drums to be presented for display in Oldham Town Hall and later in the Civic Centre.

In 1941 another incident occurred which also raised concern among former members of the 10th. The commanding officer of the 2/9th Battalion Manchester Regiment sought permission to rename his battalion the 10th Battalion Manchester Regiment. The East Lancashire Territorial Force Association asked Brigadier Chic Taylor's opinion on the subject. Taylor conferred with Hardman who argued that if they made no objection to the request, the new 10th might well lay claim to the old 10th's colours and drums. The matter was conveniently shelved.

Meanwhile the 10th's successor units were on their way to the Western Desert. The 41st left Liverpool on HMT SCYTHIA in May 1942 and, having docked *en route* at Freetown and Cape Town, disembarked at Suez in July. One squadron of the 47th, which was, like the 41st part of 24 Armoured Brigade, was temporarily detached for service in Madagascar. All of the 41st's Valentine tanks were sent forward as reinforcements and, until the replacement Shermans, Grants and Crusaders arrived, the regiment concerned itself with acclimatisation and navigation training. The 41st and 47th took a mauling during the Battle of Alamein with the result that the 47th was, like its predecessor the 2/10th, disbanded. The 41st was ordered to hand over its remaining tanks to another unit and was withdrawn into Egypt. The regiment was next equipped with Scorpion flail tanks and in February 1943 it took part in the attack on the Mareth Line. For the next 12 months while three squadrons fought in Italy, HQ Squadron was detached in Egypt. During this period the unit became known as Number 1 Scorpion Squadron. In April 1944 HQ Squadron rejoined and the regiment was redesignated 141st Assault Squadron RAC/RE. It absorbed a large number of RE personnel and equipped with Shermans, Scorpions, bulldozers and a variety of other specialist vehicles, the regiment took part in operations on the Adriatic coast. Although by this stage in its history barely recognisable as the successor unit to the Oldham Territorials, 41st RTR was kept alive in the guise of the 141st.

A more direct link was re-established following the reorganisation of the TA in the immediate post-war years. In 1947, 41st RTR was reformed and, in recognition of the contribution to the life of the town made by the regiment and its predecessors, was accorded the Freedom of the Borough seven years later. To emphasise its pedigree the unit's title was changed to 41st (Oldham) RTR (TA). In 1956 the Royal Armoured Corps underwent a further reorganisation and the 41st was amalgamated with 40th (King's) RTR based at Liverpool. This arrangement continued until 1967 when the regiment became A Squadron, Duke of Lancaster's Yeomanry (RTR). The drill hall at Rifle Street remained the unit's HQ but the unit itself was little more than a cadre. Two years later it became 75 Engineer Workshop REME (RTR) (V). The workshop detachment shared Rifle Street with the cadets (who retained a link with the tanks by wearing the Royal Tank Regiment cap badge) and with a company (later reduced to a platoon) of 4th (Volunteer) Parachute Regiment.

In 1998 the Government announced the findings of the Strategic Defence Review. This analysis of the nation's future defence requirements allowed for a cut in the size of the Territorial Army. One of the victims of the cuts is the Rifle Street drill hall. The existing workshop will move to Failsworth and the cadets will eventually be rehoused. With its regimental silver and memorial drums in the Civic Centre and its colours in the keeping of the trustees, the messes will be emptied of what memorabilia they still contain; the drill hall will resound no more to the stamp of feet, the bellowing of orders and the songs and laughter of smoking concerts. For the first time in over 90 years there will be no Territorials within the confines of Oldham town centre.

SOURCES

SEVERAL MAJOR AND MANY SMALLER collections of primary sources have been used in the compilation of this study. Notes on some of the larger ones are given below. In order to keep the text as free of clutter as possible footnotes and references have been eliminated: it is usually possible to identify the source from the accompanying text.

Published and unpublished histories of the 10/Manchester
The war diaries of the 1st and 2nd Battalions are deposited in the Public Record Office. Unfortunately there is no trace of the volume which covers the 1/10th's overseas service between September 1914 and July 1915. The diaries have a WO.95 classification: 1st Battalion, 4315, 4595 and 2658; 2nd Battalion, 3141. War diaries of other units in the 42nd Division were also consulted.

In 1919 Oldham's two papers serialised the war history of the 1st and 2nd Battalions. The *Chronicle's* version was written by the Quartermaster, Arthur Wynne, while the *Standard* used articles written by one of its own reporters, Maurice Bradbury, who had served with the 10th from 1914–1919. These articles are on microfilm in Oldham's Local Studies Library.

In addition to his articles for the *Chronicle*, Arthur Wynne produced an extensive handwritten account of the 10th's early service in Egypt and Gallipoli; this does much to replace the missing volume of the war diary. Wynne also wrote a history of the 1st Battalion probably for circulation among former members. One typed draft is with the Hardman papers in the Imperial War Museum. This version is similar to his articles in the *Chronicle* but in some sections is slightly more blunt and contains additional detail. The Hardman papers also contain a lengthy although incomplete essay written by Chic Taylor on the battalion's activities in March 1918.

Printed and personal accounts
Local newspapers
In common with many local papers across the country, until 1916 the *Chronicle* and *Standard* printed letters sent by soldiers to their families. Although subject to censorship and over or under statement, these letters provide many interesting examples of soldiers' overseas experiences. The chapters on the 1st Battalion's time in Egypt and Gallipoli have made extensive use of these sources.

The Hardman Collection

Fred Hardman of Queen's Road was commissioned into the Oldham Territorials in 1910; he served continuously until finally relinquishing command of the battalion in 1932. During the war he was an exceptionally prolific writer of letters to his wife and father. Many scores of these letters and a large selection of their replies have survived. They provide a fascinating insight into his personal relationships, his views on the fighting, the men of the battalion, his fellow officers and contemporary attitudes to the war. The collection, which is deposited in the Department of Documents of the Imperial War Museum, also contains some papers relating to the battalion's history during the inter-war period.

The Taylor Collection

J. A. C. Taylor (Chic), an architect by profession, was commissioned into the 1st Battalion in 1914. He served continuously until appointed to command a new Territorial unit established in Failsworth in 1938. During the Second World War he attained the rank of Brigadier-General.

Taylor, who originated from Waterhead, devoted much of his life to the 10th. He collected a huge assortment of newspaper cuttings, photos and memorabilia relating to the regiment. The collection is now in the care of the regimental trustees. A scrapbook containing photos and personal items also compiled by Taylor is in private possession.

The Regimental Scrapbook

According to a resolution noted in the Officers' Mess Minute Book of 1922, Lieutenant Wright was instructed to begin collecting material for a battalion scrapbook. It is unclear whether the large volume now in the Stalybridge Archive is the direct consequence of that instruction or whether it is from a different origin.

It was for many years in the possession of a former officer, Captain Alan Mellowdew. The book consists largely of newspaper cuttings but does also have a number of official papers, personal reminiscences and photos. Permission to consult the material is required from the regimental trustees.

Printed primary sources

The journal of the Manchester Regiment, *The Manchester Gazette,* volumes covering the period 1910-1939.

Minutes of the East Lancashire Territorial Force County Association, 1914-1938.

Lawson, Henry, *Vignettes of the Western Front* (Positif Press, 1979)

Collections in the Department of Documents, Imperial War Museum – Bleakley, James 96/36/1; Hardman, Fred 76/27/; Street, Jack 86/8/1

Papers and diaries in private and regimental possession

H. Clarke, T. Gorbutt, H. Hague, P. Healey, J. Humphries, A. Kirkbride, J. Openshaw, Park family, W. Swallow, J. A. C. Taylor, A. Wynne.

Various volumes of Officers' Mess Minute Books, regimental correspondence and account ledgers.

Secondary sources

There is now such an abundance of books on the Great War that it has become almost impossible to give an adequate and balanced bibliography of available volumes. The titles below provide the reader with an overview of the campaigns and areas in which the 1/10th and 2/10th fought.

Official History of the War, (various authors, HMSO)

Gibbon, F., *The 42nd East Lancashire Division* (Country Life Library, 1920)

James, R. R., *Gallipoli* (London: Pan Books, 1984)

Liddle, P. H., (ed) *Passchendaele in perspective* (Leo Cooper, 1997)

Macdonald, L., *They called it Passchendaele* (Michael Joseph, 1978)

Middlebrook, M., *The Kaiser's Battle* (Penguin, 1983)

Mitchinson, K. W., *Epéhy* (Leo Cooper, 1998)

Mitchinson, K. W., *Villers-Plouich* (Leo Cooper, 1999)

Montgomery, A., *The Story of the Fourth Army* (Hodder & Stoughton, 1919)

Moorehead, A., *Gallipoli* (Hamish Hamilton, 1956)

Steel N. & Hart P., *Defeat at Gallipoli* (Macmillan, 1994)

Toland, J., *No Man's Land* (Methuen, 1980)

Vaughan, E.C., *Some desperate glory* (Frederick Warne, 1985)

Appendix 1

The Rolls of the Fallen: Introduction

THE ROLLS OF THOSE MEN of the 10/Manchester who were killed in action, died of wounds or died of disease are taken from the post-war *Soldiers Died* and *Officers Died* registers. These give the names of those men who died as an immediate consequence of their wartime service. The registers do not list those who may have died of wounds or incapacity in the years following the armistice. This largely accounts for the incongruity between the 628 names inscribed on the memorial silver drums and the 615 in the official registers.

In the years following the war, the Commonwealth War Graves Commission relaid existing cemeteries, expanded others by concentrating the remains from small cemeteries into them and erected memorials to the missing in the theatres where British forces had been in action. On the columns of the memorials are inscribed the names of those men whose remains either could not be found or identified. Nearly 150 names of the 1/10's fatalities sustained during the Gallipoli campaign are carved on the Helles Memorial (Helles M.M.) which stands sentinel over the Dardanelles; fifty names of the 2/10th are on the panels of the Tyne Cot memorial (Tyne Cot M.M.) nestled beneath Passchendaele Ridge.

The fallen with known graves are scattered about the several cemeteries on Gallipoli and in the British-held sectors of the Western Front. Those who died of wounds or disease were buried largely in Malta and Egypt or close to the base hospitals at Boulogne, Wimereux, Rouen and Etaples. The remainder lie in the beautifully maintained cemeteries closer to the front line. The locations of those cemeteries which contain a significant number of the men of the 1/10th and 2/10th Battalions are noted overleaf. Further information can be obtained from libraries and from the Commonwealth War Graves Commission at Maidenhead.

Unless otherwise noted, all cemeteries containg the 1/10th's dead of 1914, 1915 and 1916 are on Gallipoli and those with the dead of both battalions of 1917 and 1918 in France or Belgium. Information regarding the individuals has been collected from CWGC registers, local papers and some official records.

Bancourt British: Two miles S.E. of Bapaume, S. of the N30.

Belle Vue British (Biastre): Twelve miles E. of Cambrai and two miles S. of Solesmes, W. of the D955.

Bertrancourt Military: Eight miles N.W. of Albert on the D114.

Brandhoek: Three cemeteries in close proximity. Five miles W. of Ieper on the Poperinghe road.

Cambrin Military: Between Bethune and La Bassée on the N41.

Caudry British: S.E. of Cambrai on the N43.

Couin New British: Eight miles E. of Doullens and S.W. of Souastre on the D2.

Gorre British: Four miles E. of Bethune on the Festubert road (D72).

Neuville-Bourjonval British: Twelve miles N.N.E. of Péronne, S. of Havrincourt Wood.

Sucrerie Military (Colincamps): Nine miles N.W. of Albert on the D163.

Zuydcoote Military: Between Dunkirk and Veurne.

The Rolls of the Fallen.

Part 1 - Officers

THE OFFICERS LISTED BELOW are those who are given in the official *Officers Died* register as belonging to the 10/Manchester and those who were posted to the two overseas battalions and died while serving with them. It is probably an incomplete list as the war diaries do not always note deaths of officers who were attached to the regiment from elsewhere.

Name	Rank	Fate	Notes – *Buried/Commemorated*
Ascroft, Robert	2Lt	kia 4/6/15	Age 19. Son of James and nephew of (late) Robert, a former MP for Oldham. Left Charterhouse School July 1914. Commissioned into the 10th 25/8/15 and went with it to Egypt. Worked at the family firm of Ascroft, Maw and Shimfield. – *Helles M.M.*
Baird, Leonard	Captain MC MID	kia 20/4/17	RAMC attached 10th. From Bury. – *Tincourt New British Cemetery*
Baxter, Gerald	2Lt	kia 9/10/17	To Egypt 1916. Wounded at Gillemont Farm May 1917. To 2/10th on recovery. – *Tyne Cot M.M.*
Byron, Harry	2Lt	kia 2/9/18	Probably attached to 8/Manchester. – *Manchester Cemetery (Riencourt)*
Clegg, James	Lt	dow 25/5/15	Age 27. Lived at Thornlee, Grotton. Worked at Clegg's Mumps Mill. His brother John was killed in June 1915 with the 6/Manchester. Cousin of John Hamer Clegg. – *Helles M.M.*
Clegg, John, Hamer	Captain	dow 4/6/15	Age 27. Lived at Frederick St, Werneth. Enlisted 1914 and stayed with the Home Service men when the battalion left for Egypt. Promoted Captain 28/11/14 and to Gallipoli. Managing Director of Clegg's Mumps Mill. – *Helles M.M.*
Carmichael, Gilbert	2Lt	kia 21/3/18	Attached to 2/6th Manchester. – *Pozieres M.M.*
Chapman, Henry	2Lt	kia 9/10/17	Reported wounded and missing Oct.1917 and confirmed killed in Jan.1918. – *Tyne Cot M.M.*
Cook, Frank	Lt MC	kia 20/10/18	Age 28. Husband of Nora, 14, Richmond Ave., Huddersfield. Enlisted 1/9/14. Twice wounded. – *Belle Vue British Cemetery*
Cooper, Charles	Lt	kia 20/10/18	Attached from 7/Manchester – *Belle Vue British Cemetery*

Name	Rank	Fate	Notes – Buried/Commemorated
Elliot, Frank	2Lt	kia 23/8/18	Attached from 1/Manchester. – *Sucrerie Military Cemetery (Colincamps)*
Emmott, John	2Lt	kia 4/6/15	Son of Professor and nephew of Lord Emmott. Married to 2Lt Ascroft's sister. – *Twelve Tree Copse Cemetery*
Forth, Charles	2Lt	kia 30/7/17	Age 20. – *Coxyde Military Cemetery*
Gilliat, Robert	Lt	dow 25/5/18 (as a pow)	Age 27. From Oldham. Also wounded 3/8/17. – *Rethal French National Cemetery*
Gregory, S.	2Lt	kia 8/6/18	Age 23. Son of Ernest & Catherine, 9, Market St., Northwich. – *Bertrancourt Military Cemetery*
Griffiths, Francis	Lt	dow 2/6/15	Age 27. Lived at 90, Wellington Rd., Oldham. Formerly Hulme G.S. Commissioned into 10th 1913. Promoted Lt 31/8/14 Secretary at Rutland Mill, Shaw. His brother, D.E. also went with the 10th to Egypt and Gallipoli. Their father, Cllr and Lt-Col had been CO of 3rd Battalion Manchester Volunteers at Ashton for 28 years. – *Lancashire Landing Cemetery*
Hart, Francis	Lt	died 4/7/18 (in UK)	Attached to 42nd MGC. – *Manchester Southern Cemetery*
Horncastle, Edward	Lt	kia 27/5/18	Age 36. Attached elsewhere. Husband of Rosa, Thorpe Bay, Essex. – *Soissons M.M.*
Hughes, William	2Lt	kia 26/3/18	Attached 1/9th Manchester. – *Pozieres M.M.*
Kershaw, Joseph	Lt	died 16/9/19	Age 41. Husband of Bertha, 32, Moston Lane, Failsworth. – *Kantara War Cemetery (Egypt)*
Kirk, James	2Lt VC	kia 4/11/18	Attached to 2/Manchester. Wounded May 1917. – *Ors Communal Cemetery*
Kirk, Joseph	2Lt	died 10/2/16 (motorcycle accident)	Brother of Tom. England lacrosse international. Commissioned into 10th from 6/Manchester 24/4/15. Wounded and evacuated 18/8/15. – *Willow Grove Cemetery (Reddish)*
Kirk, Tom	2Lt	kia 4/6/15	Age 25. Son of George & Jane, 5, Prince's Rd., Heaton Moor. Played tennis and lacrosse for Lancashire. Rejoined 6/Manchester on outbreak and commissioned into 10th 24/4/15. Brother of Joseph. – *Helles M.M.*
Lee, James	2Lt	dow 22/1/18.	– *Lister Lane Cemetery (Halifax)*
Lewis, Percy	Lt-Col	kia 8/9/17	Attached from Devonshire Regt. – *Ypres Reservoir Cemetery*

Name	Rank	Fate	Notes – Buried/Commemorated
Maw, Arthur	Captain	kia 21/3/18	Age 27. Possibly attached to 1/9th Manchester. Son of Walter & Lucy, Holmleigh, Windsor Rd., Oldham. To 1st Battalion in Gallipoli 1915 and invalided home. – *Pozieres M.M.*
McAdorey, John	2Lt	dow 5/5/18	Age 25. Lived at 18, Market St., Malton. – *Bagneux British Cemetery*
Nevinson, Humphrey	2Lt	dow 5/6/15	Age 23. Son of a rector from Market Harborough. Worked at Oldham Brewery. Buried at sea. – *Helles M.M.*
Norris, William	Lt MID	dow 14/10/18	Age 27. D Coy., Husband of Jeanette, Cotham, Bristol. – *Mount Huon British Cemetery*
Owen, George	Captain	kia 6/6/15	Age 32. From Warrington. Joined 2nd Volunteer Battalion, Manchester Regt. as a youth. University of Manchester OTC. Promoted Captain in 10th 31/8/14. A yarn agent in Manchester. – *Helles M.M.*
Reeder, Robert	Captain	dow 6/1/18	Age 24. Attached RFC., From Balham, London. – *Doullens Communal Cemetery Extension No.1*
Shaw, Walter	Lt MC	kia 7/11/18	Age 37. Attached from Royal Fusiliers.
Shepphard, R.	Lt	kia 13/5/17	Attached from 13/London. – *Cambrin Military Cemetery*
Spielman, Harold	Captain	kia 13/8/15	Son of Sir Isidore CMG & Lady, 56, Westbourne Terrace, Paddington. Clifton School, Trinity College, Cambridge. – *Pink Farm Cemetery*
Stott, James	Lt	kia 19/6/15	Age 18. Son of William & Helena, Westlands, Werneth. Brother of Procktor. – *Helles M.M.*
Stott, Philip	2Lt	died 21/3/15	Probably 3/10th Battalion. – *Stanton (St Michael) Churchyard, Gloucs.*
Taylor, David	2Lt	kia 9/9/16	Attached 2/5th Lancashire Fusiliers. – *Thiepval M.M.*
Thorley, Gordon	Lt	dow 7/11/18	Age 23, Husband of Gladys, 675, Oldham Rd., Newton Heath. Wounded July 1917. – *Gommegnies Communal Cemetery*
Thorp, Frederick	2Lt	dow 31/3/18	Age 24, Attached RFC, Son of Henry & Annie, 18, Granville Rd., Fallowfield. – *Aubigny Communal Cemetery Extension*
Walters, Ernest	2Lt	kia 26/9/16	Possibly attached to Lancashire Fusiliers and – erroneously inscribed on *Loos M.M.* rather than *Thiepval M.M.*
Wilson, Tom	2Lt	kia 27/9/18	Age 22. B Coy., Son of Thomas & Mary, 1, Glebelands Rd. East, Prestwich. – *Ribecourt Road Cemetery*
Yates, Samuel	2Lt	kia 22/12/17	Attached to 8/Manchester. From Newton Heath. – *Béthune Town Cemetery*

Part 2 – The 1/10 Battalion

Name	No.	Rnk	Fate	Notes – Buried/Commemorated
Adams, Robert	1491	Pte	kia 4/6/15	Born and enlisted at Oldham. – *Helles M.M.*
Addyman, William	765	Dmr	kia 13/8/15	Age 38. Son of William & Betty, 33, Boston St., Oldham. Husband of Ann, 109, Falcon St., Oldham. – *Helles M.M.*
Allen, Henry S.	376336	Pte	dow 11/4/18	Age 25. Son of Henry & Millicent of Stockport. Husband of Lucy, 46, Colwyn St., Westwood, Oldham. – *Wimereux Communal Cemetery*
Alty, Harold	2066	Pte	kia 4/6/15	Born and enlisted at Oldham. – *Helles M.M.*
Ambrose, George E.	54517	Pte	dow 31/8/18	Age 20. Lived at Woodbridge, Suffolk. (Possibly dow on 8/9/18) – *Bancourt British Cemetery*
Anderson, Harry	1943	Pte	kia 29/5/15	Born at Manchester, Enlisted at Oldham. – *Helles M.M.*
Anderton, John	965	Pte	kia 11/8/15	Age 24. Son of William and Elizabeth, 245, Rochdale Rd., Oldham. – *Helles M.M.*
Andrew, Samuel	376617	Pte	kia 24/6/17	– *Ruyaulcourt Military Cemetery*
Arundale, James	375529	Pte	dow 26/4/17	Age 20. 1, Stable St., Barry St., Oldham. – *Péronne Communal Cemetery Extension*
Ashton, Percy	2565	Pte	kia	Age 32. Son of Jane, 13, Cranbrook St., Clarksfield. – *Helles M.M.*
Ashton, Walter	2212	Pte	died 25/6/15	Age 37. 345, Rochdale Rd., Oldham. Packer at Northmoor Mill. Enlisted in August 1914 – *East Mundros Military Cemetery, Lemnos*
Aspin, Albert	2337	Pte	dow 3/9/15	Age 18. 105, Brewerton Rd., Oldham. Formerly 2/10thBattalion. – *Helles M.M.*
Aspin, James	42088	L/Cpl	kia 31/8/18	Age 20. 13, School Lane, Blackburn. Probably formerly 2/10th Battalion. – *Bancourt British Cemetery*
Bailey, Allan	44788	Pte	kia 28/9/18	Lived at Staindrop, Durham. Formerly 1730 DLI. – *Vis-en-Artois M.M.*
Bailey, Harold	201957	Pte	kia 4/8/18	Age 19. 17, Fidler St., Thatto Heath, St Helens. – *Bertrancourt Military Cemetery*
Bailey, Harry	2214	Pte	kia 4/6/15	Age 21. Son of Mary, 7, Fleet St., Ashton-u-Lyne. – *Helles M.M.*

Name	No.	Rnk	Fate	Notes – Buried/Commemorated
Bailey, John	20675	L/Cpl	kia 6/11/18	Age 25. 752, Slattocks, Castleton, Rochdale. – *Maubeuge Centre Cemetery*
Bairstow, Sutcliffe	1662	Pte	kia 4/6/15	Lived at 4, Sarah Moor, Oldham. – *Helles M.M.*
Bakewell, Herbert	376974	Pte	kia 5/4/18	Age 25. 194, Hough Lane, Barnsley. Formerly 4976 KOYLI – *Bienvillers Military Cemetery*
Bamford, James	2298	Pte	dow 16/6/15	Lived at 5, Peter St., Oldham. – *Cairo War Memorial Cemetery*
Bannister, Clarence	1234	Pte	dow 27/8/15	Age 23. Lived at 14, Chancery St., Lees Rd., Oldham. – *Lancashire Landing Cemetery*
Bannister, Samuel	3307	Pte	died 6/6/16	Age 34. Husband of Hannah, 214, Greenacres Rd., Oldham. – *Cairo War Memorial Cemetery*
Bardsley, James	870	Pte	kia 4/6/15	Born and enlisted at Oldham. – *Helles M.M.*
Bardsley, John	376307	Pte	dow 12/6/18	Age 28. Son of Andrew & Agnes, 4,Timperley St., Chadderton Rd., Oldham. – *Bagneux British Cemetery*
Barker, Albert	1945	Pte	kia 4/6/15	Age 31. Husband of Alice, 31, Burnley St., Oldham. – *Helles M.M.*
Barker, Charles	376600	L/Cpl	kia 28/3/18	Enlisted at Oldham. – *Sauchy-Cauchy Communal Cemetery Extension*
Barlow, Joseph	375947	Pte	kia 11/12/17	Lived at Patricroft. – *Gorre British Cemetery*
Barnes, James	1921	Pte	kia 4/6/15	Lived at 118, Edward St., Werneth. – *Helles M.M.*
Barratt, Samuel	2991	Pte	kia 13/8/15	Enlisted at Oldham. – *Helles M.M.*
Bates, Edward	377088	Pte	dow 5/4/18	Lived at Ashton-u-Lyne. – *Bienvillers Military Cemetery*
Bates, James	377122	Pte	kia 11/12/18	Enlisted at Hollinwood. – *Gorre British Cemetery*
Bayley, George	42717	Pte	kia 18/6/18	Age 36. Married, of 50, Pember Rd, Kensal Green, London. Formerly 33270 East Surrey Regt. – *Bertrancourt Military Cemetery*
Beaumont, Thomas	375362	L/Cpl	kia 26/6/17	Enlisted at Oldham. – *Thiepval M.M.*
Beever, Ben	2301	Pte	kia 11/12/15	Age 27. Lived at Glodwick. – *Twelve Tree Copse Cemetery*

Name	No.	Rnk	Fate	Notes – Buried/Commemorated
Beilby, Edward	2217	Pte	dow 26/11/15	Age 24. Lived at 21, Dorothy St., Oldham. To Gallipoli in November. Worked at Platts New Works. – *Helles M.M.*
Belshaw, James	546	Pte	kia 4/6/15	Born and enlisted at Oldham. – *Helles M.M.*
Belshaw, William	2789	Pte	died (enteric) 7/8/15	Age 23. Lived at 23, Culvert St., Waterhead. Piecer at Orb Mill. Enlisted 2/10th Battalion in Sept.1914. – *Pieta Military Cemetery (Malta)*
Bennett, Albert	22585	Pte	dow 2/2/18	Married, of 13, Gower St., Patricroft. – *Gorre British Cemetery*
Berry, Hubert	2078	Pte	dow 30/6/15	Age 19. Lived at 12, Trafalgar St., Oldham. Worked at Bee Mill, Royton. Wounded on 4/6/15 and evacuated to Cairo. Died on voyage to U.K. and buried at sea. – *Helles M.M.*
Berry, John	2218	Pte	dow 16/6/15	Enlisted at Oldham. – *Chatby War Memorial Cemetery (Alexandria)*
Betteley, George	252338	Pte	dow 19/10/18	Age 28. Married, of 16, Plymouth Grove West, Chorlton-on-Medlock. – *St Aubert British Cemetery*
Beverley, John	376330	Pte	dow 20/5/18	Enlisted at Oldham. – *Chadderton Cemetery*
Biram, Harry	375948	L/Cpl	kia 8/6/18	Aged 20. Son of Edward & Annie of Oldham. – *Bertrancourt Military Cemetery*
Blacas, Tom	1694	L/Cpl	dow 15/12/15	Age 22. Lived at Old Lane, Hollinwood. – *Azmak Cemetery (Suvla)*
Black, Thomas	382	Pte	dow 12/6/15	Age 36. Husband of Laura (remarried) of 25, Frankhill St.,Oldham. – *Pieta Military Cemetery (Malta)*
Blainey, David	376083	Pte	kia 24/4/18	Age 29. Son of William & Susan. Husband of Elizabeth, 9, Salt St., Littlemoor Lane, Oldham. – *Couin New British Cemetery*
Bliss, John	376961	L/Cpl	kia 14/9/17	Age 31. Lived at Middlesbrough. Formerly 8604 DLI. – *Brandhoek New Military Cemetery*
Bocking, William	1489	Pte	kia 4/6/15	Born and enlisted at Oldham. – *Helles M.M.*
Booth, Samuel	1498	Pte	dow 16/6/15	Age 21. Lived at 21, Siddall St., Oldham. – *East Mundros Military Cemetery (Lemnos)*

Name	No.	Rnk	Fate	Notes – *Buried/Commemorated*
Bould, John	376641	Pte	kia 25/9/18	Born at Macclesfield. – *Vis-en-Artois M.M.*
Bowden, Frank	1526	Sgt	kia 9/8/15	Age 19. Son of Abraham & Nancy, 38, Primrose Bank, Oldham. – *Helles M.M.*
Bowes, Herbert	1949	Pte	died (pneumonia) 19/1/16	Age 25. Lived at 39, Crompton St., Oldham.Worked for Anchor Spinning Co., Westwood. Rejoined August 1914. Died in No.15 General Hospital, Cairo. – *Chatby War Memorial Cemetery (Alexandria)*
Bowman, Joseph	375431	Pte	kia 11/12/17	Married, of 30, Evelyn St., Oldham. – *Gorre British Cemetery*
Boxwell, Jesse	277455	L/Cpl	kia 20/10/18	Born and enlisted at Bolton. Formerly 6860 Loyal North Lancashire Regt. – *Belle Vue British Cemetery*
Boyd, William	375836	Pte	kia 4/6/17	Age 25. Son of John & Mary, 4, Tunnel St., Oldham. – *Neuville-Bourjonval British Cemetery*
Boyle, John	375089	Cpl	kia 11/12/17	Age 33. Husband of Catherine, 22, Bloom St., Manchester St., Oldham. – *Gorre British Cemetery*
Bradley, Harold	2570	Pte	dow 19/8/15	Age 22. Lived at Cymbralia, Alkrington, Middleton. Buried at sea. Formerly 2/10th Battalion. – *Helles M.M.*
Brennan, Francis	252458	Pte	dow 7/11/18	Age 20. B Coy. Son of Thomas, 57, Church St., Harpurhey. – *Maubeuge Centre Cemetery*
Brierley, John	3262	Pte	dow 9/12/15	Age 39. Lived at 107, Burnley Lane, Chadderton. Five years in the Volunteers. Enlisted in 3/10th Battalion in Feb. 1915 and to Gallipoli in Oct. 1915. – *Pink Farm Cemetery*
Briggs, Harold	377226	Pte	kia 11/12/17	Age 20. Lived at Hollinwood. Son of Henry. – *Gorre British Cemetery*
Brigham, Thomas	300199	Pte	shot 4/6/18	Age 22. – *Walincourte Halte British Cemetery*
Brook, William	57466	Pte	kia 28/9/18	Age 18. 11, Charles St., Castleford. – *Vis-en-Artois M.M.*
Brown, Edward	376141	Pte	kia 6/5/18	186, Coalshaw Green Rd., Hollinwood. – *Couin New British Cemetery*
Brown, Edward	1269	Pte	kia 4/6/15	Age 21. Son of Edward & Mary, 120, Cow Hill, Chadderton.
Brown, George	276713	Pte	kia 11/12/17	Age 28. Son of George & Mary, 4, Sycamore St., Hightown, Manchester. – *Gorre British Cemetery*

Name	No.	Rnk	Fate	Notes – Buried/Commemorated
Brown, Jesse	1953	Pte	dow 6/8/15	Age 25. Lived at 24, Fulham St., Rochdale. Died in Chichester Hospital. His wife remarried. – *Chichester Cemetery, Sussex*
Brown, John	1019	Pte	kia 24/5/15	Enlisted at Oldham. – *Helles M.M.*
Brownbill, Richard	377981	Pte	kia 20/10/18	Born and enlisted at Liverpool. – *Belle Vue British Cemetery*
Buckley, Jonathan	33364	Cpl	kia 11/12/17	Age 23. Son of Jonathan & Ann of Shaw. – *Gorre British Cemetery*
Buckley, William	2224	Pte	kia 1/6/15	Age 19. Son of William & Mary, 39, Cornwall St., Werneth. – *Helles M.M.*
Burgess, John	2087	Pte	dow 10/6/15	Age 20. Son of James & Mary, 310, Higher King St., Hurst. Buried at sea. – *Helles M.M.*
Burgess, Ralph	2088	Pte	dow 29/10/15	Age 21. B Coy. Son of James & Mary, 310, Higher King St., Hurst. – *Lancashire Landing Cemetery*
Burke, John	996	Pte	dow 14/6/15	Age 23. Lived at 82, Lincoln St., Werneth. – *Lancashire Landing Cemetery*
Burrows, Harry	375839	Pte	died 23/10/18	Enlisted at Oldham. – *Mons Communal Cemetery*
Burrows, Reuben	452	Pte	died (dysentery, home) 11/12/15	Age 40. Lived at 23, Davies St., off Chadderton Rd., Oldham. – *Hollinwood Cemetery*
Bushell, Charles	18541	Pte	kia 11/12/17	Married, of 57, Romney St., Pendleton. – *Gorre British Cemetery*
Byrne, John	1862	Dmr	dow 10/6/15	Age 25. Born at Oldham. Son of Margaret of Hanley, Staffs. – *Pieta Military Cemetery (Malta)*
Cadman, John	375027	Pte	dow 6/4/18	Age 34. Husband of Elizabeth, 91, Warwick St., Werneth. – *Doullens Extension Cemetery No.1*
Calvert, Herbert	376208	Pte	kia 27/3/18	Age 23. Son of William & Hannah, 46, Chadderton Fold, Royton. – *Arras M.M.*
Carrington, Robinson	376580	Pte	kia 7/8/18	Enlisted at Oldham. – *Pozieres M.M.*
Carter, Walter	2092	Pte	dow 10/6/15	Enlisted at Oldham. – *Pieta Military Cemetery (Malta)*
Chadwick, Mansell	375336	Pte	kia 17/6/18	Lived in Middlesex. – *Bertrancourt Military Cemetery*
Chandley, Geoffrey	1900	Pte	kia 4/6/15	Age 33. Husband of Amy, 14, Iona St., Oldham. – *Helles M.M.*

Name	No.	Rnk	Fate	Notes – Buried/Commemorated
Chappell, Jonathan	375901	Pte	dow 14/9/17	Age 36. Son of Mary Ann McDermott and the late James Chappell. Enlisted at Glodwick. – *Brandhoek New Military Cemetery No.3*
Charlesworth, Joseph	2227	Pte	kia 19/6/15	Age 37. Married, of Back Hargreaves St., Oldham. Moulder at Hartford New Works. – *Helles M.M.*
Charnley, James	277563	Pte	dow 21/11/18	Age 30. Husband of Lily, 3, Ivy St., Blackburn. – *St Sever Cemetery Extension*
Cheetham, Tom	2305	Pte	kia 4/6/15	Age 22. D Coy. Son of John & Jane, 6, Armitage St., Oldham. – *Redoubt Cemetery*
Chester, Henry	245505	Pte	kia 20/10/18	Age 23. Lark Hill, Stockport. Formerly 110609 Duke of Lancaster's Own Yeomany. – *Belle Vue British Cemetery*
Claber, Thomas	2096	Pte	kia 2/6/15	Age 47. Husband of Brigit, 63, Hawksley St., Hollinwood. In the Volunteers for 19 years. Served in S.African War. Two sons in the 10th: Thomas dow 1917; James wounded June 1915. Wife remarried. – *Helles M.M.*
Claber, Thomas	375130	L/Cpl	dow 4/6/17	Age 20. D Coy. Son of Thomas & Brigit, 63, Hawksley St., Hollinwood. – *La Chapelette British Cemetery (Péronne)*
Clancy, James	2052	Pte	kia 4/6/15	Age 17. Son of James & Martha, 63, Napier St., Oldham. – *Helles M.M.*
Clark, Harry	644	Pte	kia 1/6/15	Age 21. Lived at 17, Stanley St., Chadderton. – *Helles M.M.*
Clarkson, John	376237	Pte	dow 14/7/18	Enlisted at Oldham. – *Gezaincourt Communal Cemetery Extension*
Clegg, Hugh	1837	Pte	kia 4/6/15	Lived at 15, Humphrey St., Oldham. – *Helles M.M.*
Clegg, Percy	1788	Pte	kia 12/7/15	Age 18. Lived at 71, Cowhill, Chadderton. – *Helles M.M.*
Clutton, Thomas	375154	Sgt MM	kia 31/10/18	Age 23. Son of Ellen, 17, Victor St., Hollins Rd., Hollinwood. – *Bancourt British Cemetery*
Coates, John	377151	Pte	kia 5/4/18	Age 27. Husband of Jesse (Cooke), 5, Oldham Rd., Failsworth. – *Arras M.M.*
Cocker, Harold	2906	Pte	died (pneumonia) 5/9/15	Age 35. Lived at 10, Temple St., Waterhead. Formerly 2/10th Battalion. – *Pieta Military Cemetery (Malta)*

Name	No.	Rnk	Fate	Notes – Buried/Commemorated
Colman, John	673	Cpl	dow 7/8/15	Age 24. Husband of Ellen, 10, Fountain St., Oldham. – Redoubt Cemetery
Coles, Charles	61022	Cpl	kia 20/10/18	Born and lived in Monmouth. – Belle Vue British Cemetery
Collinge, Harry	376204	Pte	kia 24/12/17	Husband of J.Gibson, 43, Napier St., Oldham. – Gorre British Cemetery
Connolly, Arthur	1740	Pte	kia 4/6/15	Age 20. Son of Mary, 98, Eldon St., Oldham. – Helles M.M.
Cook, George	2232	Pte	kia 19/6/15	Married, of 48, Edge Lane, Oldham. Enlisted in Sept.1914. Served 4 years in West Riding TF. – Helles M.M.
Cook, Wilfred	3082	Pte	kia 14/8/15	Age 23. Son of Thomas & Mary, Whams House, Den Lane, Springhead. Formerly 2/10th Battalion. – Helles M.M.
Cookes, Charles	202959	Pte	dow 27/3/18	Age 28. 47, Dorset St., Hulme. – Etaples British Cemetery
Cooper, John	2586	Pte	kia 28/9/15	Age 18. 14, Wrigley Square, Lees. – Helles M.M.
Coppins, Frederick	54213	Pte	dow 15/11/18	Born and enlisted at Gravesend. Formerly 33552 East Surrey Regt. – St Sever Cemetery Extension
Cotterall, Robert	74600	Pte	dow 20/4/18	Age 18. Son of John & Jane, 40, Lord Nelson St., Liverpool. Native of Blackburn. – Bagneux British Cemetery
Coyne, Richard	375539	Pte	kia (gas) 11/12/17	Age 40. Real name was Kilcoyne. Son of Richard & Mary of Oldham. – Gorre British Cemetery
Crawshaw, Gilbert	1624	Pte	dow 14/8/15	Age 19. Lived at 26, Albert St., Mumps. Plate moulder at Asa Lees. Formerly 2/10th Battalion. – Helles M.M.
Crew, Thomas	1470	L/Cpl	kia 4/6/15	Age 21. Son of Thomas & Louisa, 16, Rivington St., Oldham. – Helles M.M.
Crompton, Reuben	375726	Pte	kia 14/9/17	Age 22. Son of George, 4, Jane St., Chadderton. – Hooge Crater Cemetery
Crossley, Fred	74594	Pte	kia	Age 18. Son of Jeremy & Elizabeth, 96, Geraldine St., Blackburn. – Couin New British Cemetery
Culshaw, Richard	200199	Pte	dow 20/1/18	Enlisted at Leigh. – Longuenesse Souvenir Cemetery
Currie, John	1961	Pte	dow 23/5/15	Age 28. Lived at 7, Ethel St., Hathershaw. – Lancashire Landing Cemetery

Name	No.	Rnk	Fate	Notes – *Buried/Commemorated*
Currie, William	943	Pte	died 14/6/15	Age 23. Lived at 7, Ethel St., Hathershaw. – *Pieta Military Cemetery (Malta)*
Dalton, Albert	1190	Pte	kia 4/6/15	Age 19. Enlisted at Oldham. – *Helles M.M.*
Daly, John	74605	Pte	dow 16/4/18	Born and enlisted at Cardiff. – *St Sever Communal Cemetery Extension*
Darlington, Edward	375712	Pte	kia 3/4/18	Lived at 103, Greenwood St., Oldham. – *St Amand British Cemetery*
Davies, Alfred	1414	Pte	dow 25/6/15	Age 21. Lived at 19, Highfield St., Oldham. (Spelt 'Davis' in *Soldiers Died*) – *Lancashire Landing Cemetery*
Davies, John W.	245097	Pte	kia 23/8/18	Lived in Denbigh. – *Queen's Cemetery*
Dean, Charles	1259	Pte	kia 19/6/15	Age 19. Lived at 350, Shaw Rd., Hathershaw. His father was a Cpl in the 2/10th Battalion. Piecer at Tay Mill. – *Helles M.M.*
Dobson, William	33713	Pte	kia 22/8/18	Lived at Heywood. – *Sucrerie Military Cemetery (Colincamps)*
Dodgson, Francis	42569	Pte	died 4/3/19	Lived at Leeds. – *Charleroi Communal Cemetery*
Donovan, James	78	Pte	died 26/12/14	Age 34. Lived at 223, West St., Oldham. Killed by a tram in Cairo. – *Cairo War Memorial Cemetery (Egypt)*
Doran, John	1655	Pte	kia 4/6/15	Age 22. Son of Thomas & Mary, 8, Lytton St., Chadderton. – *Helles M.M.*
Drabble, Frank	1312	Pte	kia 3/6/15	Lived at 22, Church St., Oldham – *Helles M.M.*
Drayton, George	376909	Pte	kia 5/4/18	Born and enlisted at Sheffield. – *Arras M.M.*
Drinkwater, Ernest	2041	Sgt	kia 19/6/15	Age 32. Lived at 52, Littlebank St., Oldham. Wife, Jane, remarried. Joined the Volunteers aged 15. S.Africa and Long Service Medals. Resigned as Clr-Sgt in March 1914. Rejoined in Aug.1914. – *Helles M.M.*
Dunkerley, Fred	50	CSM	kia 4/6/15	Age 35. Son of Charlotte, 17, Dunkerley St., and husband of Hannah, 19, Dunkerley St., Oldham. Holder of Volunteer Long Service and Queen's S.Africa Medals. His brother CSM Cyrus also served with the battalion on Gallipoli. – *Helles M.M.*

Name	No.	Rnk	Fate	Notes – Buried/Commemorated
Dyson, Thomas	375262	Pte	kia 26/6/17	Enlisted at Oldham. – *Ruyaulcourt Military Cemetery*
Dyson, Walter	375795	Pte	dow 3/7/17	Age 19. 40, Hollin Hall St., Greenacres. – *Rocquigny-Equancourt Road British Cemetery*
Eastwood, Harold	1608	Pte	dow 5/6/15	Age 19. Lived at 267, Featherstall Rd. North, Oldham. Piecer. Buried at sea. – *Helles M.M.*
Edwards, Richard	670	Pte	dow 17/6/15	– *Addolorata Cemetery (Malta)*
Ellery, Arthur	44124	Pte	dow 28/10/17	Age 20. Son of Frank and Elizabeth, 12, Belvoir Ave., Levenshulme – *Zuydcoote Military Cemetery*
Elson, Edmund	1635	Pte	kia 19/6/15	Age 21. Son of Harold & Hannah, 94, Henshaw St.,Chadderton. Piecer at Manor Mill. – *Helles M.M.*
Elson, Tom	1785	Pte	kia 8/9/15	Son of Harold & Hannah, 94, Henshaw St., Chadderton. His brother, Frank 1788, was wounded in August 1915. – *Helles M.M.*
Etchells, Fred	376730	Pte	kia 20/10/18	Lived at Chadderton. – *Belle Vue British Cemetery*
Etchells, Joshua	375452	Pte	kia 8/9/17	Lived at Royton. – *Tyne Cot M.M.*
Evans, John	375910	L/Cpl	dow 18/4/18	Age 25. Son of Emily, 21, Vernon St., Oldham. – *Doullens British Cemetery Extension No.1*
Evans, George	302480	Pte	kia 20/10/18	Age 32. Husband of Gladys, Pear Tree House, Kendal. Native of Liverpool. – *Belle Vue British Cemetery*
Exley, Harry	2594	Pte	kia 14/8/15	Enlisted at Oldham. – *Helles M.M.*
Fallows, Samuel	1120	L/Cpl	dow 10/6/15	Age 23. Lived at 2, Kirkham St., Oldham. – *Pieta Military Cemetery (Malta)*
Fannon, Thomas	377984	Pte	dow 8/11/18	Lived at St Albans. – *Hautmont Communal Cemetery*
Fenlon, Henry	44220	Pte	kia 28/9/18	Age 34. Lived at Liverpool. Formerly 36514 King's Liverpool Regt. – *Bertincourt Chateau British Cemetery*
Finney, Arthur	758800	Pte	kia 28/9/18	Born and enlisted at Manchester. – *Vis-en-Artois M.M.*
Fisher, William	5241	Pte	kia 2/10/17	Age 20. Son of James & Ann, 1, Albany St., Oldham. Transferred to 8th Coy Labour Corps. – *Birr Cross Roads Cemetery*

Name	No.	Rnk	Fate	Notes – Buried/Commemorated
Fitton, Elijah	905	Pte	kia 25/5/15	Age 32. Married, of Lane Head, Lees. Wife remarried. Served with Volunteers and Territorials for about 15 years. His brother Albert also served in the 10th. Moulder at Platts. – *Helles M.M.*
Fitton, John	1416	Pte	kia 4/6/15	Age 21. Lived at 2, Cambridge St., Royton. – *Helles M.M.*
Fitzgerald, George	2108	Pte	kia 4/6/15	Lived at 13, Back Peter St., Oldham. – *Helles M.M.*
Fleetham, Joseph	377026	Cpl	kia 11/12/17	Married, from West Hartlepool. Formerly 9074 DLI. – *Gorre British Cemetery*
Fletcher, Albert	2314	Pte	kia 4/6/15	Lived at Chadderton. – *Helles M.M.*
Fletcher, John, E.	376311	Pte	dow 6/4/18	Age 36. Husband of Annie, 9,Salt St., Oldham. – *Doullens British Cemetery Extension No.1*
Fletcher, John, W.	203071	Pte	dow 4/4/18	Age 29. Husband of Dorothy, 1, The Meade,Chorlton. – *Doullens British Cemetery Extension No.1*
Fletcher, Leonard	5116	Pte	kia 6/11/16	Lived at Hulme. – *Kantara War Memorial Cemetery (Egypt)*
Foden, Samuel	34112	Pte	dow 16/4/18	Age 21. Lived at Congleton. – *Doullens British Cemetery Extension No.1*
Ford, John	2313	Pte	died (dysentery) 24/9/15	Age 21. A Coy. Lived at 10, Alma Place, Bankside St., Oldham. – *Chatby War Memorial Cemetery (Egypt)*
Foulkes, Thomas	43499	Pte	shot 21/11/17	Age 21. – *Loos M.M.*
Fozzard, Alfred	1609	Pte	kia 24/5/15	Age 18. A Coy. Son of Walter & Rose, 39, Mustard St., Glodwick. – *Helles M.M.*
Francis, Sam	993	Cpl	died (home) 19/11/15	Age 23. Lived at Oldham. – *Greenacres Cemetery*
Frost, William	375188	L/Cpl	kia 18/7/18	Age 23. Son of Harry & Mary, 9, Springfield St., Higginshaw Lane, Oldham. – *Bertrancourt Military Cemetery*
Gales, Martin	377011	L/Cpl	kia 24/5/17	Born and lived at Darlington. Formerly 20914 KOYLI. – *Neuville-Bourjonval British Cemetery*
Gardener, Thomas	2315	Sgt	kia 9/8/15	Age 34. Lived at 4, Bancroft St., Oldham. Formerly 2/10thBattalion. – *Redoubt Cemetery*
Gibson, William	203498	Pte	kia 23/8/18	Born and enlisted at Wigan. – *Queen's Cemetery*

Name	No.	Rnk	Fate	Notes – Buried/Commemorated
Gledhill, Harry	1722	Pte	kia 4/6/15	Age 24. Married, of 17, Peter Row, Royton. Wife remarried. – *Helles M.M.*
Goldsby, John	1560	Pte	dow 7/6/15	Age 20. Son of John & Harriet, 5, Ely St., Werneth. – *Helles M.M.*
Goodier, James	375912	Pte	kia 25/3/18	Lived at Bardsley. – *Arras M.M.*
Goodier, Wallace	78911	Pte	died 17/12/18	Lived at Stockport. – *Solesmes British Cemetery*
Gorbutt, Fred		L/Cpl	kia 4/6/15	Lived at 22, Trafalgar St., Oldham. – *Helles M.M.*
Grady, Austin	1535	L/Cpl	kia 19/6/15	Age 24. Son of Thomas & Ann, 10, Moorhey St., Oldham. Had served in the Volunteers. Piecer at Mumps Mill. – *Helles M.M.*
Greaves, Lewis	1887	Pte	kia 4/6/15	Lived at 17, Kirkbank St., Oldham. – *Helles M.M.*
Greaves, Wilfred	1201	Pte	died 30/6/15	Enlisted at Oldham. – *East Mundros Military Cemetery (Lemnos)*
Greaves, William	2456	Pte	kia 14/8/15	Age 18. Son of James & Martha, 11, Stuart St., Coppice. Formerly 2/10th Battalion. Worked at Platts. – *Helles M.M.*
Green, John A.	375123	Pte	dow 28/3/18	Age 27. Lived at 102, Trafalgar St., Oldham. – *Bucquoy Road Cemetery*
Greenwood, Fred	1258	Pte	kia 3/6/15	Age 21. Son of John & Ruth, 16, Marble St., Oldham. – *Redoubt Cemetery*
Greenwood, John	1361	Cpl	kia 9/8/15	Age 25. Lived at 2, Court St., Derker St., Oldham. – *Redoubt Cemetery*
Greenwood, William	21217	Pte	dow 8/11/18	Age 25. Lived at Todmorden. – *Hautmont Communal Cemetery*
Grundy, Herbert	203386	Pte	dow 14/11/17	Age 37. Married, of 13, Hoxton Grove, Elland Rd., Leeds. – *Adinkerke Military Cemetery*
Hadfield, Albert	2111	Pte	kia 4/6/15	Enlisted at Oldham. – *Helles M.M.*
Hadfield, Fred	1975	Cpl	kia 4/6/15	Age 45. Husband of Alice, 33, Sussex St., Oldham. Holder of Volunteer Long Service Medal. – *Helles M.M.*
Hadfield, John	823	Pte	dow 13/6/15	Enlisted at Oldham. – *Pieta Military Cemetery (Malta)*
Hadfield, Victor	3006	Pte	kia 13/8/15	Age 27. Son of James & Alice, 4, Cranbrook St., Oldham. Formerly 2/10th Battalion. – *Redoubt Cemetery*

Name	No.	Rnk	Fate	Notes – Buried/Commemorated
Hague, George	1839	Pte	dow 24/10/15	Enlisted at Oldham. – *Pink Farm Cemetery*
Hague, Harold	1314	Pte	kia 12/6/15	Age 21. Lived at 3, Brook St., Chadderton. – *Helles M.M.*
Hague, Thomas	2925	Pte	kia 30/9/15	Age 34. Lived at 1, Davison St., Werneth. – *Twelve Tree Copse Cemetery*
Hall, Joseph	47376	Pte	kia 22/6/18	Age 20. Enlisted at Manchester. Lived at 200, Hawthorne Hill, West Bromwich. – *Bertrancourt Military Cemetery*
Hallam, James	2607	Pte	kia 13/8/15	Age 18. Son of Leopold & Helen, 63, Millgate, Hollins. Formerly 2/10th Battalion. – *Helles M.M.*
Hardman, Stephen	376644	L/Cpl	kia 23/8/18	Age 34. Husband of Clara, 474, Manchester Rd.,Shaw. – *Queen's Cemetery*
Hargreaves, Alfred	11827	Pte	dow 24/10/18	Age 26. Son of John & Sarah, 83, Chadwick Rd., Eccles. – *Etaples British Cemetery*
Hargreaves, Frank	376189	Pte	kia 7/4/18	Enlisted at Oldham. – *Bienvillers Military Cemetery*
Harrison, James	3608	Pte	kia 6/11/16	Enlisted at Oldham. – *Kantara War Memorial Cemetery (Egypt)*
Harrison, Samuel	375737	L/Cpl	dow 9/9/18	Enlisted at Oldham. – *St Sever Cemetery Extension*
Harrop, James	376649	L/Cpl	kia 7/11/18	Age 29. Lived at 6, Constantine St., Greenacres. His wife remarried and emigrated to Canada. – *Maubeuge Centre Cemetery*
Hayes, George	2113	Pte	kia 4/6/15	Lived at Littleborough. – *Helles M.M.*
Healey, Dennis	22638	Pte	kia 31/8/18	Age 35. Son of Patrick, 47, Elizabeth St., Oldham Rd., Manchester. – *Bancourt British Cemetery*
Healey, Percy	376508	Pte	dow 23/11/17	Age 29. Son of George & Margaret, Darwen. – *Preston (New Hall Lane) Cemetery*
Healey, Thomas	1492	Pte	dow 3/6/15	Age 19. Enlisted at Oldham. – *Lancashire Landing Cemetery*
Henthorn, Harry	375350	Pte	kia 11/12/17	Married, of 94, Bridgewater St., Oldham. – *Gorre British Cemetery*
Hewett, William	41332	Pte	kia 17/6/18	Married, lived at Eccleston, near Chester. – *Bertrancourt Military Cemetery*
Heys, Fred	2118	Pte	dow (home)14/3/16	Age 21. Lived at 102, Roundthorn Rd., Oldham. – *Greenacres Cemetery*

Name	No.	Rnk	Fate	Notes – Buried/Commemorated
Heywood, Harry	376831	Pte	dow 10/11/18	Age 26. Lived at 117, Cambridge St., Werneth. – *Hollinwood Cemetery*
Heywood, Richard	377235	Pte	kia 11/12/17	Age 20. Son of 319, Shaw Rd., Royton. – *Gorre British Cemetery*
Highton, Harry	376355	Pte	kia 26/6/17	Age 20. Son of Betty, 55, Beech St., Shaw. – *Thiepval M.M.*
Hilton, James	2613	Cpl	kia	Age 25. Lived at 18, Carnarvon St., Hollinwood. Formerly 2/10th Battalion. – *Azmak Cemetery*
Hinchliffe, Harry	560	Sgt	kia 8/6/18	Born at Saddleworth. – *Bertrancourt Military Cemetery*
Hitchen, Alfred	1351	Pte	dow 13/8/15	Age 22. A Coy. Son of John & Mary, 29, Yale St., Oldham. – *Lancashire Landing Cemetery*
Holden, John	2472	Pte	dow 8/9/15	Age 31. Husband of Elizabeth, 23, Cottam St., Oldham. Formerly 2/10th Battalion. Buried at sea. – *Helles M.M.*
Holden, Samuel	1083	Pte	died 26/12/14	Lived at 24, Library Lane, Oldham. Killed falling from the Pyramids. – *Cairo War Memorial Cemetery (Egypt)*
Holden, Squire	1763	Pte	kia 4/6/15	Age 28. Sister lived at 79, Franklin St., Oldham. – *Helles M.M.*
Holland, Harry	1648	Pte	dow 6/11/16	Age 34. Lived at 373, Oldham Rd., Hollinwood. – *Kantara War Memorial Cemetery (Egypt)*
Holmes, Elias	375369	Pte	died 26/2/17	Lived at Hollinwood. – *Tel-el-Kebir War Cemetery (Egypt)*
Holt, George	376316	Pte	kia 26/6/17	Age 19. Son of Brierley & Emma, 32, Nile St., Oldham. – *Thiepval M.M.*
Holt, Wilfred	1866	Pte	dow 7/6/15	Age 19. Lived at 75, Nile St., Oldham. Youngest of four brothers in the 10th. Robert was invalided home in 1915. Tin plate worker. Buried at sea. – *Helles M.M.*
Hornby, William	301938	Pte	kia 20/10/18	Enlisted at St Helens. Formerly 19850 South Lancashire Regt. – *Belle Vue British Cemetery*
Horton, Ernest	1290	L/Cpl	kia 3/6/15	Lived at 14, Westend St., Oldham. – *Helles M.M.*
Howard, Charles	377189	Pte	dow 4/6/17	Age 26. Son of William & Mary, 4, Hathershaw St., Oldham. – *La Chapelette British Cemetery (Péronne)*

Name	No.	Rnk	Fate	Notes – Buried/Commemorated
Howard, Orlando	1906	Pte	kia 4/6/15	Lived at Church St., Oldham. Two brothers in the 10th and one in 2/7th West Riding Regt. Brother J.H. (1905) was wounded on 4/6/15. – *Helles M.M.*
Hoyle, Frank	2619	Pte	died (dysentery) 2/10/15	Age 25. Lived at 68, Sylvan St., Oldham. Formerly 2/10th Battalion. – *Pieta Military Cemetery (Malta)*
Hufton, William	39	Sgt	kia 9/8/15	Age 24. Son of William & Betty, 18, Anchor St., Shaw. – *Redoubt Cemetery*
Humphreys, Joseph	252374	Pte	kia 23/8/18	Lived at Salford. – *Vis-en-Artois M.M.*
Hurley, Herbert	1548	Pte	kia 4/6/15	Enlisted at Oldham. – *Helles M.M.*
Hurst, Thomas	1628	Pte	died (home) 4/5/16	Age 19. Lived at 33, Webster St., Oldham. – *Chadderton Cemetery*
Hutchins, Ernest	375343	Pte MM	kia 20/10/18	Lived at Oldham. – *Belle Vue British Cemetery*
Isherwood, James	377190	Pte	kia 18/7/18	Age 31. Son of James & Annie, Newton Heath. – *Bertrancourt Military Cemetery*
Jackson, Harry	1980	Pte	kia 4/6/15	Lived at 48, Hobson St., Chadderton. – *Helles M.M.*
Jackson, John	61252	Pte	died 22/11/18	Age 20. Born and enlisted at Oldham. Son of William & Hannah. – *Caudry British Cemetery*
Jackson, John	350641	Pte	kia 20/10/18	Enlisted at Ashton-u-Lyne. Formerly 204481 South Lancashire Regt. – *Belle Vue British Cemetery*
Jackson, John W.	376967	Pte	kia 6/9/17	Age 31. Lived at 31, Coronation Terrace, Wakefield. Born at Failsworth. – *Tyne Cot M.M.*
Johnson, Ernest	375095	Sgt	kia 24/12/17	Married, of 43, Horsedge St., Oldham. – *Gorre British Cemetery*
Johnson, John	1600	Pte	died (enteric) 24/6/15	Age 18. Born at Saddleworth. Had been wounded on 4/6/15 and evacuated. – *Pieta Military Cemetery (Malta)*
Jones, Edwin	375613	L/Cpl	kia	Age 20. C Coy Son of Robert & Annie of Oldham. – *Bertrancourt Military Cemetery*
Jones, Fred	659	Pte	kia 24/11/15	Age 33. – *Twelve Tree Copse Cemetery*
Jones, Frederick	303176	Pte	kia 31/8/18	Age 25. Born and lived in Denbigh. – *Adanac Military Cemetery*

Name	No.	Rnk	Fate	Notes – Buried/Commemorated
Jones, George Alf.	2127	Cpl	kia 9/8/15	Age 31. Lived at 161, Garforth St., Chadderton. A brother, 2128, was invalided home in January 1915. Alf was wounded on 19/6/15 and rejoined on 23/7/15. Worked at Platts. – *Redoubt Cemetery*
Jones, James	295079	Pte	kia	Age 25. Lived at 19, Price St., Ancoats. – *Arras M.M.*
Jones, Tom	377078	Pte	dow 12/12/17	Born and enlisted at Wigan, lived in Portugal. – *Merville Communal Cemetery Extension*
Jowett, Charles	220270	Pte	kia 18/4/18	Born at Wigan. – *Couin New British Cemetery*
Kelly, James	1663	Pte	kia 4/6/15	Lived at 12, Gladstone St., Oldham. – *Helles M.M.*
Kelly, James	375667	Pte	died 24/6/18 as a pow	Enlisted at Oldham. – *Niederzwehren Cemetery Cassel, Germany*
Kent, Fred	375668	L/Sgt	kia 5/8/18	Lived at Hollinwood. – *Bertrancourt Military Cemetery*
Kenworthy, Harold	3118	Pte	died (septic poisoning) 3/12/15	Age 26. Lived at 30, Sussex St.,Oldham. – *Lancashire Landing Cemetery*
Kenyon, Ernest	375165	Pte	dow 23/5/17	Age 24. Son of Clara & Ben, 94, Huxley St., Lees Rd., Oldham. – *La Chapelette British Cemetery (Péronne)*
Kerr, James	1981	Pte	died (dysentery, home) 17/11/15	Age 31. Lived at 113, Radclyffe St. Oldham. – *Chadderton Cemetery*
Kershaw, Alfred	376440	Pte	kia 31/8/18	Married, of 10, Clovelly Ave., Hollinwood. – *Bancourt British Cemetery*
Kidd, Walter	829	Cpl	kia 4/6/15	Age 22. Son of Edith, 240, Manchester St., Oldham. Former Blue Coat School. – *Helles M.M.*
King, Thomas	375212	Pte	dow (home) 26/4/18	Age 28. Lived at 22, Newton St., Oldham. – *Greenacres Cemetery*
Kirkman, Harry	375391	Cpl	kia 22/6/18	Age 24. Son of Peter & Mary of Hollinwood. – *Bertrancourt Military Cemetery*
Kirkman, James	2134	Pte	dow 22/7/15	Lived at 20, Mold St., Coldhurst. – *Lancashire Landing Cemetery*
Kite, Nathaniel	352399	Pte	kia 22/6/18	Born at Pendleton. Formerly 6291 Border Regt. – *Bertrancourt Military Cemetery*

Name	No.	Rnk	Fate	Notes – Buried/Commemorated
Kitson, Taylor	213	Sgt	kia 4/6/15	Age 33. Husband of Annie, 25, Tudor St., Coppice. – *Helles M.M.*
Knott, Harry	376150	Pte	dow 7/11/18	Age 26. Son of Joseph and Lois of Chadderton. – *Le Quesnoy Communal Cemetery*
Knott, Thomas	1917	Pte	kia 14/10/15	Age 27. Husband of 34, Edith St., Hathershaw. – *Twelve Tree Copse Cemetery*
Lally, Thomas	1832	Pte	died (smallpox) 7/3/15	Lived at 3, Renshaw St., Hollinwood. – *Cairo War Memorial Cemetery (Egypt)*
Lane, Robert	2136	Pte	kia 18/5/15	Age 32. Married, of 18, Mold St., Coldhurst. Wife remarried. – *Skew Bridge Cemetery*
Langley, Charles	375228	Sgt DCM	dow 1/9/18	Age 22. Lived at 29, Anchor St., Oldham. – *Bagneux British Cemetery*
Lawson, Walter	375809	Pte	kia 24/12/17	Age 22. Son of Charles & Amelia, 94, Goddard St. Oldham. – *Gorre British Cemetery*
Lawton, Fred	375490	Pte	dow 25/4/17	Age 21. Wounded May 1915 Son of 63, Radclyffe St., Chadderton. – *Péronne Communal Cemetery Extension*
Leach, Lester	376502	Pte	kia 31/8/18	Age 27. Son of Samuel & Eliza, 291, Featherstall Rd., Oldham. – *Manchester Cemetery (Riencourt)*
Lees, John W.	376578	Pte	kia 27/3/18	Lived at Shaw. – *Arras M.M.*
Lewis, Harvey	376354	L/Cpl	kia 22/8/18	Age 22. Son of Harvey & Clara, 1, Pink St., Godson St., Oldham. – *Sucrerie Military Cemetery (Colincamps)*
Little, Thomas	1799	Pte	dow 23/8/15	Enlisted at Oldham. – *Chatby War Cemetery (Egypt)*
Littlewood, Thomas	3020	Pte	died (dysentery, home) 11/11/15	Age 35. Lived at 12, Sarah Moor, Oldham. Formerly 2/10th Battalion. – *Netley Military Cemetery*
Littlewood, William	276072	Pte	died 28/10/18	Age 20. Son of William & Sarah, 13, Harold St., Old Trafford. – *Mount Huon British Cemetery*
Lloyd, Fred	251075	Pte	kia 7/11/18	Age 23. Enlisted at Manchester. – *Maubeuge Centre Cemetery*
Lockwood, Alexander	3611	Pte	kia 6/11/16	Age 28. Lived at 64, Vulcan St., Ripponden Rd., Oldham. – *Kantara War Cemetery (Egypt)*
Lomas, John	395012	Pte	kia 1/4/18	Lived at 13, Mornington St., Chorlton. – *Couin New British Cemetery*

Name	No.	Rnk	Fate	Notes – Buried/Commemorated
Lycett, Edward	376990	Pte	dow 29/3/18	Age 34. Born at Sheffield. Formerly 4994 KOYLI. – *Gezaincourt Communal Cemetery Extension*
Lynn, John	2264	Pte	kia 4/6/15	Married, of 17, Bankside St., Oldham. Enlisted 4/9/14. – *Helles M.M.*
Mason, James	376462	Pte	kia 8/11/17	Age 37. Husband of Rhoda, 12, Burnley Lane, Chadderton. – *Coxyde Military Cemetery*
Mason, William	2150	Cpl	kia 4/6/15	Age 37. Husband of Edna, 82, Alfred St., Werneth. – *Helles M.M.*
Massey, Samuel	2634	Pte	dow 16/12/15	Age 22. Lived at 337, Manchester Rd., Hollinwood. – *Lancashire Landing Cemetery*
Massey, James	376384	Pte	dow 26/3/18	Age 35. Husband of Clara, 31, Bridgewater St., Oldham. – *Bac-du-Sud British Cemetery*
Maxwell, John	2151	Pte	died 1/7/15	Enlisted at Ashton-u-Lyne. – *Pieta Military Cemetery (Malta)*
McConnell, Thomas	375367	Pte	kia 4/6/17	Born at Ashton-u-Lyne. – *Neuville-Bourjonval British Cemetery*
McNulty, John	375966	Pte	kia 24/4/17	Age 28. D Coy. Wife remarried (Worrall) – *Thiepral M.M.*
Mead, Joshua	2152	Pte	kia 4/6/15	Enlisted at Oldham. – *Helles M.M.*
Mellor, Alfred	1797	Pte	died 25/6/15	Born at Royton. – *Cairo War Cemetery*
Mellor, Frank	1864	Pte	kia 9/8/15	Age 21. Lived at 6, Middleton Rd., Royton. – *Helles M.M.*
Mellor, Thomas	377165	Pte	kia 5/4/18	Married, of 4, Glebe St., Chadderton. – *Bienvillers Military Cemetery*
Mewett, John	57419	Pte	kia 7/8/18	Lived at Maida Hill, London. Formerly L/46698 RFA. – *Bertrancourt Military Cemetery*
Miller, George	74506	Pte	dow 22/6/18	Age 19. Son of Robert & Eliza of Chorlton. – *Bertrancourt Military Cemetery*
Miller, Joe	4981	Pte	died (enteric) 24/4/16	Age 36. Married, of 15, Little London Place, Sheffield. Formerly KOYLI – *Cairo War Cemetery (Egypt)*
Mills, Herbert	1528	Pte	kia 4/6/15	Age 19. Born at Oldham. – *Helles M.M.*
Mills, Walter	375499	Pte VC	kia 11/12/17	Married, of 10, Smith St., Oldham. – *Gorre British Cemetery*
Mills, William	2320	Pte	kia 4/6/15	Enlisted at Oldham. – *Helles M.M.*

Name	No.	Rnk	Fate	Notes – Buried/Commemorated
Milner, Joseph	375754	Sgt MM	kia 20/10/18	Lived at Chadderton – *Belle Vue British Cemetery*
Mitchell, Walter	377180	Pte	dow 5/10/17	Age 30. Son of William & Mary of Oldham. – *Greenacres Cemetery*
Molineux, Thomas	377920	Pte	kia 23/8/18	Married, of 70, Coral St., Chorlton. Wife remarried. – *Vis-en-Artois M.M.*
Monks, George	2155	Pte	kia 4/6/15	Age 21. Lived at 21, Cecil St., Stockport. – *Helles M.M.*
Moores, John	377070	Pte	dow 13/7/18	Lived at Dyserth, Flint. Native of Longsight. – *Gezaincourt Communal Cemetery Extension*
Moran, Fred	2954	Pte	dow 14/8/15	Age 21. Lived at 27, Canal St., Hollinwood. Formerly 2/10th Battalion. Buried at sea. – *Helles M.M.*
Morecroft, William	1591	Pte	kia 4/6/15	Born at Oldham. – *Helles M.M.*
Morgan, Harry	2505	Pte	dow 24/12/15	Age 27. Lived at 4, St Stephen St., Oldham. Buried at sea. – *Helles M.M.*
Morgan, John	1252	Pte	dow 30/5/15	Age 20. Born at Glodwick. – *East Mundros Military Cemetery (Lemnos)*
Morgan, Thomas	1677	Pte	kia 4/6/15	Age 20. D Coy. Son of Thomas & Margaret, Tregarth, Bangor. – *Helles M.M.*
Morgan, William	377166	Pte	kia 4/6/17	Age 25. Son of George & Lydia of Oldham. – *Neuville-Bourjonval British Cemetery*
Murphy, John	755	Pte	kia 4/6/15	Lived at Chadderton. – *Helles M.M.*
Nanson, William	1745	Sgt	kia 4/6/15	Age 34. Husband of Margaret, 192, Horsedge St., Oldham. Served in the South Africa Campaign. – *Helles M.M.*
Needham, James	2270	Pte	dow 8/6/15	Enlisted at Oldham. – *Lancashire Landing Cemetery*
Needham, Joseph	375682	L/Sgt	kia 8/6/18	Enlisted at Oldham. – *Bertrancourt Military Cemetery*
Nelson, George	1567	Pte	kia 19/6/15	Age 22. Son of Thomas & Mary, 77, Wrigley Head, Failsworth. Worked at Moston Pit. – *Helles M.M.*
Neville, Michael	376960	Pte	kia 11/12/17	Age 25. Husband of Margaret of Prestwich, Northumberland. – *Gorre British Cemetery*
Newman, Ernest	376195	Pte	dow 7/11/18	Lived in Co. Mayo. – *Maubeuge Centre Cemetery*
Newton, Harold	376180	Pte	kia 14/7/18	Age 21. Son of William & Lizzie, 11, Westfield St., Chadderton. – *Bertrancourt Military Cemetery*

Name	No.	Rnk	Fate	Notes – Buried/Commemorated
Nicholas, David	302301	Pte	kia 20/10/18	Lived in Pembrokshire. – *Belle Vue British Cemetery*
Nicholls, Frederick	45519	Pte	dow 11/4/18	Age 20. Son of John & Martha, 2, Palm St., Oldham. – *Etaples British Cemetery*
Norcross, Henry	378008	Pte	kia 8/6/18	Age 23. Son of David & Mary, 11, Prince George St.,Oldham. – *Bertrancourt Military Cemetery*
Norman, Arthur	1431	Pte	died (enteric) 11/7/15	Age 22. Lived at 6, Tudor St., Coppice. – *Cairo War Cemetery (Egypt)*
Ogden, Arthur,	1994	Pte	kia 21/5/15	Age 23. B Coy. Lived at 50, Coppice St., Oldham. Had served three years in the battalion and rejoined in Aug.1914. Clerk at Platt Brothers. Formerly Hulme Grammar School. – *Helles M.M.*
Ogden, Ernest	375626	Pte	kia 30/1/18	Age 25. Attached to TMB. Son of Albert & Mary, 28, Radnor St., Werneth. – *Gorre British Cemetery*
Ogden, Herbert	375824	Pte	kia 1/4/18	Age 41. Wounded May 1915. Husband of Sarah Ann, 30, Mount Pleasant St., Oldham. – *Couin New British Cemetery*
Ogden, James	1451	Pte	kia 9/8/15	Age 20. Born at Heyside. – *Helles M.M.*
Olive, Edmund	1590	Pte	dow 16/5/15	Age 18. C Coy. Lived at 16, Peak St., Werneth. Employed at Platts Spindle Works. – *Skew Bridge Cemetery*
Openshaw, John	1554	Pte	kia 19/6/15	Age 22. Lived at 1, Towler St., Radcliffe St., Oldham. – *Helles M.M.*
Owen, Richard	1727	Pte	kia 13/8/15	Born at Glasgow. Enlisted at Oldham. – *Helles M.M.*
Owen, Thomas	377284	Pte	died 6/5/18	Born and enlisted at Manchester. – *Doullens Communal Cemetery Extension No.2*
Palmer, Richard	54210	Pte	kia 20/10/18	Lived in Sussex. Formerly 20714 Royal Sussex Regt. – *Belle Vue British Cemetery*
Patchett, John		Pte	kia 16/7/15	Age 20. Lived at 1, Bar Gap Rd., Oldham. – *Helles M.M.*
Percy, Cyril	303637	Pte	dow 8/11/18	Lived at Wallasey. Formerly 381389 King's Liverpool Regt. Cemetery register has him as 1/8th Manchester. – *Caudry British Cemetery*
Pickering, Harry	2273	Pte	kia 4/6/15	Age 22. D Coy. Lived at 154, Chadderton Rd., Oldham. – *Helles M.M.*

Name	No.	Rnk	Fate	Notes – Buried/Commemorated
Pickering, Thomas	303939	Pte	kia 7/11/18	Married, of 5, Barrow St., Salford. – *Maubeuge Centre Cemetery*
Pickles, Wilson	3283	Pte	dow 5/12/15	Age 18. Lived at 32, Malton St., Oldham. A postman. – *Lancashire Landing Cemetery*
Pinder, John	902	Pte	dow 6/6/15	Age 29. Husband of Minnie, 51, Constantine St., Waterhead. – *Pink Farm Cemetery*
Platt, Ernest	74517	Pte	kia 18/7/18	Age 19. D Coy. Son of John & Margaret of Oldham. – *Bertrancourt Military Cemetery*
Platt, James	375504	Pte	kia 27/3/18	Wounded July 1915. 5, Landsdowne Rd., Chadderton. – *St Amand British Cemetery*
Platts, Harold	376780	Pte	kia 28/9/18	Age 25. B Coy. Son of Fred & Mary, 3, Ashley St., Main Rd., Oldham. – *Fifteen Ravine British Cemetery*
Pollitt, James	376811	Pte	kia 9/9/17	Age 25. Son of Robert & Sarah, 43, Fields New Rd., Chadderton. – *Ypres Reservoir Cemetery*
Poole, Thomas	395001	Sgt	kia 10/9/17	Born and enlisted at Manchester. – *Ypres Town Cemetery Extension*
Powell, Harry,	1936	Pte	kia 4/6/15	Lived at 20, Cambridge St., Werneth. – *Helles M.M.*
Powell, John	252434	Pte	kia 20/10/18	Age 22. Son of John & Fanny, 23, Zacharia St., Salford. – *Belle Vue British Cemetery*
Powell, Robert	376015	Pte	dow 10/11/18	Enlisted at Oldham. – *Caudry British Cemetery*
Prescott, George	252268	Pte	dow 20/10/18	Age 40. Husband of Florrie, 46, Stonehill St., Liverpool. – *Belle Vue British Cemetery*
Pritchard, Walter	74524	Pte	kia 31/8/18	Lived at 2, Bowker St., Higher Broughton, Manchester. – *Bancourt British Cemetery*
Pye, J.S.	57357	Pte	dow 7/10/18	– *Hautmont Communal Cemetery*
Ramsden, John	2063	Pte	dow 24/5/15	Enlisted at Oldham. – *Lancashire Landing Cemetery*
Ratcliffe, Robert	2275	L/Cpl	kia 4/6/15	Lived at 205, Ripponden Rd., Oldham. – *Helles M.M.*
Rayment, Tom	376082	Pte	kia 29/3/18	Age 31. 28, Tin St., Oldham. – *St Amand British Cemetery*
Redford, Wilfred	375690	Pte	kia 15/9/17	Enlisted at Oldham. – *Hooge Crater Cemetery*

Name	No.	Rnk	Fate	Notes – Buried/Commemorated
Rees, Gwelyn	74532	Pte	dow 20/11/18	Age 19. Lived in Port Talbot. – *St Sever Cemetery Extension*
Regan, John	1919	Pte	kia 4/6/15	Age 23. Husband of Emily (remarried) 38, Mulberry St., Glodwick. – *Helles M.M.*
Rennie, John	1680	Pte	kia 4/6/15	Lived at Hollinwood. – *Helles M.M.*
Renshaw, Ernest	18697	Pte	kia 20/10/18	Age 24. Son of Charles & Susannah, 23, Milton Grove, Gorton. – *Belle Vue British Cemetery*
Richardson, John	1460	Pte	kia 14/8/15	Lived at Chadderton. – *Helles M.M.*
Riley, James	376905	Pte	died 30/5/17	Enlisted at Dewsbury. Formerly 11329 KOYLI. – *La Chapelette British Cemetery (Péronne)*
Roberston, James	375279	L/Cpl	kia 31/8/18	Born and enlisted at Oldham. – *Bancourt British Cemetery*
Robinson, Edward	376604	Pte	dow 31/8/18	Born and enlisted at Oldham. – *Adanac Military Cemetery*
Robinson, Fred	375968	L/Cpl	kia 17/6/18	Age 37. Husband of Lilian, 160, Edge Lane Rd., Oldham. – *Bertrancourt Military Cemetery*
Robinson, Frederick	375435	Pte	kia 25/10/17	Age 27. Husband of Ellen, 12, Mulliner St., Oldham. – *Coxyde Military Cemetery*
Robinson, Stanley	2169	Pte	died 23/6/15	Enlisted at Oldham. – *Cairo War Cemetery (Egypt)*
Robinson, Thomas	1617	Pte	kia 4/6/15	Age 18. Son of Charles & Mary, 2, Court, Hobson St. Oldham. – *Helles M.M.*
Roscoe, Robert	377085	L/Cpl	kia 10/9/17	Born at Wigan. – *Ypres Town Cemetery Extension*
Rose, John	342	Cpl	kia 4/6/15	Age 39. Lived at 22, Ripon St., Oldham. – *Helles M.M.*
Ross, Henry	275461	Pte	kia 17/4/18	Age 23. Lived at 17, Kenneth St., Higher Broughton. – *Couin New British Cemetery*
Rothwell, William	1805	Pte	dow 28/6/15	Son of Henry & Alice, 42, Mustard St., Oldham. Buried at sea. – *Helles M.M.*
Rourke, Granville	377161	Pte	kia 10/9/17	Age 24. Son of Patrick & Emma, 32, Lynn St., Werneth. – *Ypres Town Cemetery Extension*
Royle, Harry	2529	Pte	kia 25/10/15	Age 19. Son of Ralph & Mary, 14, Latimer St., Oldham. Formerly 2/10th Battalion. – *Azmak Cemetery*
Ryall, George	375286	Pte	dow 1/7/18	Wounded May 1915. Lived in Denbigh. – *Bagneux British Cemetery*

Name	No.	Rnk	Fate	Notes – Buried/Commemorated
Saint, Henry	2173	Pte	kia 4/6/15	Age 22. Lived at 36, Brunswick St., Oldham. – *Hellles M.M.*
Saunders, Robert	51448	Pte	dow 29/10/17	Age 24. Lived in Co. Down. Formerly 32696 Border Regt. – *Zuydcoote Military Cemetery*
Saville, George	1934	Pte	kia 14/8/15	Lived at Hollinwood. – *Helles M.M.*
Scholes, Frank	376324	Pte	dow 10/5/17	Age 26. Husband of Martha, 3/4 Court, Hobson St., Oldham. – *La Chapelette British Cemetery (Péronne)*
Scholes, Fred	375187	Pte	dow 9/11/17	Age 24. Son of Joseph, 107, Trafalgar St., Oldham. – *Zuydcoote Military Cemetery*
Schofield, Ben	2663	Pte	kia	Age 20. Son of Ann, 251, Middleton Rd., Oldham. – *Helles M.M.*
Schofield, Harry	376478	Pte	died 2/12/18	Age 25. Lived at 30, Fulham St., Oldham. – *Caudry British Cemetery*
Schofield, Herbert	2532	Pte	died (dysentery) 4/9/15	Age 21. Lived at 20, Viscount St., Oldham. Formerly 2/10th Battalion. Buried at sea. – *Helles M.M.*
Scott, Walter	295097	Pte	dow (gas) 28/9/18	Aged 27. Attached 126th LTM. Son of Mary, 4, Herbert St., Lime Bank St., Ardwick. – *Terlincthun British Cemetery*
Seville, Harold	375107	Sgt	kia 4/6/17	Born at Dobcross. Lived in Ireland, and at 7, Oxford St., Werneth. – *Neuville-Bourjonval British Cemetery*
Seville, Wilfred	1075	Pte	died (enteric) 11/9/15	Age 25. Lived at 25, Balfour St., Oldham. – *Chatby War Cemetery (Egypt)*
Shaw, George	376177	Pte	kia 4/6/17	Lived at Chadderton. – *Neuville-Bourjonval British Cemetery*
Shaw, James	1798	Pte	kia 4/6/15	Age 17. Lived at 32, Springfield St., Higginshaw Lane, Oldham. – *Helles M.M.*
Shawcross, Albert	2392	Pte	kia 6/11/16	Lived at Ashton-u-Lyne. – *Kantara War Memorial Cemetery (Egypt)*
Shepherd, Charles	376010	Pte	dow 4/3/18	Enlisted at Oldham. – *Boulogne Eastern Cemetery*
Sheppard, Lewis	42506	Pte	kia 20/10/18	Lived at Mere (Wilts) Formerly 018786 RAOC. – *Belle Vue British Cemetery*
Shires, Harry	42574	Pte	dow 22/8/18	Age 20. Lived at Hough End, Barnsley. – *Sucrerie Military Cemetery (Colincamps)*
Shirley, Joseph	303372	Pte	kia 25/3/18	Enlisted at Manchester. – *Arras M.M.*

Name	No.	Rnk	Fate	Notes – Buried/Commemorated
Slinger, Harry	2178	Pte	kia 4/6/15	Age 33. Son of Francis & Mary, 19, Anchor St., Oldham. – *Helles M.M.*
Smalley, Ernest	2179	Pte	kia 26/5/15	Age 18. Lived at 69, Hawksley St., Hollinwood. – *Helles M.M.*
Smedley, Sidney	1481	Pte	kia 2/6/15	Lived at 3, Kelverlow St, Clarksfield. – *Twelve Tree Copse Cemetery*
Smith, Frank	2282	Pte	kia 4/6/15	Age 23. Lived at 64, Blackshaw Lane, Heyside. – *Helles M.M.*
Smith, Herbert	1346	Pte	dow 31/5/15	Age 44. Lived at 33, Kirkham St., Oldham. Had served for about 8 years. Worked at Platts. – *East Mundros Military Cemetery (Lemnos)*
Smith, James	376442	Pte	kia 24/3/18	Age 28. Son of Joel, 45, Clowes St., Hollinwood. Husband of Annice, 8, Fishwick St., Hollinwood. – *Arras M.M.*
Smith, Joseph, T.	376362	Pte	dow 14/9/17	Lived at Hollinwood. – *Brandhoek New Military Cemetery*
Smith, Robert	1473	Sgt	kia 4/6/15	Age 33. Husband of Sarah, 26, Adelphi St., Higginshaw Rd., Oldham. – *Helles M.M.*
Snare, Alfred	2182	L/Cpl	dow 25/8/15	Age 35. Lived at 144, Busk Rd., Chadderton. – *Twelve Tree Copse Cemetery*
Snow, Albert	1810	Pte	dow 3/6/15	B Coy. Son of Robert & Emma. – *East Mundros Military Cemetery (Lemnos)*
Stansfield, Farrar	375162	Sgt	kia 4/6/17	Lived at 264, Middleton Rd., Royton. – *Neuville-Bourjonval British Cemetery*
Stansfield, James	375161	Pte	kia 28/3/18	Age 24. Wounded May-June 1915 Enlisted at Oldham. – *Couin New British Cemetery*
Stanton, Thomas	1333	Pte	kia 4/6/15	Lived at 38, Boardman St., Oldham. – *Twelve Tree Copse Cemetery*
Starkey, Abraham	2398	Pte	died (pneumonia) 28/10/15	Age 27. Lived at 55, Radcliffe St., Oldham. – *Chatby War Cemetery (Egypt)*
Steventon, Joseph	376169	Pte	dow 20/10/18	Lived at Newton Heath. – *Rocquigny-Equancourt Road British Cemetery*
Stockton, Arthur	376073	Pte	kia 20/10/18	Age 34. Lived at Stoke. – *Belle Vue British Cemetery*
Stott, Clifford	49280	Pte	dow 27/9/18	Born and enlisted at Shaw. – *Grevillers British Cemetery*
Stott, Ernest	1776	Pte	kia 4/6/15	Age 20. Lived at 64, Colwyn St., Oldham. – *Helles M.M.*

Name	No.	Rnk	Fate	Notes – Buried/Commemorated
Stott, Fred	1867	Pte	kia 9/8/15	Age 20. Lived at 34, Norbury St., Glodwick. Wounded on 4/6/15 and to Malta. Rejoined. Cop packer at Glodwick Spinning Co. – *Helles M.M.*
Stott, Frederick	3217	Pte	dow 17/12/15	Age 33. Husband of Phyllis, 22, Bentley St., Chadderton. – *Chatby War Cemetery (Egypt)*
Stott, James	376614	Pte	dow 3/9/18	Age 34. Son of Samuel & Ruth, Werneth. Husband of Ethel, 24, Fenny Hill, Glodwick. – *St Sever Communal Cemetery Extension*
Strachan, Thomas	1542	Pte	kia 4/6/15	Age 22. Lived at 6, Kendal St., Oldham. – *Helles M.M.*
Strafford, Claude	2542	Pte	died (enteric) 3/9/15	Age 19. Lived at 54, Hanson St., Clarksfield. Formerly 2/10th Battalion. Buried at sea. – *Helles M.M.*
Stubbs, Walter	74542	Pte	kia 22/6/18	Age 19. Son of William & Isabella, Salford. – *Bertrancourt Military Cemetery*
Styles, Harry	1611	Pte	kia 4/6/15	Age 22. Lived at 35, Marmaduke St., Oldham. – *Helles M.M.*
Sutcliffe, William	2399	Pte	died (dysentery, home) 9/1/16	Age 24. Lived at 40, Granville St., Chadderton. Landed on Gallipoli 14/8/15 and evacuated in November. Piecer at Neville Mill, Westwood. – *Chadderton Cemetery*
Sutton, Charles	377974	Pte	dow 25/11/18	Age 20. Son of Joseph & Sarah, 30, Colley St., Stretford. – *St Sever Communal Cemetery Extension*
Sutton, James	375884	Pte	kia 13/8/15	Age 19. Lived on Middleton Rd., Chadderton. A piecer at Lansdowne Mill. – *Helles M.M.*
Sykes, Fred	2873	Pte	died (dysentery) 21/8/15	Age 24. Son of William, 61, Thomas St., Lees. – *Chatby War Cemetery (Egypt)*
Taulbot, George	1386	Pte	kia 14/10/15	Enlisted at Oldham. – *Helles M.M.*
Taylor, George	375430	Pte	kia 24/6/17	Age 26. Son of George & Mary, 333, Featherstall Rd. North, Oldham. – *Ruyaulcourt Military Cemetery*
Taylor, James	1925	Pte	kia 4/6/15	Age 18. Son of John & Matilda, 1, Grantham St., Oldham. – *Helles M.M.*
Taylor, James	378020	Pte	dow 6/5/18	Enlisted at Chadderton. – *Couin New British Cemetery*

Name	No.	Rnk	Fate	Notes – Buried/Commemorated
Taylor, John	2285	Pte	kia 4/6/15	Age 24. B Coy. Lived at 79, Beever St., Oldham. – *Helles M.M.*
Taylor, Samuel	74556	Pte	dow 9/9/18	Age 19. Son of 26, Clammerclough Rd., Farnworth. – *Bagneux British Cemetery*
Taylor, William	2194	Pte	kia 4/6/15	Lived at 277, Hollins Rd., Hollinwood. – *Helles M.M.*
Taylor, William	376827	Pte	kia 24/12/17	Age 25. Son of John & Emma, 178, Hollins Rd., Hollinwood. – *Gorre British Cemetery*
Thomas, David	821	Pte	dow 10/6/15	Age 25. Lived at 24, Featherstall Rd. North, Oldham. – *Chatby War Cemetery (Egypt)*
Thorpe, John	375520	Pte	dow 11/11/18	Age 30. Husband of Clara, 18, Somerset St., Oldham. – *Caudry British Cemetery*
Titley, John	376454	Pte	kia 8/5/17	Enlisted at Oldham. – *Templeux-le-Guerard British Cemetery*
Tomlinson, Jesse	46518	Pte	kia 10/7/18	Age 23. Son of Edenfield, near Bury. Formerly 4347 Duke of Lancaster's Own Yeomanry. – *Bertrancourt Military Cemetery*
Travis, George	2196	Pte	kia 19/6/15	Age 31. Lived at 24, Bedford St., Oldham. Minder at Sun Mill. – *Helles M.M.*
Travis, Joseph	376887	Pte	kia 28/4/18	Lived at Hollinwood. – *Gommecourt British No.2 Cemetery*
Turner, Albert	1412	Cpl	kia 8/9/15	Age 22. Son of A.E.& Louisa of Ellesmere, Salop. – *Helles M.M.*
Turner, Albert	2874	Pte	died (home) 21/12/15	Age 31. Husband of Lilian (remarried) 17, Alfred St., Werneth. Formerly 2/10th Battalion. Died in Seely Military Hospital. – *Hollinwood Cemetery*
Turner, Emanuel	2969	L/Cpl	dow 13/8/15	Age 33. Lived at 51, Lansdowne Rd., Chadderton.Went with first draft from 2/10th Battalion. Served in the South Africa Campaign. Moulder's labourer at Platts. – *Lancashire Landing Cemetery*
Turner, John	1239	L/Cpl	kia 4/6/15	Age 21. Husband of Clara, 4, Lansdowne Rd., Chadderton. – *Helles M.M.*
Turner, William	2198	Pte	kia 19/6/15	Enlisted at Oldham. – *Helles M.M.*
Turnock, William	48550	Pte	kia 8/6/18	Only son of William & Betsy, 100, Chapel Lane, Wigan. – *Bertrancourt Military Cemetery*
Twigge, Frank	202172	Pte	kia 7/8/18	Age 23. Son of George & Lucy, 102, Birch St., Ardwick. – *Bertrancourt Military Cemetery*

Name	No.	Rnk	Fate	Notes – *Buried/Commemorated*
Tyson, Joseph	2199	Pte	died (accidentally killed) 21/3/16	Age 23. D Coy. Lived at 43, Horsedge St., Oldham. – *Suez War Memorial Cemetery (Egypt)*
Urmston, Ralph	1530	Pte	kia 3/6/15	Age 19. Son of Ralph & Sarah, 34, Heron St., Hollinwood. – *Helles M.M.*
Vaudrey, James	1579	Pte	kia 19/6/15	Age 35. Lived at 2, Court, Rochdale Rd., Oldham. – *Helles M.M.*
Viner, Alfred	43069	Pte	kia 29/3/18	Lived at Allesley, Coventry. A printer. Formerly 17228 Ox & Bucks L.I. – *Arras M.M.*
Wales, James	375770	Pte	kia 11/12/17	Age 33. C Coy. Husband of Mally, 157, West End St., Oldham. – *Gorre British Cemetery*
Walker, Ernest	50155	Pte	kia 31/8/18	Age 32. Lived at 118, Chadderton Rd., Oldham. – *Bancourt British Cemetery*
Walker, James	2017	Pte	kia 4/6/15	Age 28. Husband of Ellen (remarried) 3, Marple St., Coldhurst. – *Helles M.M.*
Walker, Thomas	375112	Sgt	kia 7/11/18	Age 29. Son of John & Molly, 25, Stoneleigh St., Oldham. – *Maubeuge Centre Cemetery*
Walmsley, Richard	395007	Pte	died 24/11/18	Lived at Hindley. – *Solesmes British Cemetery*
Walsh, Patrick	1632	Cpl	kia 4/6/15	Enlisted at Oldham. – *Helles M.M.*
Ward, Thomas	1236	Pte	kia 4/6/15	Age 21. Son of Emily, 57, Silver St., Oldham. – *Helles M.M.*
Wardle, Percy	376575	Pte	kia 4/4/18	62, Brunlees St., Hollinwod. – *St Amand British Cemetery*
Warrener, Elson	1094	Pte	kia 12/5/15	Age 26. Lived at 130, Ward St., Oldham. – *Helles M.M.*
Watson, Harold	1152	Pte	kia 4/6/15	Age 22. Lived at 177, Garforth St., Chadderton. – *Helles M.M.*
Whewell, George	2201	L/Cpl	kia 4/6/15	Lived at Ashton-u-Lyne. – *Helles M.M.*
Whitehead, Thomas	3035	Pte	dow 23/12/15	Age 32. Lived at 26, Bagnall St., Oldham. Formerly 2/10th Battalion. – *Lancashire Landing Cemetery*
Whitmore, Robert	376387	Cpl	kia 20/10/18	Age 24. Son of Alfred & Maria, The Spinners Arms, 107, Lees Rd., Oldham. Wife remarried. – *Belle Vue British Cemetery*
Whittaker, Robert	303943	Pte	dow 11/4/18	Age 39. Husband of Jeanie, 88, Silverdale St., Higher Openshaw. – *Etaples British Cemetery*

Name	No.	Rnk	Fate	Notes – Buried/Commemorated
Whittaker, Roland	1550	Pte	kia 13/8/15	Age 20. Lived at 27, Busk St., Chadderton. – Redoubt Cemetery
Whitworth, John	1313	Dmr	kia 4/6/15	Born at Chadderton. – Helles M.M.
Whyatt, Fred	1749	Pte	kia 4/6/15	Age 18. Son of James & Sarah, 27, Featherstall Rd., Oldham. – Helles M.M.
Wilde, Ernest	376625	Pte	kia 16/5/17	Age 19. Son of Sidney & Henrietta, 5, Hereford St., Werneth. – Templeux-le-Guerard British Cemetery
Wilkinson, William	2204	Pte	dow 18/6/15	Age 22. Enlisted at Oldham. Piecer at Borough Mill. – East Mundros Military Cemetery (Lemnos)
Wilson, Charles	34830	Pte	dow 7/11/18	Age 33. – Maubeuge Centre Cemetery
Wilson, Leonard	46812	Pte	kia 22/8/18	Age 29. 31, Alma Rd., Birkdale, Stockport. – Sucrerie Military Cemetery (Colincamps)
Wolstencroft, Stuart	375047	Sgt	kia 28/4/18	Age 27. Son of Jacob & Mary, 130, Boundary Park Rd., Oldham. – Couin New British Cemetery
Wood, Arthur	987	Pte	kia 4/6/15	Age 25. Son of George & Sarah, 18, Shaw St., Oldham. – Helles M.M.
Wood, James	376577	Pte	dow (gas)15/4/18	Age 41. Enlisted at Oldham. Son of James & Elizabeth. – Wimereux Communal Cemetery
Wood, John	2019	Sgt	kia 4/6/15	Born at Oldham. – Helles M.M.
Woods, Arthur	377847	Pte	kia 2/11/17	Age 19. Son of Alice & Albert, 204, Fairfield, Bury. More likely to have been 2/10th Battalion. – Tyne Cot M.M.
Worthington, James	1384	Pte	kia 19/6/15	Born at Oldham. – Helles M.M.
Wright, Albert	376865	L/Cpl	kia 8/6/18	Age 26. Son of George & Mary of Oldham. – Bertrancourt Military Cemetery
Wright, Herbert	74564	Pte	kia 8/6/18	Born and enlisted at Crewe. – Bertrancourt Military Cemetery
Wyke, William	201	Sgt	kia 9/8/15	Age 30. Husband of Alice, 10, Barry St., Oldham. Served in the Volunteers and TF for 14 years. Worked at Entwistle & Co. – Helles M.M.

Part 3 – The 2/10 Battalion

Name	No.	Rnk	Fate	Notes – *Buried/Commemorated*
Archbold, George	377959	Sgt	dow 15/9/17	Lived in Hertfordshire. Formerly 2568 Essex Regt. – *Ramscappelle Road Military Cemetery*
Ashton, Walter	377143	Pte	kia 9/10/17	Lived at Chadderton. – *Tyne Cot M.M.*
Atkinson, Joseph	377903	Pte	kia 9/10/17	Lived at Manchester. – *Tyne Cot M.M.*
Ball, Joseph	377631	Pte	kia 9/10/17	Age 28. Lived at 9, Smithies St., Haslingden.
Barlow, Richard	380233	Pte	kia 9/101/7	Lived at Bury. Formerly 380233 King's Liverpool Regt. – *Tyne Cot M.M.*
Bartlett, George	377562	Pte	kia 6/6/17	Lived at Bawtry. – *Cambrin Military Cemetery*
Bell, Thomas	377678	Pte	died (accidentally drowned) 27/5/17	Age 19. Lived on the Isle of Man. Attached 198 Bty. RGA. – *Gorre British Cemetery*
Bibby, John	377579	Pte	dow 30/3/17	Lived at Manchester. – *Cambrin Military Cemetery*
Bradbury, Charles	377556	Pte	kia 30/7/17	Age 30. Husband of Mary, 19, Prestage St., Longsight. – *Coxyde Military Cemetery*
Brierley, Ellis	377518	Pte	dow 8/8/17	Age 25. Married, of 7, Phoenix St., Pendleton. – *Adinkerke Military Cemetery*
Brooks, Eddie	377638	Pte	kia 9/10/17	Lived at Burnley. – *Tyne Cot M.M.*
Buckley, James	376879	Cpl	dow 6/5/17	Lived at Oldham. – *Cambrin Military Cemetery*
Carolin, Joseph	201916	Cpl	kia 9/10/17	Lived at Thornton Heath, Surrey. – *Tyne Cot M.M.*
Carr, Robert	377491	Cpl	dow 28/3/17	Age 34. Husband of Emily, 5, Clematis St., Blackburn. – *Cambrin Military Cemetery*
Castle, William	378013	Pte	kia 9/10/17	Lived at Manchester. – *Tyne Cot M.M.*
Cummins, William	377883	Pte	kia 4/4/17	Lived at Salford. – *Cambrin Military Cemetery*

Name	No.	Rnk	Fate	Notes – *Buried/Commemorated*
Cundiff, John	377341	Pte	died (pneumonia) 14/4/17	Age 34. Husband of Dorothy of Gorton. – *Chocques Military Cemetery*
Cuthbert, Robert	42557	Pte	kia 27/11/17	Lived in Northumberland. – *Tyne Cot M.M.*
Davies, Arthur	377497	Pte	dow 11/10/17	Lived at Hulme. – *Tyne Cot M.M.*
Dawson, Sidney	377936	Pte	dow (home) 14/12/17	Age 24. Lived at Waterhead. – *Waterhead (Holy Trinity) Churchyard*
Dinwoodie, Arthur	377456	Pte	kia 9/10/17	Age 20. Lived at 58, Ellesmere St., Moorside. – *Tyne Cot M.M.*
Dixon, Harry	376763	Pte	dow 10/10/17	Age 21. Son of Joseph & Ella, 41a, Rock St., Oldham. Possibly 1/10th Battalion. – *Nine Elms Cemetery (Poperinghe)*
Dolan, William	375631	Pte	kia 9/10/17	Age 33. Husband of Mary, 15, Lower Victoria St., Chadderton. – *Tyne Cot Cemetery*
Dyer, Nicholas	376805	Pte	dow 12/10/17	Age 20. Lived at Royton. – *Nine Elms Cemetery (Poperinghe)*
Eatherall, Albert	377908	Pte	kia 9/10/17	Age 22. Lived at 14, Peel St., Hulme. – *Tyne Cot M.M.*
Edwards, Joseph	377866	Cpl	dow 10/10/17	Age 25. Husband of Harriet, 5, Zetland St., Duckinfield. – *Nine Elms Cemetery (Poperinghe)*
Elliot, Frank	377747	Pte	dow 6/2/18	Age 21. Lived at Manchester. – *Lijssenthoek British Cemetery*
Ellis, Fred	201910	Pte	kia 9/10/17	Age 23. Adopted son. Lived at 25, Stirrup Brook, Boothstown. – *Tyne Cot M.M.*
Fielden, William	251219	Pte	kia 9/10/17	Lived at Manchester. – *Tyne Cot M.M.*
Fletcher, David	376802	Pte	kia 9/10/17	Age 23. Son of Moses & Jane, 16, Firwood St., Middleton Junction. – *Tyne Cot M.M.*
Fletcher, Ronald	377939	Pte	kia 13/1/18	Lived at Manchester. – *Tyne Cot M.M.*
Gamble, John	42572	Pte	dow 8/8/17	Age 32. Married. Lived at Sheffield. – *Adinkerke Military Cemetery*
Garmory, Harold	377910	Pte	kia 9/10/17	Age 19. Lived at 25, Wellington St., Moss Side. – *Tyne Cot M.M.*

Name	No.	Rnk	Fate	Notes – *Buried/Commemorated*
Gildea, Robert	377607	Pte	dow 7/6/17	Age 30. Husband of 5, Wansford St., Moss Side. – *Bethune Town Cemetery*
Hagan, James	42577	Pte	kia 9/10/17	Lived at Sunderland. – *Tyne Cot M.M.*
Hamilton, John	203070	Pte	kia 9/10/17	Lived at Preston. – *Tyne Cot M.M.*
Hanham, William	303988	Pte	dow 14/1/18	Lived at Collyhurst. – *Lijssenthoek British Cemetery*
Heald, Alfred	376878	Pte	kia 9/10/17	Age 27. Lived at 131, Glodwick Rd., Oldham. – *Tyne Cot M.M.*
Henderson, Thomas	42521	Pte	kia 9/10/17	Age 41. Lived at Newcastle-on-Tyne – *Tyne Cot M.M.*
Henson, Thomas	378022	Pte	kia 9/10/17	Age 19. Lived at 16, Park St., Hulme. – *Tyne Cot Cemetery*
Hill, Robert	376021	Cpl	kia 9/10/17	Age 26. Son of Arthur & Ann, 17, Birchenlea St., Hollinwood. – *Tyne Cot M.M.*
Hodgin, James	376725	Pte	kia 4/4/17	Age 21. Son of Annie, 60, Under Lane, Hollinwood. – *Cambrin Military Cemetery*
Hollows, James	52710	Pte	kia 13/1/18	Lived at 65, Price St., Farnworth. – *Tyne Cot M.M.*
Holmes, John	376919	Pte	died 26/4/17	Lived at Dewsbury. Formerly 11764 KOYLI. Probably 1/10th Battalion. – *Bray Military Cemetery*
Holt, Clarence	377356	Pte	kia 9/10/17	Lived at Manchester. – *Tyne Cot M.M.*
Holt, Walter	377283	Pte	kia 7/4/17	Lived at Manchester. – *Cambrin Military Cemetery*
Hoskisson, David	377325	Pte	kia 7/4/17	Age 28. Husband of Florence, 20, Amos Ave., Newton Heath. – *Cambrin Military Cemetery*
Hulme, Daniel	377611	Pte	kia 17/9/17	Lived at Manchester. – *Tyne Cot M.M.*
Hurst, James	376039	Pte	dow 29/4/17	Lived at Oldham. Attached 198th LTM Bty. – *Béthune Town Cemetery*
Jervis, Arthur	377503	Pte	kia 9/10/17	Age 37. Husband of Alice, 20, Pingstone St., Beswick. – *Tyne Cot M.M.*

Name	No.	Rnk	Fate	Notes – Buried/Commemorated
Johnson, Walter	377605	Pte	kia 31/3/17	Age 27. Son of late Clr-Sgt., 15, Needwood St., Queens Park, Manchester. – *Cambrin Military Cemetery*
Jones, Ben	303675	Pte	kia 13/1/18	Age 19. Lived at 16, Railway St., Gorton. – *Tyne Cot M.M.*
Kane, David	40307	Pte	kia 26/11/17	Lived at Manchester. Formerly 6002 Lancashire Fusiliers. – *Tyne Cot Cemetery*
Kenworthy, Fred	375865	L/Sgt	kia 9/10/17	Lived at Oldham. – *Tyne Cot M.M.*
Kenyon, John	376286	Pte	kia 9/10/17	Lived at Chadderton. – *Tyne Cot M.M.*
Kerr, Walter	203625	Pte	kia 21/11/17	Age 32. Lived at Swinton. – *Tyne Cot M.M.*
Knight, Alan	202962	Pte	kia 13/1/18	Age 19. 9, LLoyd St., Hulme. C Coy. – *Tyne Cot Cemetery*
Leach, Thomas	377699	Pte	kia 9/10/17	Age 27. Married. Lived at Liverpool. – *Tyne Cot M.M.*
Ledgerwood, John	42525	Pte	kia 9/10/17	Lived at Ashington. – *Tyne Cot M.M.*
Lees, Albert	377352	Pte	kia 9/10/17	Lived at Manchester. – *Tyne Cot M.M.*
Leonard, George	377128	Pte	dow 19/10/17	Age 24. Son of Louis & Alice of Oldham. – *Boulogne Eastern Cemetery*
McAllister, J.J.	377478	Pte	kia 9/10/17	Lived at Manchester. – *Tyne Cot M.M.*
McCarthy, Adam	377721	Pte	dow 11/10/17	Age 30. Lived at 14, Wye St., Everton. – *Nine Elms Cemetery (Poperinghe)*
Mahomet, Arthur	377376	Pte	kia 9/10/17	Age 35. Husband of Edith, 18, St Mark St., Levenshulme. – *Tyne Cot M.M.*
Mills, Herbert	375928	Sgt	kia 7/10/17	Age 22. Son of Joseph & Florence, 423, Park Rd., Oldham. – *Menin Road South Military Cemetery*
Monkhouse, William	376806	Cpl	dow 12/10/17	Age 22. Son of John & Eliza, 377, Oldham Rd., Longsight, Oldham. – *Nine Elms Cemetery (Poperinghe)*
Morris, Harry	203200	Pte	kia 9/10/17	Lived at Pendleton. – *Tyne Cot M.M.*
Moulson, Rufus	377658	Pte	kia 9/10/17	Lived at Nelson. – *Tyne Cot Cemetery*
Murphy, William	377970	Pte	kia 9/10/17	Lived at Liverpool. – *Tyne Cot M.M.*

250

Name	No.	Rnk	Fate	Notes – Buried/Commemorated
Needham, George	202835	Pte	kia 9/10/17	Lived at Manchester. – *Tyne Cot M.M.*
Nuttall, Frank	376187	Cpl	dow 17/10/17	Son of Thomas & Charlotte, 765, Middleton Rd., Chadderton. – *Wimereux Communal Cemetery*
Page, Harold	377815	Pte	dow 13/1/18	Lived at Middleton. Formerly 11853 Lancashire Fusiliers. – *Menin Road South Military Cemetery*
Parker, George	42748	Pte	kia 9/10/17	Lived at Croydon. Formerly 31774 East Surrey Regt. – *Tyne Cot Cemetery*
Parkinson, Fred	377448	Pte	kia 9/10/17	Married. Lived at 74, Westmoreland St., Harpurhey. – *Tyne Cot M.M.*
Parrott, James	277134	Pte	kia 9/10/17	Lived at Manchester. – *Tyne Cot M.M.*
Penketh, Albert	203140	Pte	kia 9/10/17	Lived at Manchester. – *Tyne Cot M.M.*
Pennington, Abel	377547	Pte	kia 6/6/17	Husband of Ethel (remarried) 14, Ward St., Blackley. – *Cambrin Military Cemetery*
Pennington, Colin	376863	Pte	kia 4/4/17	Lived at Failsworth. – *Cambrin Military Cemetery*
Pointon, William	203085	Pte	kia 21/11/17	Age 32. Husband of Marion, 26, William St., Ardwick. – *Tyne Cot M.M.*
Popplewell, Thomas		QMS	died (home) 28/2/16	Lived at Manchester. – *Borough Cemetery, Bear Rd., Brighton*
Porter, John	252606	Pte	kia 30/7/17	Age 19. Lived at Ormskirk. Formerly 5634 Kings Liverpool Regt. – *Coxyde Military Cemetery*
Potts, George	376050	Pte	kia 9/10/17	Lived at Failsworth. – *Tyne Cot M.M.*
Ratcliffe, William	303963	Pte	kia 26/11/17	Lived at Manchester. – *Tyne Cot M.M.*
Rawlings, Thomas	203537	Pte	died (home) 19/8/18	Age 42. Husband of Mary, Homerton, London. – *Abney Park Cemetery, Stoke Newington*
Redman, Robert	377666	Pte	kia 30/7/17	Lived at Nelson. – *Coxyde Military Cemetery*
Smethurst, Charles	376767	Pte	kia 9/10/17	Age 20. Son of Kate of Oldham. – *Tyne Cot M.M.*
Smith, Arthur	377621	Pte	kia 9/10/17	Age 33. Husband of Amy, 5, Moorfield Grove, Sale. – *Tyne Cot M.M.*

Name	No.	Rnk	Fate	Notes – Buried/Commemorated
Sprung, Moses	377708	Pte	kia 6/6/17	Lived at Liverpool. – *Cambrin Military Cemetery*
Stuart, William	376251	Cpl	dow 17/10/17	Age 21. Son of James & Ann, 49, Stanley St., Chadderton. – *Boulogne Eastern Cemetery*
Tansey, John	377674	Pte	kia 2/4/17	Age 30. Husband of Elizabeth, 18, Rook St., Nelson. – *Cambrin Military Cemetery*
Tinning, Alfred	50869	Pte	kia 9/10/17	Age 28. Lived in Co. Durham. Formerly 44971 Yorkshire Regt. – *Tyne Cot M.M.*
Todd, William	42541	Pte	kia 9/10/17	Age 29. Lived at Tynemouth. – *Tyne Cot Cemetery*
Turner, Robert	375889	L/Cpl	dow 24/11/17	Lived at Oldham. – *Wimereux Communal Cemetery*
Turner, William	377956	Pte	kia 10/6/17	Age 20. Son of Ada, 59, Foxdenton Lane, Middleton Jct. – *Cambrin Military Cemetery*
Vawer, Alfred	50871	Pte	kia 17/9/17	Age 19. Lived at West Hartlepool. Formerly 45104 Yorkshire Regt. – *Nieuport M.M.*
Wainman, Harry	377676	Pte	kia 9/10/17	Age 30. Married. Lived at 24, Skipton Rd., Colne. – *Tyne Cot M.M.*
Walker, John	377488	Pte	kia 10/9/17	Lived at Manchester. – *Ramscappelle Road Military Cemetery*
Wall, Thomas	50875	Pte	kia 9/10/17	Age 29. Married. Lived at Boldon, Co. Durham. Formerly 45081 Yorkshire Regt. – *Tyne Cot M.M.*
Walsh, James	376791	Pte	kia 9/10/17	Lived at Shaw. – *Tyne Cot M.M.*
Watkinson, Percy	203589	Pte	dow 23/11/17	Age 21. Lived at Atherton. – *Lijssenthoek Military Cemetery*
Waywell, William	5473	Pte	died (home) 28/12/16	Age 35. Husband of Hannah, 22, Cookson St., Ancoats. – *Philips Park Cemetery, Miles Platting*
Webb, Frank	377983	Pte	kia 4/4/17	Age 23. Son of Mary, 60, Wimbourne St., Newton Heath. – *Cambrin Military Cemetery*
Weilding, Charles	377626	Pte	kia 17/9/17	Lived at Openshaw. – *Nieuport M.M.*

Name	No.	Rnk	Fate	Notes – Buried/Commemorated
Wheatley, Sydney	42765	Pte	kia 9/10/17	Age 26. Married. Lived at Uckfield, Sussex. Formerly 3/33321 East Surrey Regt. – *Tyne Cot M.M.*
Wilcock, Thomas	376727	Pte	died (as a pow) 25/3/17	Lived at Hollinwood. – *Cologne Southern Cemetery (Germany)*
Wild, Samuel	375975	Cpl	kia 9/10/17	Lived at Bardsley. – *Tyne Cot Cemetery*
Wilkinson, John	377928	Pte	died (pneumonia) 23/9/17	Age 37. Husband of Ada, 246, Belgrave Rd., Oldham. – *Zuydcoote Military Cemetery*
Willman, Harry	377378	Pte	kia 9/10/17	Age 37. Married. Lived at 9, Blanchard St., Chorlton. – *Tyne Cot M.M.*
Wilton, Edgar	377427	Pte	dow 9/10/17	Lived at Manchester. – *Nine Elms Cemetery (Poperinghe)*
Woolley, Samuel	303837	Pte	kia 13/1/18	Lived at Manchester. – *Tyne Cot Cemetery*
Worsnop, Edward	303881	Pte	died 30/12/17	Age 25. Lived at Manchester. – *Wimereux Communal Cemetery*
Worthington, Samuel	400167	Pte	dow 5/9/17	Lived at Broughton. Formerly 1130 Lancashire Fusiliers. – *Zuydcoote Military Cemetery*

The following men were killed after having been drafted to the 1/King's Liverpool Regiment (then serving on the Somme) in 1916. They are listed as 2/10th Manchester in *Soldiers Died*. It is known that at least another 50 men of the same draft were killed by December 1916 but are listed correctly as King's.

Name	No.	Rnk	Fate	Notes
Dale, William	4217	Pte	kia 29/8/16	Lived at Hollinwood. – *Euston Road Cemetery*
Fenn, Joseph	2358	Pte	kia 28/8/16	Age 25. Son of Henry & Jane, Millgate, Hollins Rd., Oldham. Husband of (remarried) Lily. – *Thiepval M.M.*
Fletcher, Thomas	2360	Pte	kia 29/8/16	Age 36. Husband of Alice, 96, Glodwick Rd., Oldham. – *Euston Road Cemetery*
Hindley, John	4825	Pte	kia 29/8/16	Age 24. Son of John & Martha, 69, Tudor St., Oldham. – *Euston Road Cemetery*
Kelty, Frank	1714	Pte	kia 5/9/16	Lived at Oldham. – *Euston Road Cemetery*
Kilner, John	4522	Pte	kia 29/8/16	Lived at Oldham. – *Euston Road Cemetery*

Part 4: The 3/10 Battalion

Name	No.	Rnk	Fate	Notes – *Buried/Commemorated*
Cain, William	4144	Pte	died (home) 30/3/16	Age 20. – *Tidworth Military Cemetery, Wiltshire*
Cook, George	376246	Pte	died (home) 17/4/17	Age 28. Son of Charles of Hollinwood. – *Hollinwood Cemetery*
Fielding, Herbert	51	Sgt	died (home) 10/4/15	Age 29. Son of Joseph & Emma. Husband of Mary, 164, Waterloo St., Oldham. – *Chadderton Cemetery*
Hardy, Herbert	4372	Pte	died (home) 9/3/16	Age 17. Son of Mary Ellen, 26, Portland St., Oldham. – *Chadderton Cemetery*
Helliwell, Eli	3943	L/Cpl	died (home) 3/4/16	Age 29. Son of Hannah, 23, Norbury St., Glodwick. – *Greenacres Cemetery*
Horrocks, Granville	2121	Pte	died (home) 5/4/16	– *Wylye (St Mary) Churchyard, Wiltshire*
Hurst, Thomas	1628	Pte	died (home) 4/5/16	Age 19. Son of Betty, 33, Webster St., Oldham. – *Chadderton Cemetery*
Newitt, Fred	4715	Pte	died (home) 3/3/16	Age 23. Son of Sarah. – *Greenacres Cemetery*
Rothwell, William	3514	Pte	died (home) 9/7/15	Age 29. Husband of Amena, 278, Fields New Rd., Chadderton. – *Southport (St Cuthbert) Churchyard*
Wrigley, Harold	2786		dow 28/8/16	Posted to 1/King's Regiment. – *Couin British Cemetery*

APPENDIX 2

MEMBERS OF THE 6TH VOLUNTEER BATTALION WHO SERVED IN SOUTH AFRICA

THE TA CENTRE at Ardwick holds a large plaque commemorating the service of 126 men of the 6th Volunteer Battalion (Oldham) Manchester Regiment who saw service during the Boer War.

In 1900 the 1st Detachment (1st) and the 1st Section (2nd) went to the RAMC and the 1st Battalion Manchester Regiment respectively. In 1901 a half company (3rd) was also sent to the 1/Manchester, the 2nd Relief Section (4th) went to the 2/ Manchester and a further contingent (5th) was sent later in the year to the 1st Battalion. Smaller groups went to the Imperial Yeomanry (6th) and the St Johns Ambulance (7th).

Captain
    P. Bamford (2nd)

Lieutenant
    G. W. Hardman (3rd)

Sergeants:
    W. Bailey (4th)
    J. H. Barr (2nd)
    W. Chadderton (6th)
    C. Dunkerley (3rd)
    H. Jackson (3rd)
    F. Howarth (1st)
    H. Jackson (3rd)
    G. Marsden (6th)
    J. Mulcaster (3rd)

Corporals:
    A. Caley (3rd)
    W. Davies (4th)
    A. H. Priestley (6th)
    J. R. Street (3rd)

Lance Corporals:
    F. Dunkerley (3rd)
    F. Williams (3rd)

Bugler:
    J. Black

Privates:
    F. Andrew (3rd)
    J. Armstrong (3rd)
    G. W. Ashworth (3rd)
    A. Bancroft (3rd)
    H. Barber (5th)
    K. Barber (1st)
    J. H. Bardsley (5th)
    J. Bell (3rd)
    H. Belshaw (5th)
    T. Bennett (7th)
    J. Booth (1st)
    G. A. Bowden (2nd)
    J. Bowman (3rd)
    C. Buckley (3rd)
    J. Buckley (3rd)
    J. Byrom (4th)
    R. Cash (3rd)
    J. Chadwick (3rd)
    J. J. Cheetham (5th)
    W. Clegg (5th)

J. Coglan (3rd)
S. C. Cole (5th)
S. Collier (3rd)
C. Collins (4th)
A. N. Connochie (3rd)
J. Conway (3rd)
J. Cubby (3rd)
J. Curran (3rd)
G. Davies (5th)
W. Dolphyn (2nd)
E. Drinkwater (5th)
J. Ebdon (3rd)
W. Emmott (2nd)
H. Garland (3rd)
J. Gillham (5th)
A. Glover (3rd)
G. Goodwin (3rd)
J. E. Goodwin (4th)
S. Greenhalgh (3rd)
W. Halkyard (3rd)
R. Hall (3rd)
T. A. Hankinson (3rd)
F. Harding (5th)
C. Hardman (5th)
H. Harrison (5th)
J. T. Heron (3rd)
J. Hibbert (3rd)
W. Hoddy (5th)
E. Holden (3rd)
H. Hollins (7th)
J. Houlston (3rd)
W. Hoyle (5th)
O. Hunt (5th)
J. Insull (5th)
T. Kershaw (2nd)
J. Kierman (3rd)
E. Lane (3rd)
J. S. Lees (7th)
R. Lees (3rd)
T. Lewis (1st)
W. Lewis (1st)

W. Marcroft (3rd)
J. Marsden (5th)
E. Mellor (5th)
H. Mellor (5th)
R. Neilson (1st)
J. J. Nelson (1st)
C. Newton (6th)
J. Nightingale (1st)
H. Ogden (2nd)
P. W. Orriss (5th)
P. Papworth (3rd)
G. Pownall (6th)
A. Prescott (3rd)
E. Rhodes (3rd)
J. Rhodes (5th)
W. Roebuck (5th)
H. Royle (3rd)
T. Schofield (3rd)
W. H. Schofield (3rd)
J. J. Seddon (5th)
J. J. Shackleton (1st)
E. Smith (3rd)
E. Smith (4th)
E. F. Standring (5th)
W. Steeple (3rd)
H. Stott (5th)
S. E. Stott (5th)
H. V. Summersgill (3rd)
G. Tattersall (3rd)
A. Taylor (2nd)
A. F. Taylor (5th)
P. Taylor (2nd)
R. Taylor (5th)
W. Taylor (5th)
N. Turner (5th)
J. Trevitt (3rd)
T. Wadsworth (2nd)
J. Walne (3rd)
R. Waugh (3rd)
R. Weston (2nd)
T. Whitehead (3rd)

H. Whittaker (3rd)	J. Wolstencrof (4th)
W. Whyatt (5th)	J. S. Wood (3rd)
J. Winterburn (5th)	J. W. Wood (3rd)

Sgt. T. Fagan's name does *not* appear on the plaque, although he unquestionably served in South Africa and with considerable distinction ...

No. 4023. Sgt. T. Fagan, 6th Volunteer Battalion, Manchester Regiment. Award of the Edward VII D.C.M. listed in the London Gazette of 31 October, 1902. Also awarded the Queen's South Africa Medal with the bars *Cape Colony, Orange Free State, South Africa 1901* and *South Africa 1902*. Fagan's medals were sold at Spinks' Boer War Centenary Auction in October 1999.

His was the only Boer War D.C.M. awarded to the Manchester Militia and Volunteers. He was probably an Oldham man.

APPENDIX 3

THE 42ND (EAST LANCASHIRE) DIVISION

WHEN WAR BROKE OUT in 1914 the East Lancashire Division was an existing Territorial Force unit. Its infantry, artillery, field companies and field ambulances were drawn from Manchester, Salford, Bury, Rochdale, Blackburn, Burnley, Ashton-u-Lyne, Wigan and Oldham. When it left England for Egypt in September 1914 it earned the proud distinction of becoming the first Territorial division to leave the UK for foreign service.

In 1914 the division consisted of three infantry brigades, four brigades of artillery (although two remained in the UK until 1915), A Squadron, Duke of Lancaster's Own Yeomanry, Brigade Ammunition Columns, three Field Companies RE, three Field Ambulances and the Divisional Ammunition Train. At full strength the division mustered over 18,000 men.

The three infantry brigades were as follows:

Lancashire Fusilier Brigade: 5/LF, 6/LF, 7/LF, 8/LF

East Lancashire Brigade: 4/East Lancashire, 5/East
                             Lancashire, 9/Manchester,
                             10/Manchester

Manchester Brigade: 5/Manchester, 6/Manchester,
                             7/Manchester, 8/Manchester

In May 1915 the brigades were designated respectively 125, 126 and 127.

When the division went to France in March 1917 each infantry brigade had a Machine-Gun Company, the artillery was at full strength and the 19th Mobile Veterinary Section had been attached. In June the infantry brigades were each allotted a Light Trench Mortar Battery and the division received three Medium and one Heavy Trench Mortar Batteries. The 239th Divisional Employment Company was also attached.

In February 1918, like most divisions on the Western Front, the 42nd underwent a reorganisation. Each infantry brigade lost at least one battalion and their Machine-Gun Company. As a consequence 126 Brigade comprised the 5/East Lancs., 8/Manchester and 10/Manchester. The division gained a Machine-Gun Battalion and the 7/Northumberland Fusiliers as its Pioneer battalion.

In November 1914 the 2/10th Battalion was allotted to 198 Brigade 66th Division. The brigade's other infantry battalions were the 2/4th East Lancashire, 2/5th East Lancashire and 2/9th Manchester. The 2/10th remained with the brigade until the battalion was disbanded on 15 February 1918.

Appendix 4

Officers of the 1/10th Manchester

THE FOLLOWING OFFICERS left Bury in September 1914 with the 1/10th Manchester *en route* for Egypt.

Lieutenant-Colonel
  J. B. Rye VD

Majors
  P. Bamford
  G. W. Hardman

Captain & Adjutant
  E. J. de Pentheny O'Kelly

Captains:
  A. C. Booth
  D. E. Griffiths
  A. Leach
  G. R. Newton
  G. E. Stott
  L. C. Wilde

Lieutenants:
  L. Baird RAMC
  F. Hardman
  F. N. Griffiths

G. W. Owen
D. Park
G. D. Pochin
P. Stott
H. Sutcliffe
L. St. G. Wilkinson

Lieutenant & Quartermaster
  S. E. Kennedy

Second Lieutenants:
  R. G. Ascroft
  J. K. Bleakley,
  A. Butterworth
  J. Clegg
  J. B. Emmott
  A. E. Lee
  H. K. Nevinson
  J. Stott
  J. A. C. Taylor
  R. W. Wilde

On board the AVON the eight company organisation of a TF battalion was replaced by a four company system. The company commanders were as follows:

Old C & D Coys became A Coy under Major Hardman

Old H & F Coys became B Coy under Captain Wilde

Old A & B Coys became C Coy under Captain Booth

Old G & E Coys became D Coy under Captain Newton

The following officers left Egypt *en route* for the Dardanelles.

Lieutenant-Colonel:
Rye
(invalided to UK)

Major:
P. Bamford
(Senior Major, invalided to UK)

Captain & Adjutant:
E. J. de Pentheny O'Kelly
(invalided to UK)

Captains:
A. C. Booth
(to hospital)
D. E. Griffiths
(invalided to UK)
A. Leach
(Bde Machine-gun officer,
invalided to UK)
G. R. Newton
(Assistant Adjutant, invalided
to UK)
G. W. Owen (kia)
G. E. Stott
(invalided to UK)
H. Sutcliffe
(sick leave to UK)
L. C. Wilde
(to hospital)

Lieutenants:
L. Baird RAMC
J. Clegg (dow)
J. H. Clegg (dow)
F. N. Griffiths (dow)
F. Hardman
(invalided to UK)
D. Park
(invalided to UK)
G. D. Pochin
(Transport Officer, did not land)
P. Stott
(Machine-gun officer, invalided
to UK)
R. W. Wilde
(Scouts officer, invalided to UK)
L. St. G. Wilkinson
(acting QM, to hospital)

Second Lieutenants:
R. G. Ascroft (kia)
J. K. Bleakley
(invalided to UK)
A. Butterworth
(to hospital)
J. B. Emmott (kia)
T. Kirk (kia)
A. E. Lee
(invalided to UK)
H. K. Nevinson (dow)
E. Rye
(invalided to UK)
J. Stott (kia)
E. Wallwork
(invalided to UK)

Second Lieutenant J. A. C. Taylor was left in hospital and Second Lieutenant J. L. Kirk was left in charge of stores at Alexandria. Both officers subsequently served on the peninsula and both were invalided to the UK.

On 14 April 1915 the following officers joined from the 2/10th Battalion:

Lieutenant
  J. H. Clegg

Second Lieutenants:
  E. Rye
  E. Wallwork

On 24 April 1915 Privates Thomas Kirk and Joseph Kirk of the 6/Manchester were posted to the 1/10th with immediate effect as Second Lieutenants supernumerary pending War Office approval (granted).

Officers arriving at the 1/10th from the 2/10th on 18 October 1915.

Second Lieutenants:
  Beveridge
  Cooper
  Heywood
    (to hospital)
  Mercer

Rowbotham
  (to hospital)
Stanford
Sutton
  (to hospital)
Tweedie
  (to hospital)

Other officers who are known to have been invalided to the UK:

Lieutenant & QM:
  A. G. Wynne

Second Lieutenants:
  J. Boyd
  B. E. Hughes
  J. H. Kershaw

A. Maw
V. J. Matthews (attached)
F. F. Quarmby
G. Rogers
G. B. Taylor

Other officers who are known to have served with the 1/10th on the peninsula:

Captain:
  C. Eastgate-Smith
    (attached from 2/Manchester.
    To hospital)

Lieutenants:
  Gripper (attached)
  P. Truman (to hospital)

Second Lieutenants:
  Baxter
  Boyd
  Bouskill
  Faulkner
  Gardner (to hospital)
  Gillespie (to hospital)
  Hampson
  Hazelwood

Officers known to have served with the 1/10th in the desert during 1916:

Lieutenant-Colonel: Robinson

Major:
L. C. Wilde

Captains:
J. K. Bleakley
A. C. Booth
C. Eastgate-Smith
(attached. Kia 27/8/18 with 2/Manchester)

Lieutenants & 2nd Lts.:
Aves
Baxter
Beveridge
Bletcher
Bouskill
Butterworth
Candlish
Cowieson
Faulkner
Fitzgerald
Gardner
Gillespie
Gracey
Gripper (attached)
Hampson
Hardman
Hassall
W. Hazelwood
Heppard
Heywood
Horsfall
King
Knowles
Lee (wounded July 1917)
Matthews
McCombe
Rowbotham
Stanford (wounded July)
JTaylor
Thwaites
Truman
Walker
N. W. Wilkinson
L. St. G. Wilkinson
Lt. & QM. A. G. Wynne

Officers with the battalion at Hautmont, November 1918:

Lieutenant-Colonel: Peel

Captains:
Butterworth
Rowbotham
Stott
Taylor

Lieutenants & 2nd Lts.:
Beveridge
Brown
Butler
Cooper
Estelle
Fripp
Gentle
Gregory
Griffiths
Harry
Hazelwood
Howarth
Jupp
Maltby
Mathews
Matthews
Mercer
Simister
Streat
Street
Thoin
Travis
Truman
White

APPENDIX 5

THE WOUNDED, INVALIDED AND SICK OF 1915

BELOW ARE LISTS OF MEN of the 1/10th who are known to have been sent home from Egypt as unfit for further service in the desert or who were evacuated sick or wounded from Gallipoli. They have been compiled from various sources but are far from complete. For example, a nominal return for D Company dated May 1915 has some annotations which claim that for the period 9 May - 21 October the battalion suffered 92 killed, 43 died of wounds, 14 died of disease, 51 missing, 420 wounded and 165 sick. The list below gives only some 252 names. The method of reporting the wounded and sick (and indeed whether the man was in fact wounded or sick or both) does not allow for the accurate dating of a man's evacuation. The main list has therefore been compiled alphabetically rather than chronologically. Similarly, the actual departure date of a man sent back to the UK from Egypt during the period of desert training prior to the Gallipoli landing might not be totally reliable. Consequently, this list has also been compiled alphabetically. All such evacuations did however, take place between January and April 1915. Unfortunately, initials or forenames were not specified on the original lists of these 54 men.

Anderson 2068 A Coy	Cunningham 1547	Heywood 1688 B Coy
Bagley 2072 B Coy	C Coy	Hicks 267 D Coy
Bardsley 1288 B Coy	Faulkner 1459 B Coy	Higgins 1281 A Coy
Brindle 1951 C Coy	Fenn 1697 B Coy	Hilton 1929 C Coy
Binns 1119 D Coy	Fitton 1721 C Coy	Holt 1246 A Coy
Briscoe 1952 C Coy	Foy 2019 D Coy	Knight 460 B Coy
Burdock 2086 D Coy	Jones 2128 C Coy	Marland 1853 A Coy
Byrom 473 C Coy	Lancashire L/Sgt 1984	Mayers 2265 B Coy
Collins 1583 C Coy	B Coy	Norris 2158 B Coy
Connolly 2281 C Coy	Lee 2261 D Coy	Pownall 1997 B Coy
Cook 2229 D Coy	Lieboldt 2143 C Coy	Robinson 2162 C Coy
Cooper 1918 B Coy	Harrison 2247 B Coy	Robishaw 2008 C Coy
Crowther 1670 D Coy	Headland 1846 D Coy	Rose 2171 C Coy
Cullen 1572 C Coy	Heap 2115 B Coy	Schofield 1643 D Coy
	Heyes 1426 D Coy	Simpson 1850 D Coy

Smethurst Cpl 1432   Stuttard 1711 B Coy   Whittaker 1244 C Coy
   B Coy   Thorpe 59 A Coy   Wilkinson 706 C Coy
Snape 598 A Coy   Timms L/Sgt 667 D Coy
Speake 1564 C Coy   Travis 990 D Coy
Stretch 2187 A Coy   Widdison 171 D Coy

Men known to have been evacuated wounded or sick from Gallipoli

Ackroyd, H 2034	Brierley, H 2220	Dransfield, J 1793
Addison 1667	Brooks, W 2223	Duckworth, H 2106
Allen, W 1831	Brown, J 1938	Duke, A 2107
Ambler 1661	Butterworth, F 2900	Dunkerley, A 1966
Andrew, J 1899	Butterworth, H 1605	Dunkerley, N 1523
Armitage, R 1944	Cadman 225	Earnshaw, E 565
Ashton, P 2565	Cadsby, C 1971	Eames, Cpl F 521
Ashworth, S 2296	Cartledge, V 1769	Elson, F 1788
Atkins, H 1506	Catlow, G 2094	Entwistle, A 2237
Bailey, Sgt J 200	Cavaney, A 1712	Entwistle, T 2918
Bailey, R 2075	Chapman, A 748	Eyre, C 77
Barlow, W 2216	Chadwick, M 1308	Eyre, L/Cpl J 1544
Barnes, W 1417	Charnley, J 896	Faines, Cpl F 552
Barratt, Sgt	Chorlton, J 1499	Farraker, J 1713
Barratt, S 2991	Claber, J 1368	Fell, Sgt R 132
Bathe, Sgt 1336	Claber, L/Cpl T 1344	Finney, W 1337
Beaumont 1868	Clare, W 1568	Firth, C 1803
Beesley, L/Cpl W 985	Clarke, J 2099	Fitton, E 905
Benson, R 1693	Clough, J 2101	Fitton, F 935
Berry, R 1946	Coates, W 1732	Flannagan, F 1838
Best, Cpl A 3042	Collier, Sgt T 2907	Fletcher, J 2451
Birchall, J 1950	Cordingley, I 1234	Fletcher, R 2239
Bird, L/Cpl R 2035	Coyne, R 2234	Gardiner, H 1067
Bocking, W 1489	Craven, J 1304	Gartside, L/Cpl W 2243
Boon, J 1282	Crossley, T 2507	Gill, H 2601
Bowes, H 1949	Croysdale 1024	Godfrey, W 1915
Bowman, T 1868	Cunningham, J 1480	Goodall, E 2023
Bradbury 1516	Cunningham, P 2104	Goodwin, F 1046
Bradbury, H 1516	Curley, J 2800	Gorbutt, Sgt T 33
Bradbury, M	Dale, J	Green 2245
Bradley, B 800	Davies, W 2709	Greenhalgh, W 2328
Bramley, Sgt F 2201	Dockery, W 1666	Greenwood, F 1870
Brierley, D 2084	Donohue, J 1345	Greenwood, H 1786

Greenwood, J
Halkyard, Sgt W 230
Halliwell, W 1884
Hammond, A 1491
Hancock, G 1840
Harrison, F 2248
Hartley, L/Cpl J 1409
Hatch, S 2062
Hayes, S 2117
Hearne, L/Cpl J 1543
Henningham, T 1734
Henthorne 1830
Hewitt, W 1844
Hilton, E 2250
Hilton 1977
Hindley, G 1531
Hirst, H 1773
Hoddy, R 2730
Holding, H 1160
Holt 2120
Holt, J 1827
Holt, L/Sgt T 1856
Howard, J 1905
Howard 1898
Howarth, J 1301
Hufton, J 1978
Hufton, Dmr J 1298
Hughes, 1792
Hulme, H 1932
Hunt, P
Hurst, J 2125
Jackson, W 1760
Johnson, E 1158
Kelly, J 1649
Kirkham, G 2059
Keighley, E 1940
Kenny, D 2130
Kenyon, H 1317
Kershaw, C
Knowles, W 1983
Lane, F 1183

Lawton, F 1985
Lees, A 2745
Lees, R 2140
Lewis, A 511
Little, W 2144
Lockwood 1747
Lomas, L/Cpl W 2493
Lowther, D 3270
Lupton, Cpl F 658
Madden, J 2148
Marren, L 586
Martin, J 2149
Marshall, J 1787
Mason, L
Mayhew, W 1886
McArthur, H 2146
McConnell, T 1873
McCornrick, W 1656
McLynn, Sgt T 567
Meadow, H 2756
Melia, J 1134
Mellor, C 2501
Metcalf, J 653
Mills, L/Cpl 99
Mills, J 1374
Mills, J 1930
Mills, W 2154
Milner, G 2639
Minshall, F 1717
Minton, J 934
Moores, J
Moss, W
Mulliner, W 2644
Mulroy, C 1924
Ogden, G 2852
Ogden, H 1494
Ogden, H 2762
Orne, W 1501
Overton, E 1447
Palmer, W 2272
Parry 2161

Payne, H 4544
Pike, A 1616
Platt, J 2163
Pomfret, J 1348
Prestwich, F 2063
Prestwich, F 2953
Rider, G 2766
Rigby, H 2526
Riley, G 2166
Robinson, L 1718
Robinson, W 2056
Robishaw, J 1290
Rose, T 2004
Ross, G 2005 B Coy
Rowe, Dmr H 1545
Royle, J 2530
Rupton, Cpl 658
Ryall, L/Cpl 1719
Saunders, R 2278
Saunders, S 1467
Scholes, W 1025
Scott, W 1753
Seville 2064
Sewell 1750
Sharratt, J 3174
Sheridan, W 2392
Skitt, T 2177
Slater, L/Cpl E
Smart, L 1630
Smith 1436
Smith, F 1710
Smith, Cpl H 963
Smith, J 2007
Smith, T
Smith, Cpl W 1759
Stansfield, J 820
Starkey, F 1738
Stott, A 511
Stott, W 2284
Sugden, L/Cpl 1578
Summersgill, A 891

Summersgill, J 545
Summersgill, J 2183
Sunderland, E 202
Swallow, W
Tarbuck, H 1765
Taylor, J 2191
Taylor, R 2193
Todd, H 1782
Trotter, P 1685
Turner, L/Cpl J 1239
Tweedy, W 315

Vickers, T 1596
Wadsworth, Sgt
Walker, T
Walton, L/Cpl F 1362
Wardman, T 2550
Watts, L 2887
Weston, J (?)
Whittaker, R
Whittaker, W 1755
Whitworth, W 1665
Wild, C 2677

Wild, G 2407
Wild, J 1462
Wild, J 89
Wild, T
Wilkinson 1926
Williams, J 1892
Wilson, G 2048
Wood, J 1556
Wood, L/Cpl J 2292
Yates, A

Appendix 6:

Honours and Awards to Members of the 10/Manchester

Victoria Cross
375499 Private Walter Mills

Distinguished Service Order
Major L. C. Wilde
Captain J. A. C. Taylor

Bar to Distinguished Service Order
Lieutenant-Colonel W. R. Peel DSO
(Yorkshire Regiment)

Military Cross
Captain L. B. Baird (RAMC)
Lieutenant (a/Capt.) T. Bletcher
Captain A. Butterworth
Lieutenant F. E. Cook
Lieutenant G. Crawshaw
Second Lieutenant G. Fripp
Captain H.L.Hampson (att. 126thLTMB)
Captain F. Hardman
Second Lieutenant H. Hassell
Lieutenant F. Howarth
Lieutenant J. Jupp
Lieutenant (a/Capt.) J. Jones
Captain J. C. S. Rowbotham
Lieutenant W. D. Shaw (R. F.)
Captain J. A. C. Taylor DSO
Second Lieutenant J. B. Whitehead
Captain L. St. G. Wilkinson
Second Lieutenant W. Williams
Lieutenant S. Wilson

Bar to Military Cross
Captain J. A. C. Taylor DSO MC

Distinguished Conduct Medal
377044 Private C. Ayre

376870 Sergeant S. Baddeley
376329 Sergeant D. Brown
377000 Private E. Darby
39942 Sergeant M. Haskey
375228 Sergeant C. Langley
375179 Sergeant S. R. Lees MM
250888 Corporal R. Leigh
303001 Corporal O. Lloyd
376555 Lance Corporal E. Owen
350213 Lance Corporal W. Revell
375762 Corporal R. Rigby
376167 Private F. Schofield
201783 Lance Corporal J. Seddon
74549 Lance Corporal S. Spedding
375226 Sergeant J. H. Sugden
375311 Sergeant H. Tarbuck
176372 Private T. Taylor
375831 CSM K. Toogood DCM & Bar
376338 Sergeant J. Whitaker
376338 Sergeant F. Williams

Military Medal
Private W. Ashurst
Sergeant M. R. Bradbury
Lance Corporal J. Bradshaw
Private J. Bridge
Private J. Brimelow
Corporal H. Brookes
Private W. Brown
Sergeant E. Butterworth
Corporal H. Carroll
Private T. Chadwick
Private J. W. Chapman
Sergeant T. Clutton
Private G. T. Cornford
Private H. Cooke

Corporal W. R. Cowel
Sergeant F. Creswell
Private F. Critchley
Private J. Davies
Private G. Dukenson
Corporal A. Fisher
Private G. Hackney
Private A. Hancock
Private J. Hayes
Private J. R. Hayes
Private R. W. Heslop
Private S. Hulme
Private E. Hutchins
Lance Sergeant J. W. Lane
Sergeant S. R. Lees DCM
Private J. Lockhart
Private F. Matthews
Sergeant J. Milner
Sergeant H. Newton
Private W. Nicholson
Lance Corporal W. Parker
Private W. Radcliffe
Corporal B. B. Robinson
Private T. Silverwood
Private G. A. Smith
Sergeant R. S. Smith
Private E. Spink
Sergeant W. Squires
Corporal E. Stockton
Private J. Storey
Sergeant J. Sugden DCM
Private R. B. Ward
Private T. Weston
Private H. Whittaker

Bar to Military Medal
Corporal A. Fisher
Private McNamara
Sergeant W. Newton
Lance Corporal H. Rodgers

Meritorious Service Medal
375054 a/CSM S. A. Cox
375909 a/Corporal L. Dransfield
376305 Sergeant J. Gartside
375200 Sergeant P. Healey
5757 Sergeant J. E. Hollingsworth
375555 Corporal J. H. Keighley MM
375032 CSM (a/RSM) F. Miller
376223 Lance Corporal B. B. Robinson
375827 Corporal J. Scholes
375033 RQMS J. P. Trevitt

Mention in Dispatches
Lieutenant (a/Capt.) T. Bletcher
Sergeant Catlow
Regimental Sergeant-Major A. G. Chittenden
Lieutenant A. E. Lee
Sergeant N. Lewis
Second Lieutenant W. J. Norris
Corporal J. Simpson
Private G. A. Smith
Sergeant J. H. Sugden
RQMS J. P. Trevitt
Private Weston
Major L. C. Wilde DSO

Belgian Croix de Guerre
375383 Private J. Coulson
375913 Sergeant S. Haslam
Private J. Holt
295056 Sergeant N. McHugh
375774 Private Whitehead
350447 Private S. Wilde

Serbian Gold Medal of the Obolich
71 Private J. Hammond

Appendix 7

The 1955 Krithia reunion

In MAY 1955 an advertisement was placed in the *Oldham Chronicle* inviting former members of the 10th who had fought at Krithia between 4 – 6 June 1915 to attend a reunion lunch. A total of 85 Other Ranks are known to have replied. Their names and where known their rank, whether they were wounded and their addresses in 1955 are listed below.

Arnold, E.
Arnold, J.
Barnes, William 1417 28, Duke St., Chadderton. A Coy.
Beech, Herbert 155, Denton Lane, Chadderton.
Beesley, William 375074 (985) L/Cpl 9, School St., Coppice.
 B Coy. Wounded Sept.1915.
Brierley, John 1370 8, Brooklands Ave., Chadderton.
Buckley, R. 690 L/Cpl St Eval, Wadebridge, Cornwall. D Coy.
Burke, John 831 Cpl 29, Webster St., Oldham.
Butterworth, E. 1406 12, Collins St., Mumps.
Cadman, B. 285, Higginshaw Lane, Royton.
Cannon, Joseph 16, Bar Gap Rd., Oldham.
Capper, Harry 69 Sgt Moorfield Welfare Home, Greenacres Rd., Oldham.
 B Coy.
Carroll, J. 1639 24, Old Lane, Chadderton. D Coy.
Carter, T.
Cartledge, V. 1769 Wounded June 1915.
Chorlton, W. 1500 28, Lynn St., Werneth. D Coy.
 His brother J (1499) was wounded June 1915.
Chadderton, S. 187, Glodwick Rd., Oldham. A Coy.
Claber, James 1368 Wounded June 1915.
Coulson, John 375383 9, Cowper St., Oldham.
Croysdale, Lewis 1024 391, Oldham Rd., Royton. Wounded June 1915.
Cunningham, P. 375477 (2104) 3, Marple St., Oldham. Wounded June 1915.
Dawson, H. 29, Lansdowne Rd., Chadderton.
Demsley, J.
Donohue, J. 1345 106, Oxford St., Oldham. D Coy. Wounded June 1915.
Dorchester, H.
Dunkerley, W. 276, Shaw Rd., Royton.
Dyson, Harry 1603 1, Belmont St. West, Oldham. C Coy.

Eastwood, Harry 375018 43, Lyon St., Shaw. B Coy.
Edgeley, A. 15, Co-operation St., Failsworth.
Ellis, J. 46, Hive St., Hollinwood.
Eyre, J. 1544 L/Cpl Wounded Dec.1915.
Flory, Frank Braeside, 5, Thorley Close, Chadderton.
Foy, W. 169, Honeywell Lane, Oldham.
Goodwin, E. 208
Hatch, S. 2062
Haughton, Charles 38, Malton St., Oldham.
Hemmings, F. 375071 Cpl 98, Lees Rd., Oldham. C Coy.
Hewitt, J.
Horsfall, A. 5, Hathershaw Lane, Oldham. C Coy.
Horsfall, S.
Hoyle, J. 375175 Cpl 32, Manchester Rd., Werneth. A Coy.
Jennings, H. 375344 110, King St., Oldham. B Coy.
Kirkham, H. 886 55, Manley Rd., Oldham. D Coy.
Knight, W.
Lambert, F. 375069 Cpl 1, Daisy St., Westwood, Oldham.
Lees, S. DCM MM 87, Devon St., Oldham.
Lockett, Frank 29, 12th Avenue, Abbeyhills, Oldham.
Lowe, Fred 375207 80, Shaw Rd., Oldham. C Coy.
Massey, J.
McConnell, John 489, Lees Rd., Salem, Oldham.
McConnel, P. 1724
Miller, Frank
Mitchell, J. 43, Kay St., Oldham.
Moss, W. Cllr 168, London Rd., Oldham.
Newton, J. 5, House, 12, Court, Henshaw St., Oldham.
Nuttall, F.
Nuttall, J. 329 Sgt 63, Eric St., Clarksfield, Oldham.
Percival, F. 99, Stoneleigh St., Oldham.
Philburn, T.
Pike, Alfred 1616 16, Alderson St., Oldham. D Coy. Wounded May 1915.
Pratt, Walter 520, Ashton Rd., Hathershaw, Oldham.
Price, B.
Price, Richard 688, Chamber Rd., Oldham.
Pollitt, J. QMS 896, Oldham Rd, Thornham, Rochdale.
Read, William 3, Tyne St., Clarkesfield, Oldham.
Robinson, Levi, 1718 14, Mulliner St., Oldham. Wounded June 1915.
Rollinson, T.
Sewell, W.

Shaw, G. 1558 70A, Lees Rd., Oldham. B Coy.

Smith, J. 2280 20, Thatch Leach, Broadway, Chadderton. D Coy. His brother Frank was kia 4/6/15.

Starkey, F. 1738

Stott, E. 375118 42, Cowhill, Chadderton. C Coy.

Stott, Frank 99, Beever St., Oldham.

Stott, W. 375569 (2284) 34, Eldon St., Oldham. Wounded June 1915.

Street, Jack 375701 8, Butterton Rd., Rhyl.

Taylor, J. 2192 Higher Wade Farm, Dobcross, Oldham. A Coy. Wounded June 1915. His brother William was kia 4/6/15.

Taylor, James 155, Limeside Rd., Hollinwood.

Turner, S. 26, Edith St., Hathershaw.

Wadsworth, T. 2, Haven, Haven Lane, Moorside.

Webb, C.

Webb, G.

Wright, L. 22, Plum St., Oldham.

Wrigley, Fred 375035 Sgt 32, Balfour St., Oldham.

Yates, Alfred 15, Welbeck St., Oldham.

APPENDIX 8: ... AND FINALLY

IN 1962 ADVERTISEMENTS WERE PLACED in several Northern news-papers inviting former members of the Lancashire Fusiliers, East Lancashire 10/Manchester and East Lancashire Field Ambulance to apply for a small benevolence. A bequest had been made by the late Captain G. B. Jameson, who had served with the 42nd Division, for Other Ranks who had been on Gallipoli with the Division. Those former members of the 10th who responded are listed below.

Privates:
Ambler, Robert
Ashton, George William
Campbell, Albert
Carroll, John
Cartledge, Vincent
Cassidy, William
Cavanagh, Thomas
Coulson, John
Croysdale, Lewis
Cunningham, Patrick
Dawson, Fred
Donohue, James Edward
Eastwood, Harry
Eyre, Charles
Grassham, Harry
Hancock, Albert
Harrison, Harold
Hatch, Samuel
Hewitt, William
Hewlett, James
Hidderley, John William
Hipwell, Harry
Hollingworth, James Thomas
Howard, William
Howarth, Joseph
Johnson, George Nathaniel
Lees, William
Marshall, Harold
Mayall, Albert
Mellor, James
Mitchell, John
Ogden, Albert
Openshaw, Alfred

Pike, Alfred
Robinson, Levi
Scholes, Ernest
Shaw, Samuel
Simms, Henry
Smith, Sam
Stott, Elijah
Stott-Mills, Walter
Swallow, William
Taylor, William (MM)
Widdowson, James Leigh
Wild, Harold
Wright, Lawrence

NCOs:
L/Cpl Beesley, William
L/Cpl Bocking, John Arthur
L/Cpl Chadderton, Samuel
Cpl Clough, John
L/Cpl Goddard, Robert
L/Cpl Hemmings, Frederick
Cpl Hoyle, John
Sgt Johnson, Herbert
L/Cpl Kirkbride, Arthur Franklyn
Cpl Lambert, Frank
Sgt Massey, John
Cpl Moss, William
Sgt Percival, Fred
L/Sgt Read, William
Cpl Saunders, Robert
Sgt Tarbuck, Harold
Cpl Taylor, Ernest
Sgt Webb, Charles